KEY TO
SECOND YEAR LATIN

(1946 REVISION)

BY

ROBERT J. HENLE, S.J.

LOYOLA PRESS.
Chicago

LOYOLA PRESS.
3441 N. Ashland Avenue
Chicago, Illinois 60657
(800) 621-1008
www.loyolapress.com

ISBN-13: 978-0-8294-1207-9
ISBN-10: 0-8294-1207-7

Printed in the United States of America.
14 15 16 Bang 10 9 8 7 6 5 4 3 2

TABLE OF CONTENTS

ROMAN IMPERIALISM IN GAUL

INTRODUCTION

This key is intended as an aid to the busy teacher. It should serve to unlock readily and speedily whatever may be difficult or obscure, and to reassure those who wish to be certain that their own interpretations are the ones which the author himself would accept. A few points in connection with the key and its use merit a word of comment.

1. In the English translations of Latin exercises the literal meanings of Latin words and sentences are usually given, since the main purpose is to make the Latin text clear rather than to give an example of good style. Occasionally (especially when a literal translation results in pidgin English) a freer translation is added in parentheses. While it may often be necessary to demand a literal translation first, the final translation accepted by the teacher should always be pure, idiomatic English. Words added are placed in brackets: for example, "into [the territory of] the Helvetians" as a translation of "in Helvētiōs."

2. In translating English exercises into Latin this key seldom gives more than one version. "You" could often be either singular or plural; "they put" could be present, imperfect, or perfect; "I see" can be translated by three or more verbs. It would have been impossible to give every variant translation, nor would any useful purpose have been served by so doing.

3. Certain extremely simple exercises involving nothing more than a knowledge of word meanings and syntactical forms are left unanswered.

4. Numerical references such as "See No. . . . " are in all cases, without exception, to the author's LATIN GRAMMAR.

5. The author's purpose in calling for the parsing of italicized words in certain exercises is to focus attention on points of syntax requiring drill. It is understood that the amount of parsing actually done will depend on the teacher's judgment as to what the class needs and is able to do. In this key the complete parsing of every word is not given in full. It was felt that to give the parsing in full would be altogether unnecessary, almost an affront to the teacher. Comments are therefore made only when there might be some doubt as to what the author's interpretation would be or when because of some special difficulty a hurried teacher might possibly be spared the trouble of looking up the point in the GRAMMAR.

ROMAN IMPERIALISM IN GAUL

1. The Helvetian Drive to the West

The Scene of Operations (p. 17)

All Gaul (Gaul taken as a whole) is divided into three parts, of which the Belgians inhabit one, the Aquitanians inhabit another, and the Gauls the third. All of these [nations] differ among themselves (from one another) in language, laws, and many other matters. The Garonne River separates the Gauls from the Aquitanians. The Marne and the Seine separate the Gauls from the Belgians. Of all these [peoples] the Belgians are the bravest, for they are farthest from our province and merchants do not often come to (visit) them. Furthermore, they are nearest to the Germans, who dwell across (on the other side of) the Rhine, and with whom they are continually waging war.

The 'Fighting' Helvetians (p. 20)

For this reason the Helvetians also surpass the other Gauls in courage, for they often contend with the Germans. For either they are warding them off from their own territory, or are themselves waging war in their (the Germans') territory.

Orgetorix Conspires to Become Dictator of All Gaul (p. 21)

Among (of) the Helvetians the noblest and richest by far was Orgetorix. Led on by the desire of royal power, he made (instigated) a conspiracy of the nobility, for he sought command of (to become supreme in) all Gaul.

The Helvetians are held (hemmed) in on all sides by the nature of the place (natural barriers); on one side by the Rhine River, very wide and deep, which separates the Helvetians from the Germans; on another side by the very high Jura Mountains (the lofty Jura range), which divides the Sequanians from the Helvetians; and on the third side by the Lake of Geneva and the River Rhone, which separates our province from [the country of] the Helvetians. They were therefore unable easily to make war on their neighbors. They were eager, however, for war and fame.

The Helvetians Agree to the Proposal of Orgetorix (p. 23)

And so, led on by these things (induced by these factors) and stirred

1

up (influenced) by the authority (advice) of Orgetorix, they decided to go out of (set out from) their own territory with all their forces. They prepared everything that pertained to (was necessary for) their departure. They got ready the greatest possible number of yoke-animals and wagons. They prepared (amassed) a large supply of grain. With the nearest states they strengthened peace and friendship (They strengthened the bonds of peace and friendship between themselves and the states nearest them).

The Secret Diplomacy of Orgetorix (p. 23)

Orgetorix took upon himself the embassy to the neighboring states. Led on (incited) by the authority (persuasion) of Orgetorix, Casticus, a Sequanian, determined to seize power in his own state. Dumnorix, a Haeduan, also aroused by Orgetorix, determined to take command in his state. Said Orgetorix: "We can easily seize the royal power of all Gaul and obtain command. I will help you (come to your aid) with all my troops in order that you may easily seize command." Influenced by this speech, they took an oath among themselves. And so he united three very vigorous peoples in order to obtain through them command of all Gaul.

The Helvetians Continue Their Plans (p. 25)

After Orgetorix' death the Helvetians nevertheless tried to do what they had decided (tried to carry out their plans). They were preparing to set out from their own territory with all their forces. When they had made ready everything that pertained to (had made all arrangements for) their departure, they burned all their towns. Furthermore, they burned all their grain except what they had decided to carry with them. The Rauraci, the Tulingi, and the Latobrigi, their neighbors, influenced by the Helvetians, set out with them. The Helvetians joined to themselves as allies the Boii also.

They Decide to Trek through the Roman Province (p. 25)

There were in all two routes by which they could go out from (leave) home. One [was] through [the land of] the Sequanians, narrow and difficult, between the Jura Mountains and the River Rhone; the other, much easier, [was] through our province. For they could easily cross the Rhone, which flows between the territory of the Helvetians and that of the Allobroges, who had recently been pacified (subjugated) by the Romans. The most distant town of the Allobroges and the one nearest to the lands of the Helvetians is Geneva. From that town a bridge stretches (crosses over) to the [country of the] Helvetians. And so the Helvetians determined to go through the territory of the Allobroges. When they had prepared everything (made all preparations) for their departure, they set a day on which all should assemble at the bank of the Rhone.

The News Reaches Caesar. He Acts Swiftly (p. 26)

The news was reported to Caesar. He hastened to set out from the city, and hurried into Farther Gaul by the longest possible [forced] marches. He arrived at Geneva. He levied on the whole province the greatest possible number of soldiers. Altogether in Farther Gaul there was only one legion. He commanded that the bridge which crossed over to Geneva from [the land of] the Helvetians be destroyed.

The Helvetians Attempt Negotiations (p. 27)

When the Helvetians had been informed of his arrival they sent to him [as] envoys the noblest [men] of the tribe. "We will make this journey through the province," they said, "without [doing] any damage. We have no other route."

Caesar Plays for Time (p. 29)

Caesar thought he should not (did not think he should) allow this. For he remembered that the Helvetians had killed a Roman consul and had routed and overcome his army. He therefore did not think that the Helvetians would march through the province without [doing] any damage. Nevertheless, in order that some interval (time) should intervene until the soldiers whom he had levied should assemble, he replied to the envoys that he would consider the matter. "Return," he said, "on the Ides of April."

Caesar Builds a Line of Defense (p. 29)

Meanwhile, with the legion which he had with him and the soldiers who had assembled from the province, he constructed a wall and a ditch for [a distance of] nineteen miles, from Lake Geneva, which flows into the River Rhone, to the Jura Mountains, which separate the territory of the Sequanians from [that of] the Helvetians. He stationed garrisons and strengthened forts (built strong forts) so that he could more easily ward off (repel) the Helvetians.

Caesar's Answer (p. 30)

When the day had come which he had set up with (appointed for) the envoys and the envoys had returned to him, Caesar said that according to the custom of the Roman people he would not grant them any passage through the province. "If you attempt to cross the river," he said, "I will prevent (restrain) you!"

The Helvetians Attempt a Crossing (p. 30)

And so the Helvetians tried to cross the River Rhone, but were driven back by the fortification and the darts [hurled by the Romans].

The Helvetians Try the Other Road (p. 31)

There remained one [other] route, through [the country of] the Sequanians. The Sequanians, influenced by the authority (bidding, persuasion) of the Haeduans, gave the Helvetians a route (passage) through their lands. The Sequanians and the Helvetians exchanged hostages, [agreeing that] the Sequanians would not prevent the Helvetians from (forbid the Helvetians) passage, and that the Helvetians would cross over through their land without damage.

Caesar Learns the Enemy's Plans (p. 31)

Caesar was informed that the Helvetians had determined to march through the field [the land] of the Sequanians and the Haeduans into the territory of the Santones. The Santones are not far distant from the territory of the Tolosates. This state is within the province, and so Caesar perceived that great danger would be to (threatened) the province.

Caesar Raises Reinforcements (p. 31)

Because of this (consequently), he put in command of the fortification he had made (built) [his] lieutenant Titus Labienus. He himself hastened by great (forced) marches into Italy. In Italy he enrolled (enlisted) two legions, and the three [legions] which were spending the winter around Aquileia he led out of winter quarters, and where the route was nearest (shortest) into Farther Gaul through the Alps, he hastened to go (went with all possible haste) with these five legions.

He Fights His Way through the Alps and Penetrates into Non-Roman Territory (p. 33)

There the Ceutrones and others who were dwelling in the Alps tried to keep the army off the road (tried to block the advance of the army). These he repulsed in many battles and on the seventh day arrived in the province. From there he led the army into the land of the Allobroges

[and] from [that of] the Allobroges to [the country of] the Segusiavi. These are the first [people] outside the province across the Rhone. The Helvetians had already led their forces across through the defiles and through the territory of the Sequanians, and had arrived at the land of the Haeduans and were ravaging their fields. The Haeduans were unable to defend themselves and their possessions against them. They therefore sent envoys to Caesar to ask for help. "We are friends of the Roman people," the envoys said. "Our fields should not be laid waste, our children led into slavery, our towns stormed, almost within sight of your army." The Allobroges too, who have fields across the Rhone, withdrew to Caesar in flight (fled to Caesar). Induced by these happenings, Caesar decided to aid (assist) the allies and to ward off (repel) the Helvetians by force.

A Surprise Attack (p. 36)

There is a river [called the] Saone which flows through the territory of the Haeduans and the Sequanians into the Rhone. The Helvetians were crossing that river. Concerning this matter Caesar was informed by scouts that the Helvetians had already led three parts of [their] forces across that river, but that the fourth part remained [on the other side]. Having set out from the camp at the third watch with three legions, he came to that part which had not yet crossed. Having attacked (he attacked) these encumbered [soldiers and] he killed a great part of them. The others committed themselves to flight (fled) and concealed themselves in the nearest forest. After this battle, in order to be able to overtake the rest of the Helvetian troops, he made (built) a bridge across the Saone and thus led [his] army across.

Caesar Turns Aside for Supplies. The Enemy Follows (p. 37)

He was not more than eighteen miles from Bibracte, [which was] by far the largest town of the Haeduans. He therefore turned the march aside from the [direction of the] Helvetians, and hastened to go to Bibracte. This move was reported to the enemy by runaway slaves. The Helvetians, [their] plan altered and [their] route turned around (reversed), began to pursue our men in the rear.

Caesar Prepares to Fight (p. 39)

Having noticed this (when he saw what was happening), Caesar led his troops to the nearest hill. He sent the cavalry to withstand the enemy's attack. Meanwhile he himself drew up in the middle of (halfway up) the hill a triple line of four veteran legions. On the topmost ridge he stationed the two legions which he had recently enlisted in Hither Gaul, and all the reinforcements. Thus he filled the whole mountain with men. He ordered the baggage and the packs to be carried together into one place, and commanded it (this place) to be fortified by those who were in the higher line.

The Zero Hour (p. 41)

The Helvetians, having followed with all their wagons, brought their baggage together in one place. [Then] in a very compact line, when our cavalry had been hurled back and a phalanx formed, they advanced to our first line.

The Battle Begins (p. 43)

Caesar, having encouraged his men, began battle. After the soldiers had hurled their javelins from a higher position, they easily broke through the phalanx. Once it was broken, they made an attack upon them with drawn swords. At last the Gauls, exhausted with wounds, began to retreat and to betake themselves (make their way) to a mountain which was near by.

The Helvetian Rear Guard Arrives (p. 43)

When they had taken the mountain and our men were coming up, the Boii and the Tulingi, who were closing (up) the enemy's line with about fifteen thousand men and were [serving as] a guard for the rear, after they had attacked our men on the exposed flank from [their] route (without stopping), surrounded them. On seeing this, the Helvetians who had betaken themselves (made their way) to the mountain, began to renew the battle. The Romans advanced in two divisions, the first and second lines to resist (continue to engage) the conquered (those who were beaten and had withdrawn) and the third to withstand those coming [up].

The Decision of Arms (p. 44)

Thus a double action was fought long and bitterly. Finally, the enemy was no longer able to withstand the attack of our men. And some therefore withdrew to the mountain and others betook themselves (made their way) to their baggage and wagons.

Fighting Continues around the Baggage Train (p. 45)

The battle at the baggage train continued far into the night, for they had placed the wagons in front as a rampart, and were hurling darts from a higher place (position) upon our men coming (as they came up). The battle continued there for a long time. At last our men got possession of the baggage and wagons.

The Survivors Flee (p. 46)

About one hundred and thirty thousand men survived this battle and they fled (traveled continuously) throughout that whole night. In three days they came to the territory of the Lingones.

Heavy Losses Delay Pursuit (p. 46)

Our men were unable to pursue them because of the soldiers' wounds and the burial of those slain. Caesar sent messengers to the Lingones. He forbade them (the Lingones) to help the enemy with grain or anything else. After three days he himself began to follow the enemy with all his forces.

The Helvetians Surrender (p. 47)

The Helvetians, influenced by a scarcity of all things, sent envoys to him concerning (to discuss) surrender. When they came to him on the route, they cast themselves at [his] feet and, having spoken (speaking) humbly, weeping, asked (begged for) peace. Caesar ordered them to await his arrival. When Caesar had come thither he demanded hostages, weapons, and slaves.

An Attempted Escape (p. 48)

In the meantime about 6,000 men, either greatly terrified or influenced by [some] hope of safety, having (had) set out from the Helvetians' camp at dusk, [and] hastened to the Rhine and the territory of the Germans. When Caesar was informed of this move, he ordered those through whose territory they were going to lead (bring) them back. He considered them, when they had been brought back, among the number of the enemy (he treated them . . . as enemies). All the rest he received into surrender (he accepted the surrender of all the rest) when hostages, weapons, and deserters had been handed over. He ordered the Helvetians, the Tulingi, and the Latobrigi to return to their own territories. He [further] ordered that they rebuild the towns which they had burned.

Peace (p. 49)

When the war of the Helvetians was completed, envoys from almost all of Gaul, chiefs of the states, came to Caesar to congratulate him.

2. The German Peril

The war with the Helvetians over, the chiefs of the states came to Caesar to treat with him about the common welfare of the Gauls. They pointed out these facts. The Haeduans and the Arverni were (had been) contending between them for a long time for command of all Gaul. The Arverni, when they were unable to overcome the Haeduans, summoned the Germans into Gaul in order through them to hold command of all Gaul. With these [Germans] the Haeduans often contended in arms but were routed and overcome. The Germans, however, with Ariovistus as king, remained in Gaul—a large part of the territory of the Sequanians having been seized [by them]—and called other Germans from across the Rhine. Ariovistus was a barbarous man; the Gauls were no longer able to sustain (endure) his commands. When they had reported this, they finally asked help from Caesar and the Roman people, for they had no other hope.

The Battle with the Germans (p. 52)

Nevertheless Caesar decided to contend with the Germans in arms for the command of Gaul. He swiftly led [his] army into the fields which the Germans had seized and there began battle with them. The fight was long and brave. Finally the Germans, routed and thoroughly frightened, gave themselves up to flight (fled). Not many (a few) of them reached the Rhine River; they hastened to cross the river and so found safety for themselves. Among these was Ariovistus. Our cavalry killed all the rest, [who had been] pursued. Thus the Germans were finally conquered.

Disastrous Retreat of the Suebi (p. 52)

When this battle was reported across the Rhine, the Suebi, who had come to the banks of the Rhine, began to return to their own territory. When those who dwelt nearest to the Rhine perceived that the Suebi were greatly terrified, having pursued them, (they pursued and) they killed a great number of them.

Caesar's Preparations for the Winter of 58 B. C. (p. 52)

After [these] two great wars were finished in one summer, Caesar led his army into winter quarters into [the territory of] the Sequanians. He placed Labienus in command of the winter quarters. He himself set out for Hither Gaul.

3. Conspiracy among the Belgians

Caesar Learns of the Conspiracy (p. 55)

While Caesar was in Hither Gaul he was informed through messages and dispatches that all the Belgians were forming a conspiracy against the Roman people, and exchanging hostages. The Belgians, who inhabit the third part of Gaul, are the bravest of all the Gauls and the most eager for liberty and glory. They thought, now that all Gaul was pacified (subjugated), that the Roman army would come to (move against) them. They therefore prepared war against the Roman people in order to remain in (keep) that freedom which they had received (inherited) from their forefathers.

Caesar's Countermeasures (p. 55)

Aroused by these dispatches and messages, Caesar enrolled (enlisted) two new legions in Hither Gaul and when summer had begun, sent (commissioned) Quintus Pedius, a lieutenant, to lead them into Farther Gaul. He himself hastened to the army when first a supply of fodder had begun to be [collected]. He ordered the Senones and the rest of the Gauls who were neighbors of the Belgians to find out those things which (what) the Belgians were carrying on (doing) and to inform him of these things. All these announced that forces were being collected and that the army was coming together in one place. He therefore set out toward them. When a supply of provisions had been prepared, he swiftly reached the territory of the Belgians.

The Remi Submit (p. 56)

When he had arrived there, the Remi, who are the nearest of the Gauls to the Belgians, sent the most noble men of the state to say that they were ready to exchange hostages, to receive [the Romans] into [their] towns, and to aid them with grain and other things, and that they had not conspired with the rest of the Belgians against the Roman people.

The Report of the Remi (p. 57)

The Remi reported that all the Belgians were in arms and that the Germans who dwelt on this side of the Rhine had united with them. When he (Caesar) asked them which states were in arms, and how great [they were], he learned this: . . .

Caesar Acts (p. 59)

When this development was reported, Caesar, fearing a trick, held the army and the cavalry in camp. At dawn, this fact having been strengthened (confirmed) by scouts, he sent the whole cavalry to delay the enemy's last column. He ordered Titus Labienus to follow them with three legions. These [cavalry], having advanced on the last men and pursued them for many miles, without any danger (risk) [they] killed a great number of them fleeing (as they fled). Having pursued (after pursuing) them until sunset, they finally withdrew to camp.

The Plan of the Nervii (p. 61)

The enemy was holding itself in (waiting) in this forest; not many (a few) horsemen were [to be] seen in an open place. There was a river about three feet in depth.

Caesar Reaches the River (p. 63)

When the cavalry had been sent ahead, Caesar followed swiftly with all the troops. The arrangement of the column, however, was another than (different from) that which the Belgians had reported to the Nervii. For, because he was approaching the enemy, Caesar was leading six legions ready for action; behind these he had stationed the baggage trains of the whole army; then the two legions which had recently been enrolled were closing the whole line (bringing up the rear). Our cavalry, having crossed the river, began battle with the enemy's cavalry. They (the latter) withdrew to their own [forces] in the forest, but again made an attack on our cavalry from the forest.

4. Danger in the Alps

Caesar Leaves Galba in Winter Quarters (p. 68)

When Caesar was departing for Italy, he sent Servius Galba with the twelfth legion and part of the cavalry against the Nantuates, the Veragri, and the Seduni, who (whose combined lands) stretch from the territory of the Allobroges and Lake Geneva and the River Rhone to the topmost Alps. For on account of (because of the depredations of) these tribes, merchants went (traveled) by this route through the Alps with (only at the risk of) great danger.

Success of Galba's Campaign (p. 68)

Successful battles having been made (effected) and their forts stormed, and envoys sent to him from all sides, hostages given, and peace made, Galba decided to station two cohorts among the Nantuates, and to winter, himself, with the remaining cohorts of that legion in a village of the Veragri which is called Octodurus. This village is held (hemmed) in on all sides by very lofty mountains and is divided into two parts by a river. He therefore granted one part of the village to the Gauls; the other, however, left (evacuated) by them, he gave to the cohorts. He fortified that place by means of a rampart and a ditch.

Sudden Danger (p. 69)

After many days Galba was informed through scouts that everyone had fled from that part of the village which he had granted to the Gauls, and that the mountains by which the village was held (hemmed) in were being held by a great number of Gauls.

A Council of War (p. 70)

When these things had been reported [to him], Galba perceived that the danger to his men was great (extreme). For the fortifications (defenses) were not yet completed nor was there a supply of grain in the camp. For Galba had not feared a new war after the surrender was made and hostages given. And so the centurions and the military tribunes quickly came (met) together in council.

In that council they all understood that they were in the greatest danger of their safety (were faced with the gravest possible threat to their safety). For they saw that already nearly all the higher places (positions) were filled with a great (vast) number of the enemy. They perceived that they could not wait (hope) for reinforcements and that they had no supply of grain.

The Decision (p. 70)

And so, safety being almost despaired of already, some [of them] thought that, the baggage having been left, and a sortie made, they should hasten toward safety (they should leave their baggage, make a sortie, and straightway make for a safe place). [But] finally they decided in council to defend the camp.

The Sortie (p. 71)

The soldiers did what they were commanded and suddenly, when they made an attack upon the Gauls from all the gates, the enemy, thoroughly terrified, were unable to withstand [it]. Fortune thus changed (the tables turned), our men killed a large number of the enemy; they put the rest of them to flight, terrified. Now that all the enemy's forces were routed, our men withdrew into camp.

Galba Withdraws (p. 71)

And so, disturbed by this [continued] danger and the scarcity of grain, the next day, after he had burned all the buildings of that village, he hastened to return to the province; and, no enemy preventing (unhindered by any enemy), he led the legion into the [territory of the] Nantuates, then into [that of] the Allobroges, who dwell in the province, and there he placed (settled) it in winter quarters.

5. Revolt along the Seacoast

Many wars having (had) now been finished, the Belgians overcome, the Germans driven out, the Seduni conquered in the Alps, [and] Caesar thought that Gaul had been [completely] pacified (subjugated). At the beginning of summer, therefore, he set out for Illyricum, for he wanted to visit those tribes also and to learn (become acquainted with) those regions. An unexpected war, however, arose in Gaul. This was the cause of that war:

Publius Crassus, with the seventh legion, was wintering next to (near) the ocean in the [territory of the] Andes, but there was a scarcity of grain in these places. He therefore sent several captains and military tribunes away into the neighboring states for the sake of [getting] grain; in which (this) number (group) were Titus Terrasidius, sent to the Esuvii; Marcus Trebius Gallus, to the Curiosolites; and Quintus Velanius with Titus Silius, to the Veneti.

The Sea Power of the Veneti (p. 75)

The influence of this state was by far the most splendid (notable) of all these regions of the seacoast because the Veneti have very many ships (a large fleet), in which they are accustomed to sail to Britain, and because they surpass the rest in [their] knowledge and experience of naval affairs.

The Veneti Seize the Roman Envoys (p. 76)

The beginning of the war was made (brought about) by these conditions: They held Silius and Velanius, for they thought that through them they would recover [their] hostages. Their neighbors also, led on by the influence of the Veneti, held Trebius and Terrasidius for the same reason, and they formed a conspiracy among themselves, through their chiefs, envoys having been sent [around] quickly. They stirred up the remaining states, [urging them] to continue in that freedom which they had received from their forefathers. When the whole seacoast had been quickly led (brought around) to their opinion, they sent envoys to Publius Crassus. Said the envoys, "If you want to get yours back, return our hostages to us!"

Crassus Reports to Caesar (p. 77)

Caesar was informed of these things (all this) by Crassus. He ordered warships to be constructed on the Loire River, which flows into the ocean, and oarsmen to be gathered, from the province (and) sailors to be collected. After quickly managing (arranging) these matters, he himself hastened to the army, as soon as he was able through the time of year (as soon as the time of year permitted).

The Veneti Prepare to Resist (p. 78)

The Veneti and the rest of the states, learning of Caesar's arrival, decided to prepare war and to get ready those things especially which pertain to the use of ships. They were, however, relying much on the nature of the place (the terrain). After these plans were entered upon (adopted), they fortified the towns; they brought the crops in from the fields to the towns; they collected as many ships as possible at Venetia, where they thought Caesar would wage war first. In (for) that war, they joined to themselves as allies many neighboring [tribes]. [Furthermore], they summoned reinforcements from Britain, which was placed (lay) opposite those regions.

The Importance of the War (p. 80)

These were the difficulties of waging the war, which we have shown above; but nevertheless many things incited (urged) Caesar to this war—the injuries of the Roman horsemen being held, the renewal of war [made] after the surrender, the rebellion after hostages were given, the conspiracy of so many states—lest the rest of the tribes should think the same [actions] were allowed to them.

And so, when he perceived that nearly all the Gauls were eager for new things (revolution) and were being quickly incited to war, but that all men by nature strive for liberty and hate a state of slavery, he decided to distribute the army more widely before more states should form conspiracies among themselves.

Strategic Distribution of Garrisons (p. 81)

He therefore sent Titus Labienus, a lieutenant, with cavalry to the

[land of the] Treveri, who are next to the Rhine River. He ordered him
to visit the Remi and the rest of the Belgians and to hold them in
allegiance [to Rome] and to prevent the Germans who were said to be
summoned (who, it was said, were being summoned) by the Belgians
for help, if they should try to cross the river by force in ships.

Publius Crassus he ordered to set out for Aquitania with twelve
cohorts and a large number of cavalry, lest reinforcements be sent into
Gaul by these tribes and such great tribes be joined together [against
him]. The lieutenant Quintus Titurius Sabinus he sent into the [terri-
tory of the] Venelli, the Curiosolites, and the Lexovii with three legions
to isolate that band. He put Decimus Brutus in command of the fleet
and ships, which he had ordered to come together from the Pictones,
the Santoni, and the rest of the pacified (subjugated) regions, and
commanded him to set out for the Veneti as soon as he should be able
(could). He himself hastened thither with the remaining forces.

The Difficulties of the Campaign (p. 82)

Our fleet surpassed the fleet of the Veneti in speed alone and in stroke
of oars; the rest (other things) were more adapted to them [the Veneti]
because of the nature of the place (natural conditions) and the force
of the storms. For ours (our ships) were unable either to do them any
damage with the prow—so great was the solidity of these [enemy
ships]—nor was the dart hurled easily on account of their height. And
for the same reason they were less easily held in by grappling-hooks.

It was added (this was an added advantage) that, when the wind
began to rage and the ships had surrendered to (were at the mercy of)
the wind, they bore (endured) the storm more easily and rode at anchor
in the shallows more safely, and when left by the tide (when they were
left standing by low tide), they feared (need fear) no rocks. The mis-
fortune of all these things' [happening] was greatly to be feared for
our ships.

Unsuccessful Siege Operations (p. 85)

After a great many towns had been stormed, when Caesar perceived
that such great effort was taken in vain and that he could neither check
the enemy's flight after the towns were taken nor do them [any] damage, he determined to wait for the fleet.

The Fleet Arrives (p. 85)

[Now, when] it arrived and was first seen by the enemy, around two
hundred and twenty ships of theirs, completely ready and very well

fitted out with every kind of arms, having set out from the harbor, took up a position opposite ours. It was not evident enough to Brutus, who was in command of the fleet, or to the military tribunes and the centurions to whom the ships were assigned, one to each man what they should do and what plan of battle they should enter upon. For they knew that it could not be harmed (no damage could be inflicted) with the prow.

A Roman Trick (p. 86)

The rest of the contest was placed (lay) in courage, in which our soldiers easily surpassed [the enemy], and the more so because the action was carried out in the sight of Caesar and the whole army, and no deed [even] a little more brave could escape notice. For all the hills and higher places (ground), whence the view to the sea was near (clear), were held by the army.

A Complete Victory (p. 88)

And so, the sail yards cast down, the soldiers were striving with greatest (utmost) force to board the enemy's ships. After the barbarians had seen what (that this) was being done, a great many ships having been [thus] stormed, they hastened to seek safety in flight. And already, the ships turned in that direction whither the wind was bearing, such a great calm was made (came about) suddenly that they were not able to move from that place. Which (this) turn in affairs was most opportune, for ours assaulted the ships one by one so that few of all their number, with the aid (under cover) of night, reached land. The battle was fought (continued) from the fourth hour until sunset.

Unconditional Surrender (p. 88)

In this [one] battle the war of the Veneti and of the whole seacoast was finished. For all the youth, and all those of more serious (greater) age also had assembled there [for it] and they had driven all their ships into this [one] place. After these were lost, the others were unable either to withdraw to another place or to defend their towns. They therefore surrendered themselves and all their possessions to Caesar.

6. The Massacre of the Usipetes

The Arrival of the Germans (p. 90)

The tribe of the Suebi is by far the greatest (the most powerful) and the bravest of all the Germans. They were often waging war on neighboring tribes. The Usipetes and the Tencteri were no longer able to withstand the attacks of the Suebi. They therefore went out from their own territory and finally reached the River Rhine and that river they determined to cross not far from the sea into which the Rhine flows. The Menapii inhabited these regions.

The Menapii Prevent a Crossing (p. 91)

These [people] had fields and buildings on both banks of the river but, terrified by the arrival of the Germans, they fled into Gaul from those fields which they had had across the river, and, having placed garrisons on the bank, prevented the Germans from crossing.

The German Stratagem (p. 91)

When they were unable either to contend by force (attack) on account of the scarcity of boats or to cross secretly on account of the garrisons of the Menapii, they pretended to return to their own regions and, having gone a three-days' journey, returned again. Their cavalry, having completed this [return] journey in a single night, suddenly surprised the Menapii off-guard, who, having been informed by scouts of the departure of the Germans, had returned without fear to their fields across the Rhine. When they had killed these men and taken their boats, the Germans swiftly crossed the river and suddenly overwhelmed the remaining part of the Menapii. After they had seized all their buildings, they fed themselves on their supplies for the rest of the winter. Caesar, who was in Hither Gaul, was informed of these events.

Caesar Returns to Gaul (p. 92)

Caesar called the Gallic chiefs to him from all sides and, having strengthened their minds (bolstered their courage) and levied cavalry, he decided to wage war with the Germans. When a grain supply had been prepared and horsemen selected, he began to march toward those places where he had heard the Germans were. When he was not far distant from them, envoys came from them whose speech (message) was as follows: . . .

Treachery (p. 94)

The enemy, however, as soon as they had seen our cavalry, swiftly confused our men by a sudden attack. When many of our men had been cast down, they put the rest to flight and drove the terrified men so that they actually fled all the way to within sight of our column.

Caesar Seizes an Opportunity (p. 95)

Caesar ordered them to be held; he himself led all the troops from camp and ordered the cavalry to follow the column.

Caesar Moves against the Enemy (p. 96)

A triple battle line having been drawn up and the march quickly completed he suddenly came to the enemy's camp. The Germans, terrified by the swiftness of our advance and the departure of their [leaders], were violently alarmed. Our soldiers, in truth (on their part), aroused by the treachery of the Germans, broke into the camp. There, those who were able to take up arms quickly withstood our men for a little while and joined battle among the wagons and baggage; but the remaining throng of children and women—for they had gone out from home with all their people and had crossed the Rhine—began to flee. Caesar sent the cavalry to pursue and kill them. When the Germans, hearing a shout, saw their people being killed, throwing down their arms and leaving behind their standards, they hurled themselves from the camp, and when they had arrived at the confluence of the Meuse and the Rhine, and a great number had been killed, the rest cast themselves into the river and there they died of fear and by the violence of the river. All our men without exception returned safely to camp.

7. The First Invasion of Britain

Caesar's Reasons for Invading Britain (p. 101)

A small part of summer being left (when summer was all but over). Caesar, although in these parts the winters are (come) early, nevertheless hastened to set out for Britain. For he knew that in almost all the Gallic wars reinforcements had been sent from there to our enemies. He wished to visit the island, to observe the kind of men (to see what sort of men dwelt there), to learn (get information about) the places (locality), the harbors, and the approaches, nearly all of which were unknown to the Gauls. For no one except merchants went to Britain without good reason, nor was anything known [even] to them beyond the seacoast and those regions which are (lie) opposite Gaul.

His Preparations (p. 101)

And so, although he had called merchants to him from all sides, he was unable to find out the size of the island, what tribes dwelt there and how many [there were], what experience in war they had, and which harbors were suitable for a larger (rather large) number of ships. He therefore sent Gaius Volusenus ahead with a warship to find out these things. He ordered him to return to him as soon as possible, everything having been reconnoitered (after he had made a thorough reconnaissance).

He himself set out for the Morini with all his troops, for thence (at that point) the crossing to Britain was shortest. To this place he orders ships to come together from the neighboring regions on all sides, and (including) the fleet which he had made the previous summer.

An Exchange of Envoys (p. 102)

Meanwhile, his plan having become known and having been reported to the British through merchants, envoys came to him from several states of the island to promise that they would give hostages and do (obey) the commands of the Roman people. When he had heard this, having generously promised (he made generous promises), and having urged them to continue (he urged them to persevere) in that attitude, [and] sent them back home; along with them he sent Commius, whose courage and counsel (judgment) he considered good and whom he thought faithful to him, and whose influence in these regions was very great. He ordered him to visit what states he could and to encourage them to follow the faith of (to keep faith with) the Roman people, and to announce that he (Caesar) would come thither quickly (soon).

Final Preparations (p. 103)

Volusenus, having inspected the whole region, returned to Caesar on the fifth day, and gives a report on what he had seen there. . . .

The rest of the army he assigned to the lieutenants Quintus Titurius Sabinus and Lucius Aurunculeius Cotta to lead (who were to lead) it into the [territory of the] Menapii and those districts of the Morini from which no envoys had come. Publius Sulpicius Rufus, a lieutenant, he ordered to hold the harbor with that garrison which he [Caesar] thought sufficient.

The Task Force Sails (p. 105)

When these matters had been settled, and he had met with favorable weather for sailing, he put out to sea about the third watch and ordered the cavalry to set out for the farther harbor, board ship, and follow him. When this was being managed (accomplished) by whom (them) a little slowly, he himself, around the fourth hour of the day, reached Britain with the first ships and there saw the armed forces of the enemy drawn up on all the hills. Now the nature of the place was such, and the sea was held in so narrowly by mountains, that darts could be hurled down onto the beach from the places above (the heights). Having thought (thinking) this place not at all suitable for going out (disembarking), he waited until the ninth hour at anchor, until the rest of the ships should come together (while the rest of the ships gathered) there.

Meanwhile, when the lieutenants and the military tribunes had been called together, he pointed out both what he had learned from Volusenus and what he wanted done, and he warned [them] that everything should be attended to by them "smartly and at the right time." After he had sent them away, and had obtained a favorable wind and tide both at the same time, and had given the signal and lifted anchor, he set up (stationed, drew up) the ships on an open and level shore, having proceeded about seven miles from that place. But the barbarians, the Romans' plan having been learned, cavalry and charioteers having been sent ahead—a kind of troops which they were accustomed to use in battle—having followed with the remaining troops, were preventing our men from leaving the ships. (But the barbarians had learned the Roman's plan and had sent their cavalry ahead with charioteers—a kind of troops they were accustomed to use in battle—and then, following with the remaining troops, were [now] preventing our men from leaving the ships.)

Difficulties of the Landing (p. 107)

On account of (for) these reasons there was very great difficulty, because the ships on account of their size (draft) could not be placed (stationed) except in deep water, but the places being unknown to the soldiers, their hands burdened, weighted down with a great and heavy burden of arms, they had at once to leap down from the ships, find a footing in the surf, and fight with the enemy, while they [the enemy], either from dry land or having advanced a little way out into the water, all their members being unimpeded, and the places well known, were boldly hurling darts and urging on their trained horses. (There was extreme difficulty in disembarking for the following reasons: on account of their size, the ships could not be placed (stationed) except in deep water, and the soldiers, unfamiliar with the surroundings, their hands burdened, and weighted down with a great weight of armor, had at the same time to leap down from the ships, find a footing in the surf, and fight with the enemy, while the enemy, either from dry land or having advanced into shallow water, familiar with the place and with all their limbs free, were boldly hurling darts and urging on their trained horses.) Our men, terrified by these things (at this), and altogether unskilled in this kind of fight, did not use (display) the same eagerness and ardor which they were accustomed to use (show) in infantry battles.

A Hero Leads the Way (p. 110)

And, as our men were hesitating, mainly on account of the depth of the sea (water), he (the man) who was carrying the standard of the tenth legion, having called upon (prayed) the gods that this thing (venture) should turn out successfully for the legion, said, "Leap down, soldiers, unless you want to give up the eagle to the enemy. *I* certainly shall have discharged my duty to my state and my general." When he had said (shouted) this in a loud voice, he threw himself from the ship and began to carry the standard [forward] into (toward) the enemy. Then our men, having encouraged one another lest there be (not to allow) such a disgrace, all together leaped down from the ships. The others, when they had seen this from near-by ships, having followed them closely, approached the enemy.

A Desperate Struggle in the Surf (p. 111)

A fierce battle was waged on both sides. Nevertheless, our men, because they were unable either to keep ranks, maintain firmly (a firm) footing, or follow their standards, were violently disturbed. The enemy, however, all the shallows being known (since they knew all the shallows), whenever they saw from the beach any leaving the ship alone, their horses aroused (they spurred on their horses and) assailed the encumbered men, and several together hemmed in a few, [while] others hurled darts onto all from the exposed flank. When Caesar had noticed this, he ordered skiffs of (from) the warships and scouting boats to be filled with soldiers, and sent reserves to those whom he perceived to be hard pressed.

A Landing Is Effected (p. 111)

Our men, as soon as they stood firm on dry land, made an attack upon the enemy and put them to flight, but they were not able to pursue them farther (very far), because the cavalry had been unable to holds its course and take (reach) the island. This one [thing] was wanting to Caesar to his former fortune (In this one thing Caesar's usual good fortune failed him).

Peace (p. 113)

The enemy, overcome in battle, as soon as they recovered from flight (the rout), sent envoys to Caesar at once concerning (to treat of) peace; they promised that they would give hostages and do whatever he should order. Commius came together with these envoys, whom I had shown above to have been sent ahead by Caesar into Britain. They had captured him, having gone out from (when he left) the ship, (and) when he was bringing down to them Caesar's commands, and had thrown him into chains. Then, when the battle was over, they sent [him] back. In seeking peace (when suing for peace), they laid the blame for this crime upon the rabble, and on account of ignorance (pleading ignorance) they asked pardon. Caesar, having complained because, when (after) they had of their own accord sought peace from him, envoys having been sent, they had brought on war without cause, [nevertheless] said he forgave them and ordered (demanded) hostages; of which (these) they immediately gave a part (some), and said they would within a few days give a part (the rest), summoned from more remote places. Meanwhile they ordered their men to return to [their own] fields, and the chiefs began to assemble from every side and to surrender themselves and their states to Caesar.

The Cavalry Transports
Again Attempt to Reach Britain (p. 114)

Peace having been strengthened (when peace was established) by these arrangements, on the fourth day after they had come into Britain, the eighteen ships regarding which it was shown above (mentioned above), which had taken away (aboard) the cavalry, set sail from the upper harbor in a gentle wind. Which (now) when they were approaching Britain and were seen from (were in sight of) the camp, such a storm arose suddenly that not one of them was able to hold its course. Some were brought (driven) back to the same place from which they had set out and others, with their great danger (to their great peril), were hurled down to the lower part of the island which is nearer to the sunset (which lies toward the west). Which (these), however, their anchors cast (which had cast their anchors), sought the continent of necessity (had to make for the continent), since they were being filled by the waves (were shipping water).

A Disastrous Storm (p. 115)

It happened that same night that there was a full moon, which (and this) day is accustomed to cause (generally causes) very great ocean tides, and this was not known to our men. . . .

For there were no other ships in which they could be transported to Gaul, and everything useful for repairing ships was lacking and grain had not been provided in these places for the winter.

The Britons Plan a Rebellion (p. 117)

These things being known (knowing all this), the chiefs of Britain, who had gone to Caesar after the battle, conferred among themselves, since they understood that cavalry, ships, and grain were [all] lacking to the Romans, and learned (knew) from the smallness of the camp the small number of soldiers [they had]—the camp was rather narrow also, because Caesar had transported the legions without baggage—and they decided, a revolt having been made (by means of a revolt) to prevent our men [from getting] supplies and to protract the affair into wintertime, because they hoped that, with these ⌈invaders⌉ overcome and cut off from [any] return, no one afterwards would cross over to Britain for the sake of inflicting war. And so, the conspiracy formed again, they began gradually to leave camp and secretly to lead their men from the fields.

Caesar's Measures (p. 118)

But Caesar, although he had not yet learned their plans, nevertheless, both from the outcome (fate) of his ships and from ⌈the fact⌉ that they had not given the rest of the [promised] hostages, he suspected that it would be ⌈so⌉, as it happened. He was therefore preparing reserves for all ⌈possible⌉ misfortunes. For he was both carrying grain into camp from the fields daily, and was using the material (timber) and the copper of those ships which had been most seriously damaged for repairing the rest, and was ordering that those things (everything) useful for this use (purpose) be brought from Gaul. And so, since it was managed (things were worked out) by the soldiers with the greatest zeal, he brought it about that, although twelve ships had been lost, it was easily possible to sail with the rest.

The Britons Attack the Seventh Legion (p. 118)

While those things are being done, the legion which was called the seventh having been sent according to custom into the fields ⌈to get grain⌉, no suspicion of war having arisen at that time, while part (some) of the men remained in the fields and part (others) kept coming (were going and coming) to the camp, those who were on guard duty at the

gates of the camp reported to Caesar that a greater [cloud of] dust
than usual was to be seen in that direction in which the legion had
marched. Caesar ordered those cohorts which were on guard duty to set
out with him in that direction; of the rest, two to take over the guard
duty, and the rest to be armed and to follow him swiftly. When he had
gone forward from the camp a little farther (a short distance), he
noticed that his men were hard pressed and were withstanding (holding
out) with difficulty and that, the legion having been crowded together,
darts were being cast from all sides (that the crowded legion was being
showered with darts from all sides).

Caesar's Arrival Ends the Attack (p. 120)

Since our men were [thus] confused by these tactics, Caesar brought
help at the most favorable time, for at his coming the enemy halted and
our men recovered from fear. This done, having considered (judging)
the time to be unfavorable for joining battle, he restrained himself in
his place (held his ground) and after a short time led the legions back
to camp. While this is (was) being done, all of our men having been
occupied, they [the Britons] who were remaining in the fields departed.

There followed storms for many days, which (and this) both held
(kept) our men in camp and prevented the enemy from fighting.

The Britons Attack the Camp (p. 121)

Meanwhile the barbarians sent messengers in every direction and
reported to their [allies] the small number of our soldiers and pointed
out what a great opportunity was given of plunder to be made and of
themselves to be freed (of making plunder and of freeing themselves)
forever, the Romans having been driven (if the Romans were driven)
from the camp. A great multitude of infantry and cavalry having been
swiftly collected by these things (announcements), they came to the
camp. Caesar, having obtained around thirty horsemen whom Commius—of whom it has been said (we have spoken) before—had transported with him, set up the legions in battle line before the camp. The
battle on, the enemy was not able to bear the attack of our soldiers
longer (very long) and they fled. Having pursued whom (them) over
as great a space (as far) as by their running (speed) and strength they
could, they killed a great many of them; then all the buildings having
been set afire far and wide, they returned to camp.

The Enemy Sues for Peace (p. 121)

On the same day envoys sent by the enemy came to Caesar concerning (on the matter of) peace. For them Caesar doubled the number of hostages he had ordered (demanded from them) before, and ordered them to be led to Gaul.

Caesar Sails for the Continent (p. 122)

He himself, having obtained suitable weather, set sail a little after midnight; all of which (these ships) reached the continent safe and sound; but of these, two transports were unable to take (put in at) the same harbors as the rest and were carried down a little lower.

A Treacherous Attack (p. 122)

When about three hundred soldiers had disembarked from which (these) ships and were hastening to the camp, the Morini, whom Caesar had left pacified (subjugated) on setting out for Britain, led by the hope of plunder, at first stood around with a number of their men not so great (with not a very great . . .) and ordered our men to lay down their arms. But when these [our men], a circle having been formed (forming a circle), were defending themselves, about six thousand men came together at the shouting.

The Rescue (p. 123)

This thing announced (informed of this), Caesar sent the whole cavalry out of the camp as a help (to help) his men. Meanwhile our soldiers withstood the enemy's attack, and fought very bravely more than four hours and, few wounds having been taken (suffering few casualties themselves), killed a great many of them (the enemy). But after our cavalry came into sight, the enemy, weapons thrown away (throwing away their weapons), fled, and a great number of them were killed.

Punishment of the Morini and Menapii (p. 123)

The next day Caesar sent, with those legions which he had led back from Britain, Titus Labienus, a lieutenant, against the Morini who had made (instigated) the rebellion. They came into the power (fell into the hands) of Labienus almost all (almost to a man). But Quintus Titurius and Lucius Cotta, the lieutenants who had led [their] legions into the territory of the Menapii, after all their fields were devastated and their buildings burned, returned to Caesar because the Menapii had hid (gone into hiding) in the most dense [part of the] forest.

Winter Quarters (p. 124)

Caesar set up winter quarters in the Belgians (Belgian territory) of (for) all the legions. Thither two states in all sent hostages from Britain; the rest neglected [to do so].

8. Rebellion in the North

Act I, Tragedy at Aduatuca. Scene 1 (p. 128)

Arpineius and Junius report to the lieutenants what they have heard. They, disturbed by the unexpected news, even though these things were said (the statement was made) by an enemy, nevertheless considered that it must not be disregarded, and were greatly aroused by this thing, since (the fact that) the weak state of the Eburones would dare to make war on the Roman people of their own accord was scarcely to be believed. They therefore refer (submit) the question to a council, and a great dispute arises among them. Lucius Aurunculeius and a great many military tribunes and centurions of the first grade thought that nothing should be done rashly and that it should not be gone out (no departure should be made) from the winter quarters without Caesar's orders. They showed (sought to show) that even great forces of the Germans could be withstood in fortified winter quarters; that the fact that, many wounds having been inflicted (in spite of many wounds), they had actually withstood the enemy's first attack very bravely was proof [of this]; that they were not pressed for supplies; that meanwhile from the nearest winter quarters and from Caesar reserves would come (reach them); and lastly what was more light-minded and disgraceful than to make a plan, the enemy being adviser (on the advice of the enemy), in [deciding] supreme issues?

Against this Titurius exclaimed that they would do (act) too late when a greater band of the enemy, allied with the Germans, had come, or when some disaster had been taken (experienced) in the winter quarters nearest [them]. There was short (little) time for taking counsel; he thought that Caesar had left for Italy; and otherwise the Carnutes would not have made the plan of killing Tasgetius, nor would the Eburones, if he (Caesar) were present, have come to the camp in such contempt of us. He himself had regard, not for the enemy as instigator, but for the fact(s): the Rhine was close at hand, the death of Ariovistus and our former victories were for (a matter of) great sorrow to the Germans; Gaul was aflame, so many (at all) the indignities received (suffered) [since being] brought under the power of the Roman people, their former renown in military matters destroyed.

Finally, who was persuading himself of this, that Ambiorix had resorted to such a plan without certain hope [of success]? His own opinion was safe in either direction (either event): if nothing very serious was (occurred), they would reach the next legion without any danger; if all Gaul agreed (was in league) with the Germans, the only safety lay in speed. Indeed, what outcome might the plan of Cotta and those who were disagreeing with him have? In which (in this plan), if [there was] no present danger, yet certainly starvation was to be feared from a long (prolonged) siege.

The argument for each side having been had (discussed), since it was opposed sharply by Cotta and the first order of centurions, Sabinus said (cried), "Conquer (have your way) if you so will," and that in a rather loud voice, so that a great part (most) of the soldiers might hear; "Nor am I the sort of man," he said, "who would be the most seriously terrified of [all of] you by the danger of death. These men will understand; if anything rather serious should happen, they will demand of you the explanation; who (but they), if it be permitted through you (if you allow them), joined with the next winter quarters on the day after tomorrow, might sustain (would have) a common chance with the rest and not, driven back and removed far from the others (their comrades), perish either by the sword or from starvation."

They rise from the council; they grasp both [officers] and pray that they may not lead the affair to very great danger (may not utterly endanger the issue) by their disagreement and obstinacy: the thing is easy (there is no difficulty) whether they remain or depart, if only all feel (share) and approve one [plan]; on the contrary, they saw no safety in disagreement. The affair is prolonged by discussion until midnight. Finally Cotta, influenced (convinced), gives hands (yields): the opinion of Sabinus conquers (prevails).

Scene 2 (p. 136)

It is announced that they will leave at dawn. The remaining part of the night is consumed (spent) in watches (wakefulness), while each soldier looked around for his own things, what he could carry with him, and what out of the equipment of the winter quarters he would be forced to leave. At dawn they depart from the camp as men to whom it had been persuaded (who were persuaded) that the advice had been given not by an enemy but by a most friendly man, in a very long column and with heavy baggage.

Scene 3 (p. 137)

But the enemy afterwards, from the nocturnal din and watches (wakefulness), perceived (were aware of) their departure; (with) ambushes placed (posted) in the woods in two parts in an advantageous and hidden place about two miles away, they awaited the arrival of the Romans, and when the greater part of the part of the column had descended into a large defile, they showed themselves suddenly on both parts (sides) of that valley and began to press (harass) the last men (the rear guard) and to prevent the first (the vanguard) from the ascent, and to join battle in a place most unfavorable to our men.

Scene 4 (p. 138)

But a plan was not wanting to the barbarians. For their leaders ordered [it] to be announced in the whole line that no one should leave his place; that the plunder (booty) was theirs and whatever the Romans left was reserved for them; accordingly they should think (remember) that all was placed in (depended on) victory. Our men put all hope of safety in courage, though they were abandoned by their leader and by fortune, and as often as each cohort charged, a great number of the enemy fell in that section. This thing having been noticed (noticing this), Ambiorix orders it to be announced that they should hurl [their] darts from a distance and not approach nearer, and give way in whatever direction the Romans made an attack, and [then] pursue them again withdrawing (as they withdrew) to [their] standards. Which command having been obeyed by them (obeying this command) most carefully, whenever one cohort or other had withdrawn from the circle and had made an attack, the enemy very quickly withdrew. Meanwhile it was necessary for that part (flank) to be exposed and to take the darts on the exposed flank. Again, whenever they had begun to return to that place from whence they had gone forward, they were surrounded both by those who had given way and by those who had stood nearest; if, on the other hand, they chose to hold their ground, no place (opportunity) was left for courage nor, crowded together, were they able to avoid the darts hurled by such a multitude. Nevertheless, distressed by so many disadvantages, having suffered many wounds (with many men wounded), they were resisting (they stood firm), and [although] a great part of the day was consumed (spent), since the fight lasted from dawn until the eighth hour, they did nothing that was unworthy of them.

Scene 5 (p. 142)

Disturbed by these things (this), Quintus Titurius, when he had observed Ambiorix at a distance encouraging his men, sent his interpreter Gnaeus Pompeius to him to ask that he spare him and [his] soldiers. He (Ambiorix), called upon, responded [thus]: if he wished to confer with him, it was allowed (he could); he hoped what pertained to the soldiers' safety could be obtained from the multitude, [but] nothing would harm [Sabinus] himself, and for that he interposed (pledged) his own faith (and that he guaranteed). He (Sabinus) communicates with (suggests to) the wounded Cotta that if, he approved, they withdraw from the battle and confer together with Ambiorix; he hoped that it could be obtained (they would be able to obtain assurances) about their own and the soldiers' safety. Cotta said that he would not go to an armed enemy, and persisted in that [decision].

Scene 6 (p. 143)

Sabinus orders the military tribunes whom he had around him at the moment and the centurions of the first order to follow him and, when he had approached closer to Ambiorix, having been ordered to throw down his arms, does [the thing] commanded and orders his men to do the same. Meanwhile, while they are treating between them of terms and a longer speech is being set up (made) by Ambiorix deliberately, surrounded little by little, he is killed. Then indeed they shout out (acclaim) the victory and raise a yell according to their custom, and confuse our ranks, an attack having been made (by an attack). There Lucius Cotta, with a great part (proportion) of the soldiers, is killed fighting. The rest withdraw to the camp whence they had gone out. Out of (among) whom Lucius Petrosidius, a standard-bearer, when he was pressed hard by a great throng of the enemy, casts the standard within the rampart: he is killed fighting very bravely before the camp. They (the others) withstand the assault with difficulty until night; in the night—safety despaired of—they kill themselves to a man. A few, who had slipped away from the battle, come (make their way) by uncertain routes through the forest to Titus Labienus, a lieutenant, into the winter quarters, and inform him of the things done (of what has happened).

Interlude: Ambiorix Incites the Aduatuci and Nervii to Attack Cicero's Camp (p. 145)

Ambiorix, elated on account of this victory, immediately sets out with the cavalry for the [territory of the] Aduatuci, who were next to his kingdom. He delays neither night nor day (he marches without a break both night and day), and orders the infantry to follow him. The battle pointed out and the Aduatuci stirred up (having reported the battle and stirred up the Aduatuci), he comes the next day into the [territory of the] Nervii and exhorts [them] not to dismiss (let slip) the opportunity of freeing themselves forever and of punishing the Romans for those injuries which they have received. He points out that two lieutenants have been killed and that a large part of the army has perished; it would not be a difficult matter for the legion which was wintering with Cicero, surprised (if taken by surprise) to be killed (cut down). He declares himself assistant (offers his own assistance) for that purpose. By this speech he easily persuades the Nervii.

Act II, Gallic Successes Grow. Scene 1 (p. 147)

Messengers therefore having been sent at once to the Ceutrones, the Grudii, the Levaci, the Pleumoxii, and the Geidumni, who were all under their [the Nervii's] power, they collect as great bands as possible and suddenly rush on the winter quarters of Cicero, to whom the report of Titurius' death had not yet been conveyed. It happens to him also, what was necessary (as was inevitable), that some soldiers who had gone into the forest for the procuring of (to procure) wood and defenses, are cut off by the unexpected arrival of the cavalry. After these are surrounded, in a large band the Eburones, Nervii, Aduatuci, and the allies and dependents of all these begin to assault the legion. Our men swiftly rush to arms, [and] mount the rampart. That day is scarcely endured (they scarcely hold out that day), because the enemy were placing all their hope in speed and were trusting that, having gained this [initial] victory, they would be victors forever (to the end).

A dispatch is immediately sent to Caesar by Cicero, with great rewards offered if they succeeded in delivering them. (But) all the roads (are) blocked, (and) those sent are killed. By night, from that material which they had collected for defenses, they erect as many as one hundred and twenty towers. With extraordinary speed they finish what seemed to be lacking to (they rectify all apparent deficiencies in) the fortifications. On the next day the enemy, a much greater force having been collected (with a far greater force which they have assembled), assault the camp, and fill in the ditch. It is resisted by ours (our troops resist) in the same way as the day before. This same thing is done in turn on the remaining (following) days. For not a moment of the night-time is there a break in the work; no opportunity for rest is given to sick or wounded.

Scene 2 (p. 151)

Then the leaders and chiefs of the Nervii, who had some access of speech (some opportunity to speak with) and cause (basis) of friend-ship with Cicero, say they wish to confer [with him]. When the oppor-tunity (permission) is given, they mention the same [argument] which Ambiorix had done (presented) to Titurius: all Gaul, they said, was in arms; the Germans had crossed the Rhine; the winter quarters of Caesar and of the others are being stormed. They add [the news] of Sabinus' death; they exhibit (bring forward) Ambiorex for the sake of making faith (as an assurance of their sincerity). They say they (the Romans) are mistaken if they hope (expect) any protection from those who lack confidence in their own affairs (those who are themselves in a desperate situation); that they themselves are in this mind (of this attitude) toward Cicero and the Roman people, that they object to nothing except [to having] winter quarters [in their territory] and do not wish this custom to become established; that it is permitted to them to (that they may) depart safely out of the winter quarters through them (by their permission) and without fear set out in whatever direc-tion they wish. To this Cicero replies one thing (makes only one answer): that it is not the custom of the Roman people to accept an agreement (terms) from an armed enemy; if they would depart from (lay down) their arms they might use him as assistant (his assistance) and send envoys to Caesar; he hoped that through his fair dealing they would obtain what they sought.

Scene 4 (p. 153)

But so great was the courage of the soldiers and such their presence of mind that, although they were scorched by the flame on all sides and were being pressed hard by the vast multitude of darts, and knew that all their baggage and all their fortunes were burning up, not only did no one leave the rampart, but scarcely anyone even looked back and at the time all were fighting very fiercely and bravely. This day was by far the most serious for our men, but nevertheless it had this outcome, that a vast number of the enemy were wounded and killed that day, as they had pressed closely under the very rampart and the last (those in the rear) gave no [chance of] retreat to the front lines.

Scene 5 (p. 156)

The more serious and violent was the siege from day to day, and especially because, with a great part (proportion) of the soldiers exhausted (disabled) by wounds, the responsibility had come (fallen) on a small number of defenders, so much the more frequent were the dispatches and messengers sent off to Caesar; of whom a part (some), captured [by the enemy], were put to death with torture within sight of our men. There was one Nervian within, by the name of Vertico, born in a distinguished place (of high rank), who had fled to (taken refuge) with Cicero from the first (beginning of the) siege, and had [since] shown faith (loyalty) to him. This man persuades a slave by the hope of liberty and by rich rewards to carry a dispatch to Caesar. He brings it out attached to a javelin, and being a Gaul among Gauls, he arrives (gets through) to Caesar with no suspicion (all unsuspected). The danger of Cicero and the legion is made known through him.

Act III, The Reversal of Fortunes. Caesar to the Rescue
Scene 1, The Camp of Caesar (p. 157)

When he has received the dispatch about the eleventh hour of the day, Caesar immediately sends a messenger into the [territory of the] Bellovaci to Marcus Crassus, a quaestor, whose winter quarters were twenty-five miles distant from him; he commands the legion to set out at midnight and come to him quickly. Crassus goes out with the messenger. He sends another to Gaius Fabius, a lieutenant, that he may lead his legion into the lands of the Atrebates, where he knew he himself would have to march. He writes to Labienus to come with his legion up to the boundaries of the Nervii if he can do [it] in accord with the interests of the state. For the remaining part of the army he does not think he ought to wait, because it is a little farther (too far) away; he collects about four hundred cavalry from the nearest winter quarters.

About the third hour he is informed by forerunners of Crassus' arrival (approach), and that day advances about twenty miles. He puts Crassus in charge of Samarobriva and assigns him a legion because he was leaving there the baggage of the army, the hostages of the states, public letters (documents), and all the grain which he had brought thither for the sake of the winter to be endured (for their sustenance during the winter). Fabius, as ordered, having delayed not much (with little delay) meets him on the march with [his] legion. . . .

He comes by forced marches into the territory of the Nervii. There he learns from prisoners what is going on with (in regard to) Cicero, and in how (what) great danger the situation is. Then he persuades a certain one of the Gallic horsemen by means of rich rewards to carry a letter to Cicero. He sends this written in Greek letters lest, if the letter be intercepted, our plans be learned (discovered) by the enemy.

He advises (instructs) him, if he cannot approach [closely], to cast within the fortfications a dart with the letter tied to the thong. In the dispatch he writes that he has set out with the legions, and will quickly (soon) be near; he urges [him] to keep up [his] original courage. The Gaul, having feared the danger (fearing the danger), threw the javelin as had been commanded. This by chance clung to a tower, nor having been noticed (but being unnoticed) by our men for two days, is seen on the third day by a certain soldier and, removed, is brought to Cicero. He reads aloud in an assembly of the soldiers [the message which he has already] read through, and it affects them all with very great joy. Then, the smoke of the fires is seen from a distance, which thing (and this) drives out every doubt of the coming of the legions.

Scene 2 (p. 161)

The Gauls, the news being learned through scouts, leave (give up) the siege; they hasten toward Caesar with all [their] forces. These were [amounted to] around 60,000 armed men. The opportunity having been given (when the chance arises), Cicero asks again for a Gaul from that same Vertico whom we have mentioned above, to deliver a dispatch to Caesar. He warns him to make the journey cautiously and carefully. He writes in the dispatch that the enemy has retired from him and has turned all (the whole host) against him (Caesar). This dispatch having been brought about midnight, Caesar informs his men and encourages them to fight with spirit. The next day at dawn he moves camp and having advanced about four miles, he observes a multitude of the enemy across a large (broad) valley and a stream. It was a matter of great danger to struggle in an unfavorable place with such large forces; then, because he knew that Cicero had been freed from the siege, with composure (without anxiety) he thought he should leave off from (lessen his) speed. He halts and fortifies a camp in the most level place possible and this camp, although it was small in itself—scarcely of seven thousand men, especially with no baggage—he nevertheless drew it together as much as possible by means of narrow streets, with that plan, that he come into the greatest possible contempt to the enemy (with the purpose of making the enemy underrate him as much as possible). Meanwhile, scouts sent off in every direction, he finds out by what route he can most advantageously cross the valley. . . .

At dawn the enemy's cavalry comes to the camp and joins battle with our cavalry. Caesar deliberately orders the cavalry to yield and to withdraw into camp, and at the same time, orders the camp to be fortified on all sides with a higher rampart and the gates to be blocked up, and it to be run about as much as possible in these things to be managed and [the work] to be done with pretense of fear (and as much confusion and pretense of fear as possible to be shown in the execution of these arrangements).

The enemy, invited (led on) by all these things, lead their troops across and set up a battle line in an unfavorable place, but our men having been led down even from the rampart, they approach closer and hurl darts within the defenses from every direction, and, heralds sent about, they order it to be announced that if anyone, whether Gaul or Roman, wishes to cross over to them (their side) before the third hour, he may do so without danger, [but] after that time there would be no opportunity.

Scene 3 (p. 166)

Then Caesar, a sortie having been made from all the gates and the cavalry sent forth, quickly put the enemy to flight, so that not a man remained behind to fight at all, and he kills a great number of them and strips them all of their arms.

Having feared (fearing) to follow them farther, because woods and marshes lay between, he reaches Cicero that same day with all his men safe. He admires the towers erected, the sheds, and the fortifications of the enemy. The legion having been led out, he learns that not [even] every tenth soldier is left without a wound; from all these things he judges with how (what) great danger and with how (what) great courage the operations have been managed (carried out). Cicero he praises highly for his merit, and the legion [likewise]; he calls upon the centurions and the military tribunes one by one, whose courage, he had learned from Cicero's testimony, was remarkable. He learns more surely (exactly) of (from) the prisoners about the fate of Sabinus and Cotta.

Epilogue (p. 168)

The next day, an assembly having been made (called), he explains the action [which has been] carried on and comforts and encourages the soldiers; what damage (the damage which) was received (suffered) through the fault and rashness of the lieutenant, that [damage] he shows (explains) should be borne with the greater composure because, the disaster avenged by the favor of the immortal gods and by their [own] courage, neither joy of long duration is left to the enemy nor a very long (enduring) grief to them.

9. All Gaul in Arms

Part 1, Secret Councils in Gaul (p. 169)

Moved by this opportunity, the chiefs of Gaul began to enter upon plans of war more freely and boldly. Councils having been called (calling councils) together in wooded and remote places, they lament the death of Acco. They point out that this [same] fate may befall them. They bewail the common fate of Gaul. They ask for those [volunteers], with (offering) every reward, who will make a beginning of war and recover in danger of their own heads (at the risk of their lives), the liberty which they have received from [their] forefathers. They say that among the first things, a plan must be had whereby Caesar may not come to (may be prevented from reaching) [his] army. This was easy, [they said], because neither would the legions dare, in the absence of their commander, to go out of winter quarters, nor could the commander get through to the legions without a garrison. Lastly, [they say], it is better to be killed in the battle line than not to recover the ancient warlike glory and freedom which they received from [their] forefathers.

The Carnutes Volunteer to Lead the Rebellion (p. 171)

These things having been said (at these words), the Carnutes declare that they refuse (will shirk) no danger for the sake of the common safety and they promise that they the first of all will make war, and since they cannot exchange hostages lest the matter be made known (lest the news get out), they ask that it be sanctioned by an oath and (of) loyalty [given] with all the military standards gathered together, lest, the war begun, they be deserted by the others. Then, after the Carnutes are highly praised, and an oath given by all who were present, and the time for this affair decided, it is departed from the council (the council is adjourned).

Massacre of Roman Civilians at Cenabum (p. 172)

When that day came, the Carnutes at a given signal, rushed on Cenabum, and kill the Roman citizens who had stood (settled) there for the sake (purpose) of carrying on business, and take their goods. The news is swiftly conveyed to all the states of Gaul.

The Man of Destiny (p. 172)

Informed of the slaughter of the Romans, Vercingetorix, an Arvernian and a man of the greatest power, calls his clients and easily sets them on fire. His plan having been made known, they rush together to arms. He is prevented (opposed) by Gobanitio and the rest of the chiefs. He is driven out of the town of Gergovia. Nevertheless he does not give up but holds in the fields a levy of needy and desperate men. When this band has been collected, he brings over to his own opinion whomsoever from the state he approaches. He urges them to take up arms for the cause of the common freedom. When great forces have been collected, those by whom a little [while] before he had been driven out, he drives from the state. By his own men he is called king. He sends envoys in every direction; he urges them to remain in (keep) faith. He swiftly joins to himself many neighboring states and all those who are near the ocean.

Vercingetorix Is Made Commander in Chief (p. 173)

By the consent of all command is brought to (conferred upon) him. Which (this) power having been obtained, he levies hostages on all these states. He commands a certain number of cavalry to be led to him swiftly. . . .

An army having been assembled quickly by [fear of] these punishments, he sends Lucterius, a Cadurcan, a man of the greatest daring, against the Ruteni; he himself sets out against the Bituriges. At his coming the Bituriges send envoys to the Haeduans, with whom they were in alliance, to ask for help in order to withstand more easily the enemy's forces. The Haeduans send troops of cavalry and of infantry to help the Bituriges. Who (these), when they had come to the river Loire which separates the Bituriges from the Haeduans, having delayed there a few days and not daring to cross the river, they return home, and report to our envoys that they had returned, having feared (because they feared) treachery. When the Haeduans had gone, the Bituriges immediately join themselves with the Arverni.

Caesar's Difficulty (p. 175)

These things (all this) having been reported to Caesar in Italy, he set out for Farther Gaul. When he had arrived there, he was affected by (faced with) a great difficulty as to what way (how) he could reach the army. For, if he summoned the legions into the province in his absence, he knew they would have to fight a battle on the way; if he himself should hasten to the army he saw that not even to those who seemed to be pacified at that time could his safety be entrusted without fear.

The Revolt Spreads (p. 176)

Meanwhile Lucterius, the Cadurcan, sent to the Ruteni, won that state over to the Arverni. Having gone forward to the Nitiobroges and Gobali, he accepts hostages from both, and a great band having been collected, he hastens to make a sortie into the province towards Narbo. When this was reported, Caesar hastened to set out for Narbo. When he had arrived there, he strengthens the fearing (fearful); he sets up garrisons among the Provincial Ruteni, the Volcae Arecomici, the Tolosates, and around Narbo, which places were next to the enemy (which were the lands bordering on enemy territory); part of the troops from the province and the reinforcements which he had led (brought) from Italy, he orders to come to the [territory of the] Helvii, who are neighbors to the Arverni. When these things (defenses) were prepared, Lucterius having been restrained and removed (gotten out of the way) because he did not dare to lead forces into the (that) garrison, Caesar sets out for the Helvii.

Caesar Strikes across the Mountains (p. 177)

Although the Cevennes Mountains, which separate the Arverni from the Helvii, impeded (blocked) the road with very deep snow in the most severe time of the year, nevertheless, the snow cleared away and the roads opened by the supreme effort of the soldiers, he came to the lands of the Arverni. Which (these) being suddenly surprised, because they thought themselves to be fortified by the Cevennes as by a wall, Caesar orders the cavalry to roam about as widely as possible, and inflict fear on (terrorize) the enemy to the utmost [of their ability].

Rumor and reports [of all this] are quickly brought to Vercingetorix, whom all the Arverni, terrified, stand around and beseech him to take counsel for their fortunes and not to allow them to be torn asunder by the enemy, especially since he sees the whole war to be brought over to (shifted toward) them. Moved by which (these) entreaties, he moves camp from the Bituriges over toward the Arverni.

Caesar Reaches the Army (p. 180)

But Caesar, having delayed in these places for two days, left the army on pretext of collecting reinforcements and cavalry; he places Brutus in command of these troops; he advises him that the cavalry should roam (to keep the cavalry roaming) about in every direction as widely (extensively) as possible; [he says] that he will take pains not to be absent from camp more than three days. These things having been decided, he came to Vienne by forced marches. There having found the new cavalry which he had sent ahead many days before, the march having been interrupted neither by day nor by night, he hastens through the territory of the Haeduans, into the Lingones where two legions were wintering. When he had arrived there, he sends [word] to the other legions, and collects them all in one place, before [news of] his arrival could be reported to the Arverni.

Vercingetorix Attacks the Boii (p. 180)

This having been learned (on learning this), Vercingetorix led [his] army back again into the [land of the] Bituriges, and having set out from there, he determines to attack Gorgobina, a town of the Boii.

This affair was bringing (causing) great difficulty to Caesar in making a plan. For he feared that, if he should keep the legions in one place for the remaining part (remainder) of the winter, Gorgobina having been taken by storm (with the fall of Gorgobina), all Gaul would revolt; but if he should lead the legions out of winter quarters too early, he would be in difficulty over the supply of grain (would suffer from lack of grain).

Caesar Marches to the Relief of Gorgobina (p. 182)

It seemed better, however, to endure all the difficulties than to alienate the good will of all his [allies] by tolerating so great an injury. Having therefore urged the Haeduans to supply provisions, he sends messengers to the Boii to inform them of his coming and to urge them to continue in faith (remain loyal) and withstand the enemy's attack with great courage. Having left (leaving) two legions and the baggage of the whole army at Agedincum, he sets out for the Boii. The next day, when he had reached Vellaunodunum, a town of the Senones, he decided to storm it lest he should leave any enemy behind him (in his rear), and in two days surrounded it with a rampart. On the third day, envoys having been sent from the town regarding surrender, he orders arms to be brought together, beasts of burden led forth, and six hundred hostages given. He leaves Gaius Trebonius, a lieutenant, to accomplish these (this); he himself in order to make the march as soon as possible sets out for Cenabum of the Carnutes.

He arrives there in two days. Camp having been pitched before the town, he puts off the siege to the next day, orders the soldiers [to do] whatever may be useful for the [coming] action and, having feared (fearing) that the inhabitants of Cenabum might flee by night from the town, he orders two legions in arms to keep guard.

He Captures Cenabum (p. 183)

The Cenabenses, having gone out from the town silently a little before midnight, began to cross the river. Which having been reported (when this was reported) by scouts, Caesar sent in, the gates having been set afire, the legions which he had ordered to be light-armed (ready for action), and gets possession of the town, almost all the enemy having been taken, because the narrow place (narrowness) of the bridge and the road had hindered the flight of the multitude. He pillages and burns the town. He gives the booty to the soldiers. He leads the army across the Loire and arrives in the territory of the Bituriges.

Vercingetorix, when he learned of Caesar's coming, gave up the siege and sets out to meet Caesar. The latter began to storm Noviodunum, a town of the Bituriges, placed along the way (lying along his route). From which (this) town, when envoys had come to him regarding surrender, in order to accomplish the thing as swiftly as possible, he orders arms to be brought, horses to be led forth, and hostages to be given.

The Sudden Arrival of Vercingetorix (p. 184)

A part of the hostages having been already handed over, while the rest (remaining affairs) were being managed, centurions and a few soldiers having been sent in, the enemy's cavalry, which had gone before the army of Vercingetorix, is seen afar off. As soon as the townspeople saw which (it) and came into (saw) hope of aid, they began to take arms, a shout having been raised, and to close the gates, and fill the wall. The centurions in the town, when they had understood that some new plan was being entered upon (adopted) by the Gauls, seized the gates with drawn swords and withdrew all their men safely.

Caesar orders the cavalry to be led out from camp and begins a cavalry battle. He sends about four hundred German horsemen as relief to his own men [who were] in difficulty. The Gauls were unable to withstand their attack and, thrown into flight, having lost many men, they withdrew to the column.

Who (these) having been driven back, the townspeople, again terrified, led out to Caesar those by whom they thought that the multitude had been aroused to arms [and whom they had] arrested. Which (these) things having been accomplished, Caesar set out for the town Avaricum, which was the greatest and most fortified in the territory of the Bituriges, because, this town taken, he was confident that he would bring the state of the Bituriges under his power.

The Gauls Change Their Strategy (p. 186)

Vercingetorix, so many disasters having been taken (after suffering so many disasters) at Vellaudunum, Cenabum, and Noviodunum, calls his men together in council. He shows that the war must be waged by a far different plan than the one by which it had been carried on before. In every manner it must be striven after this thing (they had to see to it) that the Romans were warded off from (were prevented from obtaining) supplies. This was easy, [he said], because they were superior in cavalry and because they were assisted by the time of year; fodder could not be cut; the scattered enemy [must] necessarily seek it from buildings (granaries); all these could be killed daily by the cavalry. Besides, he said, for the sake of the common welfare the benefit of property must be disregarded. The villages and buildings must be burned wherever the Romans might seem to be able to go for fodder. An abundance of these things is at hand for them because those in whose lands the war was being waged were assisting them with their resources. The Romans either would not bear the scarcity, or would go forward farther from the camp with great danger (to their peril). Furthermore, those towns ought to be burned which were not [made] safe from all danger by fortification or by the nature of the place (by natural conditions). If these things seemed severe, these things ought to be considered much more severe, that their children and wives be led into slavery, and they themselves killed; which (and this) is certain to happen to the conquered.

This opinion having been approved by the agreement of all, in one day more than twenty cities of the Bituriges were burned. The same was done in the rest of the states. In every direction fires are seen.

It is deliberated (they deliberate) about Avaricum in common council, whether it seemed good that it be burned or defended (whether it should be burned or defended). The Bituriges fell down at the feet of all the Gauls, [begging] not to be forced to burn with their own hands the most beautiful city in almost all of Gaul, which was the [chief] garrison and ornament of the state. They say they can defend [it] easily by the [very] nature of the place because, surrounded on nearly all sides by a river and a marsh, it had [only] one narrow entrance. The favor is granted to those asking (who ask). Suitable defenders for (of) the town are chosen.

The Romans in Desperate Need of Supplies (p. 191)

He does not cease to urge the Boii and the Haeduans [to act] in regard to a supply of grain. Some of whom (these), because they acted with no eagerness, were not helping much, others, not in (not having) great resources because the state was small, quickly used up what they had. The army having been affected by the extreme difficulty [in the matter] of provisions—because of the poverty of the Boii, the negligence of the Haeduans, and the cities burned (destroyed by fire)—to such a point that the soldiers were actually without grain for a great many days and had come to extreme famine. Nevertheless not a word was heard from them unworthy of the honor of the Roman people and former victories. . . .

When the towers had approached (been moved up) close to the wall, Caesar learned from prisoners that Vercingetorix, his provisions used up, had moved camp nearer Avaricum and that he had set out thither with cavalry and light-armed troops for the purpose of ambush, where he thought that our men would come on the following day to forage.

Caesar Attemps a Surprise Attack on the Camp of Vercingetorix (p. 192)

Which things having been learned (after this was learned), having set out silently at midnight, he came to the enemy's camp in the morning. The arrival of Caesar having been swiftly learned through scouts, they hid their wagons and baggage in very dense woods and drew up all [their] forces in a high and open place. . . .

Finally the Gauls, because nothing had come up (succeeded), on the next day made a plan to flee from the city, Vercingetorix encouraging and commanding (under the encouragement and leadership of Vercingetorix). By night they were already preparing to do this, when the matrons rushed forward and, having cast themselves weeping at the feet of their men, begged [them] with all [their] prayers not to surrender themselves and their common children (the children who belonged to them in common) to the enemy for punishment, whom weakness of nature and of strength would hinder from taking flight. When they saw them persisting in the opinion (plan), because very often in supreme danger fear does not take (does not admit feelings of) compassion, they began to cry out and make signs to the Romans about the [proposed] flight. The Gauls, terrified by the fear that the roads were taken possession of by the cavalry of the Romans, gave up the plan.

The Romans Storm Avaricum (p. 197)

On the next day Caesar, a tower having been moved forward and the works completed which he had begun to make, when a great storm had arisen—and he considered the weather not disadvantageous for making (carrying out) this plan, because he saw the guard on the wall was rather incautiously distributed—he ordered his men to engage in [their] work rather sluggishly too, and showed what he wanted done, the legions having been prepared in secret within the sheds; and then having encouraged them [with the reminder] that at length they would receive the fruit of victory for such great efforts, he offered rewards to those who should go up the wall first, and gave the signal to the soldiers. They suddenly flew [together] from all sides and quickly filled the wall.

The enemy, terrified by the new action, [and] having been cast (driven) down from the wall and the towers, stood firm in open places in wedge-shaped masses, with this mind (intention), that, if from any side it was (anyone should) come against [them], they would fight, a l'ne having been drawn up (in battle line).

When they saw that no one let himself (leaped) down onto the level place, but on every side on the whole wall it was (they were) being surrounded, having feared (fearing) that hope of flight would be altogether taken away, arms having been cast away (they cast away their arms and) swiftly sought the farthest parts (corners) [of the city], and there a part (some) were killed by the soldiers as they were pressing one another in the narrow gates, a part (others) by the cavalry, having (when they had) gone out from the gates. Nor was there anyone who was eager for plunder. Thus, aroused by the slaughter at Cenabum and by the effort of the work, they spared neither those worn out with age, nor women, nor [even] infants.

Part 2

Vercingetorix Encourages the Gauls. His Popularity (p. 199)

The next day Vercingetorix, a council having been called (calling a council), comforted and encouraged them not to be very much cast down in spirit, nor to be disturbed by the disaster. [He said] the Romans had not overcome because of courage nor in battle line, but in the science of siege, in which they themselves were unskilled. They make a mistake, (he said), if any wait for (expect) in war [that] all outcomes of actions [will be] favorable. It had never seemed good to him that Avaricum be defended (to defend Avaricum); of which thing (of this) he had them as witnesses; it was brought about by the imprudence of the Bituriges and the excessive compliance of the rest that this injury (loss) was received (sustained). Nevertheless he would swiftly (soon) refresh it (set the matter right) by greater advantages. For those states which disagreed with the rest of the Gauls, these by his care he would unite, and make one council of all Gaul, whose agreement (union) not [even] the world could oppose; and he himself had nearly brought it about already. Meanwhile it was right for it to be asked (to ask) of them for the sake of the common welfare, that they should begin to fortify the camp, in order more easily to withstand the sudden attacks of the enemy.

This speech was not displeasing to the Gauls, and especially because he was not cast down, so great an injury having been received (in spite of such a terrible disaster), nor had he hid in a secret place nor fled the sight of the multitude; and he was thought to foresee in mind the more (to be more foresighted) because at the outset he had thought Avaricum should be burned, and afterwards, that it should be abandoned. And therefore, as unsuccessful things (reverses) impair the influence of other generals, so day by day the dignity of this [one] increased, an injury having been received (after he suffered a mishap).

The Gauls Reorganize (p. 201)

First the Gauls began at this time to fortify the camp and these men unaccustomed to toil are so disturbed in mind they thought (think) everything should be suffered and carried through which was ordered. Nor was Vercingetorix working less hard than he promised, in order to unite the remaining states, and was winning over their chiefs by every means. He levies a certain number of soldiers from the states, and commands all the archers, of whom there was a great number in

Gaul, to be sent to him. By these things (this means) that which had been (was) lost at Avaricum is filled out (made up for) quickly.

Caesar Opens a New Campaign; He Sends Labienus into the North and Himself Advances against the Main City of the Arvernians, Gergovia (p. 201)

Caesar, having delayed at Avaricum for many days, and having obtained there a very large supply of grain and of other provisions, refreshes the army (provides the army with refreshment) from toil and want. Winter having now been nearly finished (since winter is now nearly over) and since by the very season of the year he is called (invited) to carry on the war, he determined to set out against the enemy. . . .

The army he divided into two parts. He gave four legions to Labienus to be led against the Senones and the Parisii; he himself led six against the Arverni to the town of Gergovia along the Elaver River. Part of the cavalry [also] he assigned to him, and a part he left for himself.

Vercingetorix Attempts to Keep Caesar on the East Bank of the Elaver (p. 204)

This thing having been learned (when he got this news), Vercingetorix, all the bridges of that river having been destroyed (destroyed all the bridges of that river and) begins to march along the other side of the river. When each army was in view of the other, Vercingetorix pitched camp nearly opposite Caesar's camp, scouts having been stationed so that the Romans could nowhere, a bridge having been built (by building a bridge), lead troops across.

Caesar Dupes Vercingetorix (p. 204)

This situation (turn of affairs) was in (a matter of) great difficulty to (for) Caesar, lest he should be hindered from [crossing] the river for the greater part of the summer, because the Elaver is not accustomed to (cannot) be crossed by a ford (fording) before nearly autumn. Lest this should happen, therefore, the camp having been pitched in a wooded place, opposite one of those bridges which Vercingetorix had taken care to destroy, he remained in a place of concealment with two legions the next day; the remaining forces, with all the baggage, he sent [out] as he had been accustomed (as usual), certain cohorts having been cut in half, so that the number of the legions would seem to stand [as before]. These having been ordered (he ordered these) to advance as far as possible, (and) when now from the time of day he could make inference (he could infer) that they had come to the camp, Caesar begins to rebuild the bridge with those piles the lower part of which was entire. The work having been swiftly done and the legions led over, and a suitable place (site) chosen for the camp, he recalled the remaining troops. Vercingetorix, the move having been learned (on learning this), in order not to be forced to fight against his will, went ahead by forced marches.

The Situation at Gergovia (p. 205)

Caesar reached Gergovia from that place in five marches, and after a light cavalry battle had been made (fought) on that day, the site of the city having been viewed (and he had seen the site of the city), which placed (situated) on a very high mountain, had all the approaches difficult (was difficult of access), so that he despaired of a siege; he decided that nothing regarding the siege must be done before the matter of provisions had been arranged. But Vercingetorix, camp having been pitched (when he had pitched camp) on a mountain near the city, stationed forces of the single states separately around him at moderate intervals and, all the hills of this ridge having been seized, he furnished (presented) a dreadful appearance (aspect), and the chiefs of those states which he had chosen for making a plan (plans) with him he ordered to come to him daily at dawn whether (in case) it seemed that anything had to be communicated or anything had to be taken care of; nor did he scarcely put a day between (let a day intervene) but that, archers having been put between (interspersed) in (for) cavalry battle, he would test what there was of spirit and courage in each of his men (and he scarcely let a day pass without making test of the spirit and courage of his men by means of cavalry skirmishes in which archers were interspersed).

A Strategic Hill (p. 206)

There was opposite the city a hill below the very roots (foot) of the mountains admirably fortified and cut off from every direction (in entirely open country), which (and) if our men held it, it seemed they would prevent (cut off) the enemy from a large part of the water [supply] and prevent them from free foraging. But that place was held by them with a garrison, not [however] very strong. Nevertheless Caesar, having gone out from camp in the silence of the night, before reserves could come from the city, the garrison having been cast down (overthrew the garrison), having got possession of the place (got possession of the place) [and] he stationed two legions there; and he [then] constructed a double ditch twelve feet wide from the greater camp to the lesser (the new camp), in order that they (the soldiers) could safely cross over even one by one from (in case of) a sudden attack of the enemy.

The Leaders of the Haedui Conspire against Caesar (p. 208)

While these things were being carried on at Gergovia, Convictolitavis, an Haeduan, instigated by the Arvernians with money (bribed by the Arvernians, confers with certain young men of whom Litaviccus was the leader and his brothers, young men born from (of) a most splendid (an illustrious) family. He imparts (divides) the reward (money) with these and exhorts them to remember that they are free and born to power. [He says] that the state of the Haeduans is the only one which holds apart (stands in the way of) the most certain victory of Gaul; the rest were being restrained (held back) by its influence; which state having been led over (if this state was won over), there would not be a place in Gaul for the Romans of standing (to stand). He had been affected by (received) some favor of Caesar, nevertheless [only] so that he held a most just cause before him (but only because he had obtained from Caesar a decision required by justice), but he renders more (would rather give his services) to the common liberty. But why should the Haeduans come (appeal) to Caesar as judge concerning their own justice and laws, rather than the Romans to the Haeduans? The young men having been quickly led away (brought to this opinion) by the speech of the magistrate and by the reward (bribe), when they declared that they would be leading men (leaders) of this plan, a manner of achieving it was sought, because they did not hope (were not relying on the possibility) that the state could be led to undertake war rashly. It was decided that Litaviccus should be appointed over those ten thousand who were being sent to Caesar for the war, and take care of leading them, and that his brothers should precede [him] to Caesar. They decide in what way it seems best [for] the rest to be done.

The Troops of the Haedui Are Tricked into Revolt (p. 209)

Litaviccus, the army having been taken charge of [by him], when he was about thirty miles distant from Gergovia, [and] the soldiers having (have) been suddenly called together, says, weeping, "Whither are we going, soldiers? All our army, all our nobility have perished. Eporedorix and Viridomarus, leaders of our state, charged with treason, have been killed by the Romans [with their] cause unheard. Learn this from these (men) who have fled from the very slaughter; for I, my brothers and all my relatives killed, am prevented by grief from announcing what things have (what has) been done." Those are led forth whom he had taught what he wanted said, and they explain to the multitude that same thing which Litaviccus had announced: that all the Haeduan cavalry were killed because they were said to have conferred (conspired) with the Arverni; they themselves had hid among a multitude of soldiers and had escaped from the midst of the slaughter.

The Haeduans shouted out and begged Litaviccus to take counsel for them. "As if indeed," he said, "it were a matter of (for) consideration, and not necessary for us to hasten to Gergovia and join (ally) ourselves with the Arverni. Or do we doubt that, an impious crime having been committed, the Romans are already gathering to kill us? Hence, if there is anything of spirit (any spirit) in us, let us avenge the death of those who perished most unworthily and let us kill these robbers." He pointed out the Roman citizens who were [standing] together in trust of (relying upon) his protection. Forthwith he plundered a great number (amount) of grain and provisions; them (the Roman citizens) he kills with torture. He sends messengers throughout the whole state of the Haeduans; he incites (raises an alarm) by the same lie about the slaughter of the cavalry and the leading men; he urges that in like manner as he has done, they avenge their injuries.

Eporedorix, an Haeduan, a young man born in very high place (of noble birth) and [a man] of the greatest power at home, and together with [him] Viridomarus, his equal in age and favor but unequal in race (lineage), had come in (among) the number of horsemen, having been called by name by Caesar. There was a contest with these among themselves over the chief position, and in that dispute of (over) the magistrates, the former had fought with all his resources for Convictolitavis, and the latter for Cotus.

Caesar Learns of the Conspiracy (p. 212)

Of these, Eporedorix, the plan of Litaviccus having become known, reports the matter to Caesar at (when it was) nearly midnight. He begs him not to allow the state to fall away from the friendship of the Roman people by (through) the perverse plans of young men, which he foresees [will happen] if so many thousands of men have joined the enemy, whose safety their relatives could neither disregard nor the state consider as of no moment.

Caesar, affected with (feeling) great anxiety in (at) this message, because he had always been particularly indulgent to the state of the Haeduans, no hesitation having been placed between (with no hesitation), leads out of the camp four light-armed legions and all the cavalry; nor was there an interval at such a time (nor was there time) for drawing (to draw) the camp together because the affair seemed placed (to depend) on speed. He leaves Gaius Fabius, a lieutenant, with two legions as a garrison for the camp. When he had ordered the brothers of Litaviccus to be arrested, he finds out that they have fled to the enemy a little before. Having urged the soldiers not to be influenced by the hardship of the march in this pressing time, all [being] most eager, having proceeded twenty-five miles, he sees the Haeduans' column; the cavalry having been sent against [it], he delays and hinders their march; he prohibits [them] all to kill anyone.

The Haedui Discover Their Error (p. 213)

Eporedorix and Viridomarus, whom they thought were killed, he orders to remain (move about) among the cavalry and to call their [countrymen] by name. These [two] having become known and Litaviccus' deception perceived, the Haeduans begin to extend their hands and to indicate surrender, and, their arms thrown (cast down), to ward off death (plead for their lives) by earnest prayer.

Litaviccus flees with his clients (adherents) to Gergovia. Caesar, messengers having been sent to the state of the Haeduans, to show [them] saved by his favor whom by right of war he could have killed, and three hours having been given to the army for rest, he moves camp toward Gergovia.

Meanwhile the Camp at Gergovia Is Assaulted (p. 213)

About the middle of the march horsemen sent by Fabius explain in how much (what great) danger the affair has been. They point out [that] the camp [has been] stormed by very great forces, since fresh [troops] frequently came up to (relieved) those worn out, and [thus] tired out our men by incessant effort, for on account of the size of the camp the same men had to remain continuously on the rampart. [They said that] many were wounded by the multitude of arrows and of every kind of dart; for resisting these the *tormenta* were of great use. Fabius, in their absence, two gates having been left [open], was blocking up the others and placing screens on the rampart and preparing himself for a similar event on the next day.

These things known, Caesar by (because of) the very great eagerness of the soldiers, arrives at the camp before sunrise.

First Reports Arrive among the Haedui (p. 214)

While these things are being carried on at Gergovia, the Haeduans, the first messages having been received from Litaviccus, leave (allow) themselves no interval for finding out (verifying the reports). Greed leads some on, anger and rashness others, which (and the latter) is especially innate to (in) that kind of men, so that they hold light hearsay for a thing found out for certain (for assured fact). They plunder the goods of the Roman citizens; they make slaughters (commit wholesale murder); they drag [some] away to slavery. Convictolitavis helps the thing already bent forward (helps events onward in the direction in which they are tending) and incites the multitude (mob) to frenzy, so that, the outrage [once] committed, it would shame them (they would be ashamed) to return to sanity.

They lead out of (banish from) the town of Cavillonum Marcus Aristius, a military tribune, marching (making his way) to [his] legion, faith having been given (although a pledge of safety had been given); they force those to do the same who had set up (settled) there for the sake of trade. Having attacked these continually on [their] journey, they despoil [them] of all [their] baggage; they besiege them fighting (as they fight) back night and day; many on both sides having been killed, they stir up (summon) a larger multitude to arms.

New Reports Arrive (p. 215)

Meanwhile, a message having been brought that all their soldiers were held in Caesar's power, they rush to Aristius. They point out (plead) that nothing was done by public plan. They order an inquiry concerning the plundered goods. They confiscate the goods of Litaviccus and [his] brothers. They send envoys to Caesar for the sake of exonerating themselves. They do these things for the sake of recovering their [soldiers], but, terrified, they begin secretly to enter upon plans of war and to stir up the remaining states. Although Caesar knew which (these) things, he nevertheless addresses the envoys as gently as possible; and says he does not at all judge more seriously (harshly) of the state because of the fickleness of the multitude.

The Assault; Orders Miscarry (p. 218)

The signal having been given, the soldiers swiftly reach the fortification and, having crossed it, get possession of three camps. Having accomplished what he had planned, Caesar ordered it to be sounded for retreat (a retreat to be sounded) and set up the standards of the tenth legion with which he was.

But the soldiers of the remaining legions, the sound of the trumpet not having been heard because a large enough (rather large) valley intervened, nevertheless were being held back by the military tribunes and the lieutenants; but elated by the hope of swift victory and the flight of the enemy and by the favorable battles of former times, they thought that nothing was so difficult for them that they could not accomplish [it] by courage, and they did not make an end of following (cease the pursuit) before (until) they approached the wall and the gates of the town.

But then a shout having arisen from every part of the city, those who were rather far away having been (being) terrified by the sudden uproar, since they thought the enemy was within the gates, cast themselves (fled) from the town. . . .

Meanwhile those who, as we have shown above, had come together (assembled) on another side of the town for the sake of defense, (when) the first shout having been (was) heard, afterward also incited by numerous messages, [that] the town was held by the Romans, having sent the cavalry forward, hastened thither with great running (in wild career). As soon as each one of them had come, he took a position at the foot of the wall and increased the number of those fighting.

The Romans in Desperate Straits (p. 220)

It was an equal struggle for the Romans neither in place (position) nor in number; for, tired out by the running and the extent (length) of the fight, they did not easily withstand [those who were] new and fresh.

Caesar, when he saw it to be fought (that the fighting was) in an unfavorable place, and that the forces of the enemy were being augmented, apprehensive for his men, sent [word] to Titus Sextius the lieutenant, whom he had left in the smaller camp as protection (a guard), to lead the cohorts forth from the camp quickly and set [them] up at the lowest [part of the] hill, on the right side (flank) of the enemy, so that, if he should see our men cast down from that place, he might hinder the enemy from pursuing [them] freely. He himself, having gone forward a little from that place where he had set up (taken a stand) with the legion, awaited the outcome of the battle.

Fresh Disorders; The Haeduan Reinforcements Mistaken for Foes (p. 220)

When it was being fought (they were fighting) fiercely hand to hand, the enemy trusting in place (position) and number, our men in courage, the Haeduans are suddenly seen on the exposed flank by our men, whom Caesar had sent from the right side by another ascent. These [Haeduans] terrified our men violently by the likeness of [their] arms (because their weapons resembled those of the enemy) and, although they were noticed with (to have their) right shoulders uncovered, which was accustomed to be the (the customary) sign of the pacified, the soldiers nevertheless thought that very thing done (this was being done) by the enemy for the sake of (with intent of) deceiving them. At the same time, Lucius Fabius, a centurion, and those who had ascended the wall together with [him], surrounded and killed, were hurled down from the wall.

Marcus Petronius, a centurion of the same legion, when he tried to hew down the gates, having been pressed hard by the multitude and despairing of himself, many wounds having been already received (since he was already badly wounded), says to his common soldiers who had followed him, "Since I cannot save myself together with you, I will certainly provide for your life (lives) whom I, influenced by the desire of fame, have led into danger; (when) the opportunity having been (is) given, take care of yourselves."

At the same time he rushed into the midst of the enemy, and two men having been killed, he drove back the rest a little from the gate. To those of his men trying (who tried) to help him, he said, "In vain do you try to help (save) my life, whom blood and strength now fail. Go therefore, while the opportunity is [yours], and betake yourselves (get back) to the legion." Fighting thus, he fell after a little and was as a safety (the salvation of) his men.

The Romans Retreat (p. 222)

Our men, when they were being pressed hard on all sides, were hurled down from [their] place (position). But the tenth legion, which had stood firm in a little more favorable place as a reserve, hindered the Gauls, pursuing (prevented the Gauls from pursuing) more violently (too eagerly). The cohorts of the thirteenth legion took this up again (support this legion), which, having been led from the smaller camp with Titus Sextius the lieutenant, had taken the higher place (position). The legions, when they had first reached the plain, stood firm, [their] hostile standards against the enemy (with standards in battle array). Vercingetorix led his men back into the fortifications from the roots (foot) of the mountain. On that day a little less (somewhat fewer than) seven hundred soldiers were lost. . . .

This assembling having been held (after this assembly) and the soldiers encouraged to the greatest degree not to be affected (disturbed) in mind on account of this cause (affair) and not to assign to the courage of the enemy that which the disadvantage of the place had brought about, thinking the same concerning a departure that he had felt before (of the same opinion as before about a departure), he led the legions out of the camp and set up a battle line in a suitable place. When Vercingetorix, however, did not descend to the level place (ground), a light cavalry battle having occurred and this [being] favorable, he led the army back into camp.

Caesar Withdraws to the Territory of the Haedui (p. 224)

When this same thing had been done (repeated) on the next day, thinking that enough had been done for (toward) lessening Gallic pride and encouraging the soldiers' minds, he moved camp into the Haeduans (Haeduan territory).

Fresh Rumors of Rebellion among the Haedui (p. 224)

The enemy having followed not indeed (even) then, on the third day he came to the Elaver River; he refreshes (rebuilds) the bridge and leads the army across. There, having been called upon by Viridomarus and Eporedorix, the Haeduans, he learns that Litaviccus has set out with all the cavalry to stir up the Haeduans and that it is necessary that they themselves go before to strengthen the state. Although in many affairs he had the treachery of the Haeduans already perceived (he clearly perceived the treachery of the Haeduans) and thought that the desertion of the state would be hastened by the departure of these two men, he nevertheless thought that they should not be held back, lest he might seem either to inflict an injury or give some indication of fear. To these (those) departing he briefly explained his own services to the Haeduans.

Caesar's Most Important Allies Join the Revolt (p. 225)

Noviodunum was a town of the Haeduans placed (situated) in an advantageous place on the banks of the Loire. Caesar had brought hither all the hostages of the Gauls, grain, the public money, and a large part of his own baggage and that of the army. He had sent hither a great number of horses bought in Italy and Spain for the sake of this war. When Eporedorix and Viridomarus had come thither and had learned of the condition of the state, that Litaviccus had been taken back by the Haeduans into Bibracte, which is a town of the greatest authority (importance) among them; that Convictolitavis, the magistrate, and a great part of the Senate had come to him; that envoys had been sent in the name of the state to Vercingetorix to win peace and friendship; they thought so great an advantage should not be overlooked. Therefore the guards of Noviodunum and those who had come there for the purpose of trading having been killed, they divided the money and horses among themselves. They took care that the hostages of the state should be led to the magistrate at Bibracte. The town, which they decided could not be held by them, they burned, lest it be of any use to the Romans. They carried away suddenly (immediately) in ships what of grain (whatever grain) they could; they destroyed the rest in the river and by fire. They began to collect forces from the neighboring regions, to station garrisons and guards at the banks of the Loire, and to display cavalry everywhere for the sake of inspiring fear, so that they could prevent the Romans from [obtaining] a supply of grain. To this hope it was helping much (in this hope they were much helped) that (by the fact that) the Loire had increased from (been swollen by) snows, so that it seemed that it could not altogether (possibly) be crossed by a ford.

Part III, The Crisis of the War (p. 227)

Therefore, very long marches having been made day and night, he came to the Loire against (contrary to) the expectation of all, and a ford having been found by the cavalry opportune for the need (emergency), so that at least the soldiers' arms and shoulders could be free from (remain clear of) the water for sustaining (supporting) [their] arms (weapons), [and] the cavalry having been stationed [in such a way as] to diminish the force of the river, and the enemy having been confused (thrown into disorder) at the first sight [of the Romans], he led the army across safe and sound.

Having obtained grain in the fields and a supply of cattle, he began to march toward the Senones.

The Campaign of Labienus (p. 228)

While these things are being done (going on) under (as regards) Caesar, Labienus, that reinforcement which had lately come from Italy having been left at Agedincum that it might be a protection for the baggage, sets out for Lutetia with four legions. That (this) is a town of the Parisii placed (situated) on an island of the Sequana River. Whose (his) arrival having been learned by the enemy, a large force came together from the neighboring states. The sum total of (chief) command is handed over to Camulogenus, one of the Aulerci, who, nearly worn out with age, has nevertheless been called forth to this honor because of his extraordinary knowledge of military affairs. He, when he had noticed that there was a continuous marsh which flowed (opened) into the Sequana and greatly impeded (obstructed) all that place, took up a position here and determined to ward our soldiers off from the passage (prevent our soldiers from crossing). Labienus at first tried to do (make) sheds, and by wickerwork and a mound to fill up the marsh and to construct a road. After he noticed that this was (would be) rather difficult, having gone out of camp silently during the third watch, he arrived at (went to) Metiosedum by the same route by which he had come. That (this) is a town of the Senones placed (situated) on an island in the Sequana, as we have [also] said of Lutetia a little before (just above).

About fifty ships having been seized and quickly joined together, and soldiers having been placed thereon and the townspeople terrified by the novelty of the thing, a great part of whom had been called out to war, he obtained possession of the town without a struggle. The bridge having been refreshed (rebuilt) which on preceding days the enemy had destroyed, he leads the army across. He begins to march to Lutetia, with the stream favorable (downstream). The enemy, the news having been learned from those who had fled from Metiosedum, orders Lutetia to be burned and the bridges of that city to be destroyed. Having set out themselves from the marsh, they take up a position on the bank of the Sequana opposite Lutetia opposite (facing) the camp of Labienus.

News from the South Forces Labienus to Take Defensive
Measures. His Difficulties in Returning
to His Base (p. 229)

Already Caesar was heard to have departed from the neighborhood
of Gergovia; already messages were being brought concerning the desertion of the Haeduans and the successful rebellion of all Gaul; and
the Gauls were affirming that Caesar, cut off from [his] route and the
Loire, [and] forced by a scarcity of grain, had hastened into the
province. The Bellovaci, however, the desertion of the Haeduans having been learned, who before were faithless themselves, began to collect
troops and to prepare war openly. Then Labienus in so great a change
of affairs perceived that some other far different plan should be undertaken by him than [that which] he had thought (considered) before,
nor did he think now that he should acquire (give thought to acquiring)
anything or provoke the enemy by battle, but that he should lead the
army back safe(ly) to Agedincum. For from one side the Bellovaci,
which state has the very greatest reputation in all Gaul for courage,
were preparing war; the other [side] Camulogenus was holding with a
ready and equipped army. Then the legions were cut off from the garrison and the baggage by a very great river. Such great difficulties having suddenly been thrown in the way, he saw that aid must be sought
from courage of mind (they must rely on a courageous heart).

Labienus Crosses the Seine by a Stratagem (p. 231)

And so, toward evening a council having been called, having urged
[them] to do carefully those things which he had ordered, he assigns
each of the ships which he had led (brought) from Metiosedum to
Roman cavalry and orders them to go forward silently, the first watch
having been finished (at the end of the first watch) four miles downstream and await him there. He leaves five cohorts, which he thought to
be (considered) least strong for fighting, as a garrison for the camp;
he commands the remaining five cohorts of the same legion to set out
in the middle of the night with all the baggage with the river opposed
(upstream) in a great uproar. He hunts up skiffs also; these he sends
off in the same direction aroused (moved) with a great sound of oars.
He himself having gone out in silence after a little with three legions,
seeks (makes for) that place to which he had ordered the ships to be
brought together. When he had come thither, scouts of the enemy, as
they were stationed in every part of the river, unawares because a great
storm had suddenly arisen, are overwhelmed by our men; the army and

the cavalry were swiftly transported, the Roman horsemen whom he put in charge of that affair managing [it]. Nearly at one (the same) time, toward daybreak, it is announced to the enemy that a disturbance beyond custom (a greater disturbance than usual) is being made in the camp of the Romans and that a great column is going with the stream opposed (upstream), and that the sound (splash) of oars is heard in the same direction, and a little below soldiers are being transported (ferried across) in ships (boats). Which things having been heard (hearing all this), because (since) they thought that the legions were crossing in three places and that all [were] disturbed by the desertion of the Haeduans [and] were preparing (considering) flight, they too distributed (divided) their troops into three parts. For, a garrison having been left opposite the camp and a small band sent toward Metiosedum to go as far as the ships had advanced, they led the remaining troops against Labienus.

Labienus Clears the Road Southward by Battle (p. 233)

At (by) dawn all our soldiers had been transported, and the battle line of the enemy was seen. Labienus urged the soldiers to keep the memory of their former courage and of so (their) many very successful battles, and to think (imagine) Caesar himself to be present, of (under) whose command they had often overcome the enemy. He gives the signal of (for) battle. At the first onset, on the right flank, where the seventh legion had stationed [itself], the enemy is repulsed and thrown into flight; on the left, which place (position) the twelfth legion was holding, when the first ranks of the enemy had fallen, pierced through by javelins, the rest nevertheless were resisting very fiercely, nor was anyone giving an indication of flight. The leader of the enemy, Camulogenus himself, had gone to (among) the soldiers and was encouraging them. But also (even) now the outcome of victory being uncertain, when it was announced by the tribunes of the seventh legion what was being done (happening) on the left flank, they show (spread out) the legion behind at the back (on the rear) of the enemy and carry the standards forward (attack). Not in that time indeed (not even then) did anyone yield, but all were surrounded and killed. Camulogenus bore (met) the same fate. But those who had been left opposite Labienus' camp as a protection, when they had heard that the battle was (had) begun, went as (to the) aid for (of) their men and took a hill, but were not able to withstand the attack of our victors (victorious) soldiers. So, mingled with their own fleeing [soldiers], those whom the woods and mountains did not hide were killed by the cavalry. This business (affair) having been completed, Labienus returns to Agedincum, where the baggage of the whole army had been left. From there he comes to (goes to meet) Caesar with all [his] forces.

The Fire of Revolt Envelops All Gaul (p. 234)

The desertion of the Haeduans having been learned (being known), the war is increased (spreads). Embassies are sent around in every direction. As much (in so far) as by favor, authority, or money they may be influential [they can], they strive to stir up the states. Having obtained hostages whom Caesar had deposited among them, they terrify the hesitating by the punishment of (by punishing) these. They (the Haeduans) ask of Vercingetorix that he come to them and impart (share his) plans for waging the war. The thing having been obtained (their object obtained), they contend that the whole of (chief) command [should] be handed over to them, and, the matter having been led (brought) into dispute (when this led to a dispute), a council of all Gaul is convoked at Bibracte. They came together in great numbers from all sides. The matter is given over to the votes of the multitude. To a man they all approve Vercingetorix as commander. The Remi, the Lingones, and Treveri were absent from this council; the former because they were following the friendship of (were loyal to) the Romans; the Treveri because they were rather far away and were being hard pressed by the Germans, which was the reason why they had been absent during the whole war and were sending help to neither [side].

The Haedui Are Disaffected by Their Failure to Gain the Leadership of the Rebellion (p. 235)

The Haeduans bore it with great sorrow that they were cast down from the chief position (deprived of supremacy). They bewail [their] change of fortune and desire again of Caesar (miss Caesar's) clemency for themselves; but nevertheless, the war having been undertaken, they dare not separate [their] plan (course) from the rest (dare not refuse to remain with the others). Reluctant(ly) [those] young men of the greatest hope (expectations), Eporedorix and Viridomarus, yield to Vercingetorix.

Vercingetorix's Plan: Starvation of the Forces in Gaul, Invasion of the Roman Province (p. 235)

He levies hostages on the rest of the states and sets a day for that affair. Finally he orders all the cavalry, fifteen thousand in number, to assemble here swiftly; he says he will be satisfied with the infantry which he had before, nor would he test fortune or fight in battle line, but that it was easily done to (easy to) prevent the Romans [from obtaining] grain and provisions, provided only that they themselves with a calm mind destroy their own crops and burn the buildings; in this way they will gain permanent power and freedom. These things having been decided, he orders from the Haeduans and the Segusiavi, who are next to the province, ten thousand infantry; to these he adds eight hundred cavalry. He places in charge of these the brother of Eporedorix and orders [him] to inflict war upon the Allobroges. On the other side he sends the Gabali and the nearest cantons of the Arverni against the Helvii; the Ruteni and the Cadurcans, however, he sends to ravage the territory of the Volcae Arecomici. He nevertheless stirs up the Allobroges by messengers and embassies, whose minds he hoped had not yet become calm (recovered) from a former war. He promises money to their leaders, but to the state (he promises) command of (supreme power in) the whole province.

The Provincial Defenses (p. 236)

For all these crises a garrison of twenty-two cohorts had been provided which, collected in the province itself by Lucius Caesar, a lieutenant, were being placed on every side. The Helvii, having met with the neighboring [tribes] in battle of their own accord are repulsed, and Gaius Valerius Domnotaurus, the son of Caburus, a chief of the state, and many others having been killed, are driven [back] into [their] towns and fortifications. The Allobroges, numerous garrisons having been stationed at (along) the Rhone, guard their territory with great care.

Cut Off from the Province, Caesar Raises Troops in Germany (p. 237)

Caesar, because he knew that the enemy was superior in cavalry and [because], all the routes having been (being) cut off, he could in no way be assisted (get aid) from the province or from Italy, sends across the Rhine to Germany to those states which he had pacified (subjugated) in previous years and summons from them cavalry and the light-armed infantry which was accustomed to fight among them. On their arrival, because they used less suitable horses, he takes horses from the military tribunes and the other Roman horsemen and distributes them to (among) the Germans.

The Gallic Host Assembles (p. 237)

Meanwhile, while these things are being done (happening), the forces of the enemy from the Arverni and the cavalry which had been levied on all Gaul, assemble. A great number of these having been collected, when Caesar was marching toward the Sequanians through the outermost territory of the Lingones so that he could more easily bring aid to the province, Vercingetorix encamped in three camps about ten miles from the Romans and, the captains of the cavalry having been called together in council, he points out that the time (hour) of victory had (has) come; the Romans were fleeing to the province and were leaving Gaul. That was enough for them for obtaining present (immediate) freedom; it would not be very useful for peace for the remaining time (would do little to ensure peace in the future); for, greater forces having been collected, the Romans would return, nor would they make an end of warring. Hence, let them attack the encumbered ⌜soldiers⌝ on the march. If the infantry brings help to its [men], and delay in (for) that, they cannot make (continue) the march; if, that which he more (rather) expects will be (will happen), the baggage having been left (they abandon the baggage and) they consult (consider only) their own safety, they would be despoiled both of the use of necessary things and of dignity (honor). For concerning (as regards) the enemy's cavalry, not even they themselves ought to doubt that not one of them would dare even to advance beyond the line of march. In order that they might do it with greater spirit (zeal) he would have the troops all (displayed) before the camp for a terror to (as a means of terrifying) the enemy.

The Attack on Caesar's Column (p. 239)

This matter having been announced, Caesar orders his own cavalry, also divided into three parts, to go against the enemy. It is fought (they fight) all together on every side. The line halts; the baggage is taken back within the legions. If our men were seen to be in difficulty on any side or to be rather hard pressed, Caesar ordered the standards to be carried forward to that place and the battle line to be turned around (an advance to be made in that sector); which (this) action both hindered the pursuing enemy and encouraged our men with the hope of help. Finally, the Germans on the right wing, having obtained possession of the topmost ridge, cast the enemy down from [that] place; they pursue and kill many fleeing (as they flee) up to the river, where Vercingetorix had taken up a position with troops on foot; which thing having been noticed (noticing this), having feared (fearing) lest they be surrounded, the rest (the troops at the river) commit themselves to flight. There was slaughter in every place. Three very renowned Haeduans [who were] captured are led to Caesar.

Vercingetorix Retreats to Alesia (p. 239)

The whole cavalry having been driven back, Vercingetorix led his troops back as they had been stationed before the camp and immediately began to march to Alesia, which is a town of the Mandubii, and ordered the baggage to be brought swiftly from the camp and to follow him. Caesar, [his] baggage having been led away (brought) to the nearest hill, [and] two legions left as protection, having followed the enemy as far as the time of day allowed, about three thousand of the enemy having been killed in the rear line, on the next day he made (pitched) camp at Alesia.

Cavalry Skirmishes (p. 240)

The work (siege-work) having been built, an equestrian battle happens (occurs) on that plain which, as we have pointed out above, extends three miles in length, unbroken by hills. Both [sides] strive with the utmost force. Caesar sends the Germans as aid to our men in difficulty. He sets up the legions before the camp, lest any attack be made suddenly by the enemy's infantry. The protection of the legions having been added, the spirit is increased in our men. The enemy, thrown into flight, hinder themselves by [their] great number, and are crowded together in the rather narrow remaining gates. The Germans pursue more fiercely up to the fortifications. A great slaughter is made (follows). Some, their horses left (abandoned), try to cross the ditch and climb over the wall. Caesar orders the legions which he had set up before the rampart to be moved forward a little. The Gauls who were within the fortifications were no less disturbed. Thinking it is to be immediately come (thinking that an immediate attack is to be made) against them, they shout (sound a call) to arms. Some, terrified, rush into the town. Vercingetorix orders the gates to be closed lest the camp be stripped. Many having been killed, and a large number of horses captured, the Germans withdraw.

Vercingetorix Issues a Universal Call to Arms (p. 241)

Vercingetorix makes a plan to send all the cavalry away from him by night before the defenses are completed by the Romans. He commands those departing, that each one of them visit his own state and collect for war all those who can by [their] age (are of an age to) bear arms. He puts forward (reminds them of) his own services to them and entreats them to have reason (regard) for his safety and not surrender him to the enemy for torture deserving the best (who had done such good work) for common liberty. Because if they should be somewhat negligent, he points out that eighty thousand men would perish with him. This plan having been gone into (a calculation is made and he says) they have scarcely [enough] grain for thirty days, but that they can hold out a little longer by sparing (using it sparingly). These commands having been given, he dismisses the cavalry silently during the second watch, in that direction (where) our work had been interrupted (was incomplete). He orders all the grain to be brought back to him. He sets up the death penalty for those who will not obey. The cattle, of which a great supply (herd) had been collected by the Mandubii, he distributes to each one. The grain he determines to be (to have) measured out sparingly, little by little. All the troops which he had stationed before the town he [now] takes back into the town. By these plans (means) he prepares to await the aid of Gaul and to manage (wage) the war.

He Constructs Defense Works behind His Own Lines to Meet the Relieving Force (p. 244)

These things having been finished, having followed territory as level in proportion to the nature of the place (as the natural terrain allowed), having enclosed (enclosing) fourteen miles, he built like defenses of the same kind, facing in the opposite direction, opposite the enemy outside, so that the garrisons of the defenses could not be surrounded even by a great multitude; lest, however, it be forced (they be forced) to go out of the camp with danger, he orders all to have fodder and grain collected for thirty days.

The Gauls Outside Hold a Council of War (p. 245)

While these things are being done at Alesia, the Gauls, a council of the chiefs having been called, determine that not all should be called out who could bear arms, but that a certain number should be levied on each state, lest, so great a multitude having been brought together, they can neither control nor keep their own apart, nor manage the matter of grain. From (of) those [nations] on whom the soldiers had been levied, the Bellovaci did not bring together their number because they said they would carry on the war with the Romans in their own name. Nevertheless, asked by Commius, they sent two thousand for the sake of his friendship. Caesar, as we have shown before, had employed the faithful and useful service of this Commius in Britain in previous years and for which (these) services had ordered his state to be free (made his state free), had restored [its] rights and laws, and had assigned (made subject) to him the Morini. Nevertheless, so great (absolute) was the agreement of all Gaul for the claiming of freedom and the recovery of the original renown of (in) war, that they were moved neither by favors nor the memory of friendship, and they all devoted themselves to that war both in spirit and in resources.

The Great Army Gathers (p. 247)

Eight thousand cavalry and about two hundred fifty thousand infantry having been collected, these were reviewed in the territory of the Haeduans, and the number was gone into (an enumeration was made). Officers were set up (appointed). All, eager and full of confidence, set out for Alesia, nor was there any one of them all who thought that even the sight of so great a multitude could be withstood, especially in a double battle, when it would be fought by (there would be) a sortie from inside the town and outside such great forces of cavalry and infantry would be seen.

A Desperate Council within Alesia (p. 247)

But those who were being besieged at Alesia, the day having passed on which they had awaited (expected) help from their men, (and) all the grain being used up, not aware of what was happening among the Haeduans, having assembled a council, were considering the outcome of their fortunes. And diverse opinions having been spoken (given), of which a part (some) decided (advised) surrender, a part (some) a sortie while strength held out, it seems that the speech of Critognatus ought not to be passed over on account of its extraordinary and wicked cruelty. This [man], born in (of) the highest place (rank) among the Arverni and looked upon as a man of great authority said, "I will say nothing of the opinion of those who call the most shameful slavery by the name of surrender, [for] I consider that they should neither be held in the place of (regarded as) citizens nor brought into (admitted to) the council. Let the affair for me (my stand) be with those who approve (propose) a sortie; in whose (their) plan, by the agreement of all (you will all agree), [some] memory of former courage seems to remain. It is weakness of soul, not courage, to be unable to bear want for a little while. [Those] who voluntarily offer themselves to death are more easily found than those who would bear pain patiently. But I would approve this opinion—so influential is honor with me—if I saw that nothing except the sacrifice of our life (lives) would happen (result); but in making a plan let us consider all of Gaul, which we had stirred up for our help (called to our assistance). Eighty thousand men having been killed in one place, what do you think there will be [left] of courage in the relatives and those of the same blood (our relatives and kinsmen) if they are forced to contend in battle almost over our very corpses? Do not strip (deprive) of your help those who have disregarded their own danger for the sake of your welfare, nor by your folly and rashness or weakness of mind prostrate all Gaul and subject [it] to everlasting slavery. Or because they did not come to the (on the appointed) day, do you doubt their faith and steadfastness? What, [then]? Do you think that the Romans are daily being exercised (kept at work) on those farther (outer) fortifications [only] to amuse themselves? If you cannot be encouraged by their messengers, every approach being blocked up, use them [the Romans] as witnesses [that] their coming is near. Terrified (struck) by fear of which (this) circumstance, they [the Romans] engage in the labor day and night. What then is my plan (advice)? To do what our forefathers did in the by no means equal war of the Cimbri and the Teutones; who, driven into the towns and forced by a similar scarcity, held out (sustained) life with the bodies of those who seemed by [reason of] age useless for war, nor did they hand themselves over to the enemy. [Indeed], if we did not have a precedent of (for) this action, I would nevertheless judge it most glorious to be set up (instituted) for the sake of freedom and recorded (handed down) to posterity. For what was there like that war? Gaul laid waste, and a great disaster inflicted, the Cimbri indeed departed at last from our territories and sought other lands; rights, laws, fields, and freedom they left to us. But the Romans, what do they seek or want except, induced by envy, to settle in the fields and states of those whom they know by report [to be] noble and powerful in war, and to impose on them everlasting slavery? For they have never waged war on any other condition (terms). For if you are ignorant of those things being done in remote tribes, look at neighboring Gaul, which, reduced to a province, its rights and laws altered, made subject to the axes (lictors), is pressed (oppressed) by perpetual slavery."

The Decision of the Council (p. 251)

These opinions spoken (expressed), they decide that those who by state of health or age are useless for war should depart from the town and all things should be tried before they resorted to the opinion of Critognatus; nevertheless they must employ his plan if the situation forces (requires it) and reinforcements are delayed, rather than that a condition of surrender or of peace should be endured. The Mandubii, who had received them into the town, are forced to depart with [their] children and wives. These, when they had approached the fortifications of the Romans, weeping, prayed with every entreaty that they would help them, taken into slavery, by means of food. But Caesar, guards having been stationed on the rampart, prevented [them] from being received.

The Relieving Force Arrives (p. 252)

Meanwhile Commius and the rest of the leaders to whom the sum total of (chief) command had been entrusted arrive at Alesia with all [their] forces, and an outer hill having been taken, they halt not more than a mile from our fortifications.

The Gauls Attack from Both Sides (p. 252)

The next day, the cavalry having been led out of camp, they fill all that plain, which we have shown to extend three miles in length; and the infantry troops, led away a little from that place, they place in higher places (positions). [Now] there was a view [down] onto the plain from Alesia. These reinforcements having been seen, they run (crowd) together. Rejoicing is done among them (they congratulate one another), and the souls of all are aroused to joy. And so, the troops led forth, they take a position before the town and fill the nearest ditch with fascines and a mound and prepare themselves for a sortie and every crisis. Caesar, the whole army distributed on both sides of the defenses in order that, if need should arise, each man might have his own place and know [it], orders the cavalry to be led from camp and a battle begun. There was a view from all the camps, which held the highest ridge on all sides, and all the soldiers, intent, were awaiting the outcome of the battle. The Gauls had placed among the cavalry scattered archers and (light-armed) ready troops of light equipment, who would assist [their] men giving way (if they gave way) and withstand the charge of our cavalry. Many, wounded by these [troops] unexpectedly, withdrew from the battle. Since the Gauls were trusting (confident) that their [men] were higher (superior) in the battle, and saw our [men] hard pressed by the multitude from every side, both those who were held within the fortifications and those who had come as reinforcements encouraged the spirits of their [men] by shout and yell. Because the affair was carried on in the sight of all, no deed whether done well or basely could be concealed, and both the desire of glory and the fear of dishonor were exciting both sides to courage. When the battle had continued from noon to nearly sunset, with the victory still doubtful, the Germans on one side made attacks against the enemy in compact squadrons and routed them; which (and these) having been thrown into flight, the archers were surrounded and killed. In like manner in the other directions, our men having followed [those] yielding even up to the camps, gave them no opportunity of rallying. But those who had gone forward from Alesia, dejected—now that victory is nearly despaired of—withdraw to the town.

The Leaders of the Relieving Force Again Deliberate (p. 255)

Driven back twice with heavy loss(es), the Gauls consult (consider) what they should do. They bring in those familiar with the places (region). From these they learn the site and defenses of the higher camp. There was a hill on the north which because of the greatness of the (its great) circumference, our [men] had not been able to fill (enclose) with the work (siege-works), and almost of necessity they had made camp in an unfavorable place. This Gaius Antistius Reginus and Gaius Caninius Rebilus, lieutenants, were holding with two legions.

A Stratagem (p. 255)

The regions having been learned through (explored by) scouts, the leaders of the enemy choose sixty thousand from the total number, from those states which had the greatest reputation of (for) courage; they decide secretly among themselves what it seems good to be done (to do); they set up the time of attack when it is seen to be noon (determine to attack at noon). They place over these forces Vercassivellaunus, an Arvernian, one of four leaders and near to (a relative of) Vercingetorix. He, having departed from camp during the first watch, the march nearly completed toward daybreak, concealed himself behind a mountain and ordered the soldiers to refresh themselves from the nocturnal effort (effort of the night). When midday seemed to be approaching, he hastened to that camp which we have pointed out (mentioned) above; at the same time the cavalry began to approach (march on) the level defenses (defenses on the plain), and the rest of the troops [began] to show themselves before the camp. Vercingetorix, having caught sight of his men from the citadel of Alesia, went out from (moved out of) the town; he brings along from the camp the long poles, the hooks, and the rest [of the things] which he had prepared for the sally. The battle rages everywhere at once, and all [expedients] are tried. [At] whatever part seems least strong, thither they rush. The band of Romans is held apart (strung out) in such [long] fortifications and (that) it does not easily meet [the attack] in many places. The shouting which arose (was raised) by those fighting in the rear was much influential (helped much) to terrify our men, because they see that their own danger depends on other's bravery; for generally all things which are absent (everything out of sight) disturb(s) men's minds more violently. Caesar, having obtained a suitable place, learns (knows) what is done in each direction (sector); he sends help to those in difficulty.

The Supreme Moment (p. 256)

To both it occurs to the soul (both sides feel in their hearts) that [this] is the one time when it is fitting to battle hardest (they ought to make their greatest effort). The Gauls, unless they break through the fortifications, despair of all safety; the Romans, if they should obtain (gain) the action, expect an end of all [their] efforts. There is a struggle especially at the higher fortifications, to which we have shown Vercassivellaunus was sent. The uneven downward slope of the place had great importance. Some throw darts, others advance, a testudo having been made (some form a testudo and advance to the fortifications); fresh men come up to (relieve) in turn those tired out. The earth thrown by all upon the fortifications both gives (provides) an ascent to the Gauls and covers up those things which the Romans had hidden in the land (ground); neither arms nor strength are at hand (sufficient) for our men now. These things having been learned (seeing this), Caesar sends Labienus with six cohorts to aid those in difficulties; he orders that, if he cannot withstand, he should fight in a sally, the cohorts having been led out; that (but this) he must not do unless [it be] necessary. He himself goes to the rest, and encourages [them] not to yield to the effort (strain); the fruit of all [their] former struggles, [he says], remains in (depends upon) that [very] day and hour. Those within, the level places (plain) having been despaired of on account of the extent of the fortifications, try the broken off (steep) places by (in) an ascent; here they bring those things which they had prepared. They dislodge from the towers by a great number (shower) of weapons those attacking; they fill the ditches with earth and wickerwork; they cut down the rampart and the breastwork with hooks. Caesar at first sends Brutus, a young man, with cohorts, and afterwards Gaius Fabius, a lieutenant, with other [cohorts]; at last he himself, when the struggle was becoming more violent, leads up fresh [troops] to help.

Caesar Enters the Fight (p. 258)

The battle renewed and the enemy repulsed, he hastens to that place where he had sent Labienus. He leads four cohorts down from the nearest fort. He orders part of the cavalry to follow him, part to go around the outer fortifications and to assail the enemy from (in) the rear. Labienus, when neither the mounds nor the ditches were able to withstand the force of the enemy, eleven cohorts having been collected which, led from the nearest garrisons, chance offered, informs Caesar through messengers what he thinks should be done. Caesar hastens in order to be present at the battle. His arrival having been learned from the color of his clothing, which signs (identification) he was accustomed to use in battle, and the squadrons of cavalry and cohorts which he had ordered to follow him having been seen, the enemy begins battle.

A shout having been raised on both sides, the shout is taken up again from the rampart and from all the fortifications. Our men, [their] javelins let fall (thrown down), carry on with swords. Suddenly the cavalry is seen at the rear; the other cohorts approach.

A Roman Victory (p. 259)

The enemy turn [their] backs; the horsemen meet them fleeing (as they flee). A great slaughter is made (follows). Sedulius, leader and chief of the Lemovices, is killed; Vercassivellaunus, the Arvernian, is taken alive in flight; military standards, four and seventy, are brought to Caesar; few from so great a number withdraw safe(ly) to camp. Having seen from the town the (this) slaughter and flight of their men, safety despaired of, they draw the troops back from the fortifications. This news having been heard, a flight is immediately made from the camp of the Gauls. And unless [our] soldiers had been exhausted by the frequent reserves [coming against them] and the effort of the whole day, all the forces of the enemy could have been killed. At midnight the cavalry, having been sent on, pursued the rear line. A great number were taken and killed; the rest retired (escaped) from the flight (rout) into [their own] states.

The Surrender of Vercingetorix (p. 259)

On the next day Vercingetorix, a council having been called together, points out that he has undertaken that war not for the sake of his own needs but for the common liberty, and that, because they must yield to fortune, he offers himself for each (either) alternative, whether they wish to satisfy the Romans by his death, or to hand [him] over alive.

Envoys are sent to Caesar concerning this matter. He orders arms to be handed over, the leading men to be led forth. He himself took a position (seated himself) on the rampart before the camp. There the leaders are brought. Vercingetorix is surrendered; arms are thrown down. Making an exception in favor of the Haeduans and the Arverni, [to see] if he could through them recover [their] states, he distributes from the rest of the prisoners heads (persons) one by one to the whole army as booty.

These affairs having been finished (when these details had been carried out), he sets out for the Haeduans; he takes back [that] state. Envoys having been sent there from the Arverni, they promise to do what he shall have ordered (he orders). He levies a large number of hostages. He sends the legions into winter quarters. He returns to the Haeduans and the Arverni about twenty thousand of the prisoners. He orders Titus Labienus to set out for the Sequanians with two legions and the cavalry, and he stations the remaining legions in separate places. He himself decides to winter at Bibracte.

These things having been learned from the dispatches of Caesar, a public prayer of twenty days is rendered (decreed) at Rome.

10. The Civil War (p. 262)

When Caesar was leading the army into Italy, Pompey transported his own forces into Greece. Italy having been swiftly taken, Caesar, having set out for Spain, overcame the lieutenants of Pompey who were holding those regions. Having turned about from there to Italy, he transported great forces into Greece and there contended in battles (struggled) with Pompey for a long time. Finally, the battle of Pharsalus having been fought (in a battle at Pharsalus), he overcame Pompey and either captured or killed a great number of his soldiers.

11. Caesar's Death (p. 264)

So Caesar, all enemies conquered, held alone supreme power in the state. The Roman people having been almost exhausted by wars and dangers, he was strengthening peace in Italy and the provinces. He was managing everything very carefully, both at Rome and in the provinces. He himself did everything.

There were many, however, who took great sorrow from this fact (who resented this). For some remembered the liberty which they had received (which had come down to them) from their forefathers and they wanted to recover and keep [it]. Others were angry because Caesar had not given them rewards. To others it was a great sorrow (others lamented the fact) that all power was [vested] in one man. Besides, they thought that Caesar desired not only the power but also the name of king.

And so they conspired against Caesar. The leaders [of the conspiracy] were Brutus and Cassius. Both were friends of Caesar. Brutus had been placed by Caesar in command of the fleet which he had made (built) during the war of the Veneti. Caesar often came into the Senate without arms (unarmed). And so, on the day appointed, the conspirators came into (entered) the Senate and awaited Caesar's arrival. He was warned of the danger on the way, for a certain friend gave him as he was going into the Senate a letter written about this matter. Caesar nevertheless did not read it but was holding it in [his] hand. When he had come into (entered) the Senate [chamber], [and was] surrounded by them, he says, "What do you want?" Next, when he had seen the swords, "Who will defend me against the force of these [men]?" Nevertheless no one came to his aid. The conspirators immediately attacked him with [their] swords. At first Caesar defended himself bravely. When, however, he saw his friend Brutus among [his] enemies, he said, "You too, Brutus," and no longer tried to resist.

So was killed Julius Caesar, the greatest and most valiant of the Romans.

JESUS CHRIST, KING OF KINGS

2. Christ, Asked about His Kingdom, Replies to Pilate (p. 272)

Pilate said to Jesus, "Are you king of the Jews?" Jesus replied, "Do you say this of yourself, or have others told it to you of me?" Pilate answered, "Am I a Jew? Your people and your priests have handed you over to me. What have you done?" Jesus answered, "My kingdom is not from (of) this world. If my kingdom were of this world, my servants would certainly struggle that I might not be handed over to the Jews; now, however, my kingdom is not hence." So Pilate said to him, "Are you then a king?" Jesus answered, "You say that I am a king. I was born unto this and for this have come into the world, that I should give witness to the truth; everyone who is of the truth, hears my voice."

For discussion, p. 273.—1. Did Christ say He was a king? 2. Did Christ say that His kingdom was like other kingdoms? 3. Why did Christ come into the world? 4. Is His kingdom the kingdom of truth?

Box, p. 273.—King of Kings and Lord of rulers (lords)—to him [be] glory and power forever.

Box, p. 273.—Come, let us adore Jesus Christ, King of Kings.

3. My Kingdom Is Not of This World (p. 274)

For Christ is not king for the purpose of exacting tribute or for assembling an army and overcoming visible enemies, but He is king because He rules minds, because He leads to the kingdom of heaven those who believe, hope, and love. He who was called King of the Jews on earth, in heaven is king of the angels. But is Christ king only of the Jews or of the nations also? Indeed (especially), of the nations.

For discussion, p. 274.—1. In what ways does Christ differ from other kings? 2. Why did Christ come into the world? 3. What Christian virtues should they have whom Christ leads to heaven? 4. Of whom is Christ king?

4. From the Preface of the Mass of Christ the King (p. 275)

It is truly meet and just, right and salutary for us always and everywhere to give thanks to You, holy Lord, almighty Father, eternal God, who have anointed with the oil of exaltation Your only-begotten Son, our Lord Jesus Christ, eternal priest and king of all; in order that, offering Himself on the altar of the cross, a pure and peacemaking victim, He might perform (complete) the mysteries of human redemption; and that, all creatures having been subjected (made subject) to His power, He might hand over (proffer) to Your infinite Majesty an eternal and universal kingdom. A kingdom of truth and life; a kingdom of holiness and grace; a kingdom of justice, love, and peace.

5. Prayer from the Mass of Christ the King (p. 277)

Almighty, everlasting God, who in Your beloved Son, King of all [creation], wished to renew (restore) all things; gracious(ly) grant that all the families of nations, separated (disunited) by the wound of sin, may become subject to His most gentle power. Who lives and reigns with You in the unity of the Holy Spirit throughout all ages. Amen.

Box, p. 277.—Hail, Christ the King

6. The Laws of Christ's Kingdom (p. 278)

A. The Great Commandment.—St. Mark: Jesus, however, answered him, "The first commandment of all is: Hear, O Israel, the Lord is thy God, the Lord is one, and thou shalt love the Lord thy God with thy whole heart, and with thy whole soul, and with thy whole mind, and with all thy strength. This is the first commandment. The second, however, is like to this: Thou shalt love thy neighbor as thyself. No other commandment is greater than these."

St. Matthew: And one of them, a teacher of the Law, asked Him, tempting Him: "Master, which is the greatest command in the Law?"

Jesus says to him: "Thou shalt love the Lord thy God from thy whole heart, and in thy whole soul, and in thy whole mind. This is the greatest and the first commandment. The second, however, is like to this: Thou shalt love thy neighbor as thyself."

B. The Program of Christ.—Jesus, however, seeing the crowd, went up into a mountain, and when He had sat down His disciples came to Him, and opening His mouth, He taught them, saying:

"Blessed [are] the poor in spirit, for theirs is the kingdom of heaven.

"Blessed [are] the meek, for they shall possess the land.

"Blessed [are] those who mourn, for they shall be comforted.

"Blessed [are] those who hunger and thirst for justice, for they shall be satisfied.

"Blessed [are] the merciful, for they shall gain (obtain) mercy.

"Blessed [are] those with a clean heart, for they shall see God.

"Blessed [are] the peacemakers, for they shall be called the sons of God.

"Blessed [are] those who suffer persecution for justice, for theirs is the kingdom of heaven.

"Blessed are you when they shall have reviled you and persecuted you, and lying, shall have said every bad [thing] against you on account of Me: rejoice and exult, for your reward is very great in heaven; for so they persecuted the prophets who were before you. . . . So let your light shine before men that they may see your good works and may glorify your Father, who is in heaven. . . . You have heard that it is said: You shall love your neighbor and hate your enemy. But I say to you: Love your enemies, do good to these who hate you; and pray for those persecuting and calumniating you; that you may be sons of your Father, who is in heaven; who makes His sun rise over the good and the bad. . . . For if you love those who love you, what reward will you have? . . . Be therefore perfect, as your heavenly Father is perfect."

7. The Commission to the Apostles to Spread Christ's Kingdom (p. 282)

And Jesus, coming [up] to [them], spoke to them, saying, "All power is given to Me in heaven and on earth. Going, therefore, teach all nations, baptizing them in the name of the Father, and of the Son, and of the Holy Spirit; teaching them to keep whatever I have entrusted to you. And behold, I am with you all days up to the end of the world."

8. Christ Himself (p. 283)

He did all things well.

"Come to me all [ye] who are in difficulty or are burdened and I will refresh you."

"I am the way, the truth, and life."

"I am the resurrection and life; he who believes in Me, even if he were dead, shall live."

"Follow Me; I am the light of the world; he who follows Me does not walk in darkness but will have the light of life."

"I am a good shepherd. A good shepherd gives his life for his sheep."

"Greater love than this no one has, that a man lay down his life for his friends."

9. The Soul's Answer to Christ's Call (p. 285)

"I live in the faith of the Son of God who loved me and handed Himself over for me."

"He who finds Jesus finds a good treasure, indeed, good above every [other] good. And he who loses Jesus loses exceedingly much and more than the whole world. Very poor is he who lives without Jesus; and very rich [is] he who is well (on good terms) with Jesus.

"Let all be loved for Jesus, Jesus however for Himself [alone]. Jesus Christ only must be loved alone, who alone is found good and faithful before all [other] friends. Because of Him and in Him let both friends and enemies be dear to you; and we must beseech [Him] for all these, that they may all know and love Him.

" 'Follow Me: I am the way, the truth, and life. Without a way, you cannot go; without the truth, you cannot know; without life, you cannot live. I am the way which you ought to follow, the truth which you ought to believe, the life which you ought to hope for. If you wish to reign with Me, carry the cross with Me. For only the servants of the cross find the way of happiness and of true light.'

"Come, brothers, advance together. Jesus will be with us. For Jesus we have taken upon ourselves this cross, for Jesus let us persevere in the cross.

"Behold, our King goes before us, who will fight for us. Let us follow manfully, let no one fear terrors; let us be ready to die bravely in [this] war."

10. The World's Greatest Short Story (p. 287)

A certain man had two sons, and the younger of them said to the father, "Father, give me the share of [your] substance which falls to me." And he divided between them the substance (inheritance). And not many days afterward, all having been gathered together, the younger son set out abroad for a distant region, and there squandered his substance by living riotously. And after he had used up everything, a great famine occurred in that region, and he began to be in want. And he went away, and clung to one citizen of that region, and he sent him to his country estate to feed hogs. And he desired to fill his belly with the husks which the hogs were eating; and no one gave [any] to him. Having turned to himself, however, he said, "How many hired servants in my father's house abound in bread; but I perish here of hunger! I will arise, and go to my father, and say to him, 'Father, I have sinned against heaven and before you; now I am not worthy to be called your son; make (treat) me as one of your hired servants.' " And arising, he came (went) to his father.

When he was as yet far away, however, his father saw him and was moved with compassion, and running [to him] he fell on his neck and kissed him. The son said to him, "Father, I have sinned against heaven and before you, [and] now I am not worthy to be called your son." But the father said to his servants, "Quickly bring forth the first (best) robe and put it on him, and give [him] a ring on (for) his hand, and shoes on (for) his feet; and lead on a fatted calf and kill [it], and let us eat and dine; because this my son was dead, and has come to life; he was lost, and is found." And they began to dine.

But the older son was in the field; and when he came and drew near the house he heard music and a [choral] dance, and he called one of the servants and asked what these things were (meant). That one said to him, "Your brother has come, and your father has killed a fatted calf, because he has received him back safe." But he was indignant and was unwilling to go in. His father, therefore, having gone out, begins to ask (question) him. But answering, he said to his father, "Behold I serve you so many years, and have never transgressed your command, and you have never given me a kid in order that I might dine with my friends; but after this son of yours who devoured his substance with prostitutes has come, you have killed for him a fatted calf." But he said to him, "Son, you are always with me, and all mine (my possessions) are yours. But it is fitting to dine and to rejoice, because this your brother was dead, and has come to life again; he was lost, and is found."

11. "Never Did Man Speak as This Man!" (p. 291)

Then the Pharisees going away entered upon a plan to take Him in conversation. And they send to Him their own disciples with the Herodians, saying (to say), "Master, we know that You are truthful, and teach the way to truth, and have no care for anyone; for You do not consider the person of men. Tell us therefore what You think—is it lawful to give tribute to Caesar or not?" But Jesus, having known (knowing) their wickedness, says, "Why do you tempt Me, you hypocrites? Show Me the coin of the tribute." But they offered Him a denarius. And Jesus says to them, "Whose image and superscription is this?" They say to Him, "Caesar's." Then He says to them, "Render therefore to Caesar [those things] which are Caesar's, and to God [the things] which are God's." And hearing [this] they admired (were in admiration), and having left Him, went away.

12. The Greatest Christmas Hymn of All (p. 293)

Be present (come), ye faithful, joyful [and] triumphing (triumphant), come, come to Bethlehem, see the (new) born King of angels. Come let us adore, come let us adore, come let us adore the Lord.

Behold, the flock having been left, the humble shepherds, having been called, hasten to the crib; let us also hasten with joyful step. Come let us adore, etc.

With star as guide, the Magi, adoring Christ, give gold, incense, and myrrh as gifts; let us offer to the Infant Jesus our hearts. Come let us adore, etc.

The eternal Father's eternal splendor we shall see veiled under flesh, God an infant wrapped in bands. Come let us adore, etc.

Poor for us, lying on straw, let us fondle [Him] with pious (reverent) embraces. Who would not love in return [one] loving us so? Come let us adore, etc.

Let now the choir of angels sing hymns, all the court of heavenly [spirits] sing: Glory, glory to God in the highest! Come let us adore, etc.

Therefore, O Jesus, who was born today, to You be glory, Word of the eternal Father made flesh. Come let us adore, etc.

13. "And the Kings of the Orient Came . . ." (p. 296)

When therefore Jesus was born in Bethlehem of Juda, in the days of King Herod, behold, Magi came from the East to Jerusalem, saying, "Where is [He] who was born king of the Jews? For we have seen His star in the East, and have come to adore Him." Hearing [this], however, Herod the king was disturbed, and all Jerusalem with him. And gathering together all the leading men of the priests (the chief priests) and the scribes of the people, he inquired of them where Christ was to be born. But they said to him, "In Bethlehem of Juda; for so it was written by the Prophet: 'And you Bethlehem, land of Juda, [are] not at all the least among the princes of Juda; for out of you will come the leader who shall rule My people Israel.' " Then Herod, the Magi having been called (summoned) secretly, carefully learns from them the time of the star which appeared to them. And sending them to Bethlehem, he said, "Go, and ask carefully concerning the Child; and when you have found [Him], report to me, so that I too, coming, may adore Him."

Who when they had heard the king, went away. And behold, the star which they had seen in the East went before them, until coming it stood above [the place] where the Boy was. But seeing the star they rejoiced with exceedingly great joy. And entering the house, they found the Boy with Mary His mother, and falling down they adored Him; and, their treasures opened, they offered Him gifts, gold, incense, and myrrh. And an answer received (receiving an answer) in dreams [that they were] not to return to Herod, they returned by another route to their own region (land).

14. The Feast of the Holy Innocents

Then Herod, seeing that he had been deceived by the Magi, got exceedingly angry. And sending [soldiers], he killed all the boys who were in Bethlehem and in all its territories (neighborhood), from two years old and under.

Hail, flowers of the martyrs, whom on the very threshold of light Christ's persecutor put under (snatched away) as a whirlwind snatches away budding roses.

You, the first victims of Christ, tender flock of the immolated, simple [children] you play with your palm and crowns under (at the very foot of) the altar.

What does such an enormity profit, what (how) does [this] crime help Herod? Alone, among so many deaths, Christ is safely taken away.

15. Tantum Ergō

This great Sacrament, therefore, let us venerate, bending low. And let the ancient teaching yield to a new rite; faith furnishes help to the weakness of the senses.

To the Father and the Son [be] praise and rejoicing; salvation, honor, and power also, as well as blessing; to the One who proceeds from both be equal praise. Amen.

16. Ō Salūtāris Hostia

O saving Victim, who opens the gate of heaven, hostile wars oppress us; give [us] strength, bring help.

To the one and triune Lord be everlasting glory, and may He bestow upon us life without end in [our] fatherland.

17. The Student's Lament

Our senses already languish, and in us already grows cold the heat (fire) of genius; if it is asked, "Who did this?" we answer, "The crowded (constant) effort of study has affected us."

EXERCISES BASED ON CAESAR

Lesson 1

Exercise 1.—See Introduction, 3.

Exercise 2.—See Introduction, 3.

Exercise 3.—1. *Patris; mātris.* (These nouns and many of the others in the exercise could be either singular or plural.) On account of the death of father, mother, and brothers. 2. *Nōmine.* In the name of God. 3. *Auctōritātem.* On account of the authority of God. 4. *Timōre.*

With fear. 5. *Classī* or *classe*. In the fleet. 6. *Timōrem*. Because of fear the leader was not with the cohorts. 7. *Itinere*. Part of the enemy was on the march. 8. *Cōnsulēs*. Caesar and Bibulus were consuls. 9. *Mīlitibus*. The general will be with the soldiers in the mountains. 10. *Flūmine*. The enemy's column was on (in) the river. 11. *Hominum*. On account of (for) the salvation of men. 12. *Lībertātem*. On account of the liberty of the Gauls. 13. *Hominum*. Christ is king of men. 14. *Cōnsule*. The cohorts were with the consul. 15. *Cīvitāte*. After the victories of the Romans there was no liberty in the Gauls' state.

Exercise 4.—1. Christ is our hope. (*Spēs*, pred. n.) 2. By the grace of God you and I are Christians. (*Sumus*, pl. v. with a compound sub.; the first person is preferred to the second.) 3. You and the consuls were in the city. (*Erātis*, pl. v. with a compound sub.; the second person is preferred to the third.) 4. You and I are Christians. (*Sum*, sing. v., agreeing with the nearest word of a compound sub., or because it stands between the subjects.) 5. There are liberty and peace in our state. (*Est*, sing. v., agreeing with the nearest word of a compound sub., or because it stands between the subjects.)

Exercise 5.—1. There was not (no) liberty in the states of the Gauls after Caesar's victory. (*Lībertās* is placed last for emphasis.) 2. Christ came into the world for our salvation. (*Vēnit*, ordinarily the verb is last.)

Exercise 6.—1. The sign of Christians is the sign of the holy cross. 2. In the cross of Christ is our salvation. 3. In the will of God is our peace. 4. Christ is the light of the world.

Christian Prayers, p. 308.—*The Sign of the Cross*. In the name of the Father and of the Son and of the Holy Spirit. Amen. *The Doxology*. Glory be to the Father and to the Son and to the Holy Spirit, as it was in the beginning, is now and ever shall be, world without end. Amen.

Lesson 2

Exercise 7.—See Introduction, 3.

Exercise 8.—(All the predicate and all the attributive adjectives agree with their nouns in gender, number, and case.) 1. Very many men are good. (*Bonī* agrees with *hominēs*.) 2. The Gauls were barbarian. (*Barbarī* agrees with *Gallī*.) 3. The Roman empire was strong. (*Rōmānum* agrees with *imperium*; *firmum* agrees with *imperium*.) 4. The state of the Americans is strong. (*Firma* agrees with *cīvitās*.) 5. The life of men is short. (*Brevis* agrees with *vīta*.) 6. The journey was difficult. (*Difficile* agrees with *iter*.) 7. The life of brave men is renowned (glorious). (*Fortium* agrees with *hominum*.) 8. Not all laws are severe. (*Omnēs* agrees with *lēgēs; gravēs* agrees with *lēgēs*.) 9. The army's march will be short and easy. (*Breve* and *facile* agree with *iter*.)

Exercise 9.—1. Via Crucis brevis et difficilis erat. 2. Hominēs fortēs nōbilēs erunt. 3. Cīvitās firma nōn semper erat. 4. Agmen breve nōn est. 5. Iter difficile erit. 6. Plūrimī hominēs barbarī sunt. 7. Cohors Rōmāna magna nōn erat.

Exercise 10.—1. Very many [men] are eager for fame. (*Glōriae,* gen. w. *cupidī.*) 2. Wars are full of dangers. (*Perīculōrum,* gen. w. *plēna.*) 3. The Mexicans are next to us. (*Nōbīs,* dat. w. *fīnitimī.*) 4. Caesar's camp was often next to (beside) a river. (*Flūminī,* dat. w. *proxima.*) 5. The camp was full of arms (*Armīs,* dat. w. *plēna.*)

Exercise 11.—1. Collis ad castra (castrīs) idōneus est. 2. Helvētiī proximī prōvinciae Rōmānae fuērunt. 3. Plūrimī hominēs pācis cupidī sunt. 4. Marīa "grātiā (grātiae) plēna" erat. 5. Rōmānī glōriae cupidī erant. 6. Vītae plūrimōrum hominum labōris plēnae erant. 7. Omnēs hominēs lībertātis cupidī sunt.

Exercise 12.—The path of virtue is easy for the brave (To the brave, the path of virtue is easy).

Box, p. 312.—Precious in the sight of the Lord is the death of His saints!

Lesson 3

Exercise 13.—See Introduction, 3.

Exercise 14.—**A.** 1. He is pacifying (conquering) Gaul. 2. They dwell in Gaul. 3. He is making a journey (He is marching). 4. He warns the leader. 5. They are making (building) a bridge. 6. He is fleeing. 7. They fear death. 8. They aid [their] friends. 9. They seek fame. 10. They hurl the darts. 11. He fortifies the camp. 12. They hear cries. 13. They are withstanding the attack. 14. He hears shouting. 15. They are building a road. 16. They desire power. 17. He is taking the city.

B. 1. The Romans pacified (subjugated) Gaul. 2. The Gauls, brave men, dwelt in Gaul. 3. The leader made many marches. 4. The good slaves warned [their] leader. 5. Caesar made (built) a bridge on (across) the river. 6. The barbarians were fleeing into the great forest. 7. Bad men fear death. 8. Strong and brave friends will help [their] friends (each other). 9. Kings eager for glory seek wars. 10. The barbarians were hurling very many darts. 11. The general was fortifying the camp. 12. The soldier heard the enemy's cries. 13. Strong soldiers will with-

stand the attack. 14. The Romans heard the shouting of the enemy.
15. The Romans built roads through the provinces. 16. Kings and emperors desired power. 17. The Romans captured many great cities.

C. 1. The Romans, eager for power, pacified (conquered, subjugated)
Gaul. 2. The Gauls, men barbarian (barbarous) but brave, inhabited
Gaul. 3. The Roman leaders, brave men, made many great marches.
4. Good servants will warn a good leader. 5. Caesar, a great man, made
(built) a bridge over the deep and wide river. 6. The rest of the barbarians had fled into the forest on account of (through) fear of the
cavalry. 7. Strong and brave men will not fear death. 8. Caesar always
helped [his] friends. 9. The kings, eager for victory and glory, did not
seek peace with neighboring tribes. 10. The enemy [soldiers] hurled
darts from all sides against the Roman camp. 11. The Roman general
fortified the camp on account of the great number of the enemy. 12. The
soldiers [constantly] heard the cries and shouting of the wretched
slaves. 13. The legions withstood strongly the attack of the brave
barbarians. 14. The Roman general heard the speech of the chiefs.
15. The Roman leaders on account of (because of their) fear of war
were building long roads through the provinces. 16. Bad men violently
desire power. 17. The Roman generals were capturing very many cities
and towns of the foreign tribes.

Exercise 15.—1. Galliam pācāvit. 2. Prīmā lūce fūgērunt. 3. Mīlitēs
victōriam cupiunt. 4. Tēla jēcērunt. 5. Rēx bonus rēgnum bonum facit.
6. Virtūs vītam sānctam facit. 7. Collem cēpērunt. 8. In montēs fugiē-
bant. 9. Urbem capit. 10. Vīdistīne agmen? 11. Post proelium corpora
in flūmine et in colle erant. 12. Impetum sustinuērunt. 13. Nauta portum
cupit. 14. Cum barbarīs pugnābant. 15. Barbarī tēla jaciēbant. 16. Gallī
signa legiōnis Rōmānae vīdērunt. 17. Servī in castrīs erant. 18. Multī
hominēs bonī Galliam incoluērunt. 19. Imperium cupīvit. 20. Barbarī
oppidum capient. 21. Legiō in perīculō gravī erat. 22. Mīles barbarōs
pācābit. 23. In prōvinciam iter faciēbant. 24. In castra tēlum jēcit.
25. Pars agminis in ponte erat.

Exercise 16.—A. 1. What do all Christians desire? (To be united
with God in heaven.) 2. In whom is the hope of all Christians? (In
Christ.) 3. To whom does God give grace? (To all men.) 4. Who was
Pilate? (Pilate was the Roman procurator of Judea who gave Christ
up to be crucified.) 5. Who waged war with the Romans in Gaul? (The
Gauls.) 6. To whom do we give thanks for all things? (To God.)
7. With whom did they lead Christ to death? (With two thieves.)
8. Whose name do we always praise? (God's name.) 9. Whom did

Caesar pacify (subjugate)? (The Gauls.) 10. Whose hostages did Caesar kill? (The enemy's.)

B. 1. Quibuscum Caesar bellum gessit? (Caesar cum Gallīs bellum gessit.) 2. Quōs Caesar laudāvit? (Caesar mīlitēs fortēs laudāvit.) 3. Quid Caesar cupīvit? (Caesar imperium cupīvit.) 4. In quō spem pōnimus? (In Chrīstō omnem spem pōnimus.) 5. Quī Gallōs vīcērunt? (Caesar Gallōs vīcērunt.) 6. Quōrum agrōs Caesar vastāvit? (Caesar agrōs Gallōrum vastāvit.) 7. Cum quōrum mīlitibus Gallī contendēbant? (Gallī cum mīlitibus Rōmānōrum contendēbant.) 8. Quī Galliam incolēbant? (Gallī Galliam incolēbant.) 9. Quibus Chrīstus magna praemia dabit? (Chrīstus hominibus bonīs magna praemia dabit.) 10. Quem omnēs laudātis? (Omnēs Deum laudāmus.)

Exercise 17.—A. 1. Why do we praise God? 2. Did Caesar pacify (subjugate) Gaul? 3. Caesar was a great man, wasn't he? 4. The Gauls did not conquer the Romans, did they? 5. Where is the Mississippi River? 6. We always praise a strong (faithful, steadfast) friend, don't we?

B. 1. Ubi Rōmānī incolēbant? 2. Jēcistīne tēlum? 3. Num fugiēs? 4. Nōnne mīlitēs victōriam semper cupiunt? 5. Cūr Caesar in Galliam iter fēcit? 6. Cēpēruntne Rōmānī multās urbēs? 7. Nōnne omnēs Marīam laudāmus? 8. Num hostēs Americānōs vīcērunt? 9. Vīdistīne montēs? 10. Pugnābantne Gallī cum Rōmānīs? 11. Pugnābisne semper prō lībertāte?

Box, p. 317.—Laws are silent (cease to be effective) in the midst of arms.

The Roman Empire, p. 318.—All men always praise liberty and peace, have always praised [it], will always praise [it]. For they are all eager for liberty and peace. But men do not keep the laws of God. They desire the glory of war and of power; they desire foreign fields and the good things of others. And so they prepare troops of soldiers; they lead an army into foreign territories; they wage war with the nearest tribes; they lay waste and burn fields and cities; they storm cities; they capture children and slaves and either conquer or kill all the enemy. And so men are often wretched because they have not kept the laws of God.

Quotation from Tacitus, p. 318.—They make a desert [and] they call it peace!

Answer in Latin, p. 318.—1. What do all men praise? (Omnēs hominēs lībertātem atque pācem laudant.) 2. Are all men eager for peace? (Omnēs hominēs lībertātis et pācis cupidī sunt.) 3. Nevertheless what do men desire? (Bellī atque imperiī glōriam cupiunt.) 4. Why do they lead an army into foreign territory? (Exercitum in fīnēs aliēnōs ducunt quod agrōs aliēnōs et bona aliēna cupiunt. 5. Why are men often wretched? (Saepe miserī sunt hominēs quod lēgēs Deī nōn servāvērunt.) 6. Did the Romans praise peace and liberty? (Rōmānī pācem et lībertātem laudāvērunt, sed pācem et lībertātem Rōmānam.) 7. Did they conquer Italy? (Italiam vīcērunt.) 8. The tribes and nations waged war with the Romans, didn't they? (Gentēs et populī cum Rōmānīs bellum gessērunt.) 9. They did not desire a Roman peace, did they? (Pācem Rōmānam nōn cupīvērunt.) 10. They remembered [their] liberty, didn't they? (Lībertātem memōriā tenēbant et prō eā vehementer pugnābant.)

Answer in English, p. 319.—1. What was the Roman Empire? (Italy, and all the other lands around the Mediterranean and some distant regions such as southern England.) 2. Who kept (preserved) peace in almost all the nations? (The Romans imposed the Pax Romana throughout the empire.) 3. Why did the kings and leading men of the barbarians (barbarian tribes) wage war with the Romans? (They fought to preserve their ancient liberties.)

Lesson 4

Exercise 18.—See Introduction, 3.

Exercise 19.—See Introduction, 3.

Exercise 20.—1. Let us make an attack. 2. Let us not fight in an unfavorable place. 3. Let us draw back the cavalry. 4. Let us drive back the enemy. 5. Let us not flee to camp. 6. Let us hurl back the javelins. 7. Let us desire grace. 8. Let us praise God. 9. Let us release the slave. 10. Let us restrain the slaves. 11. Let us live in the grace of God.

Exercise 21.—1. Obsidēs redūcāmus. 2. Pīla rejiciāmus. 3. Hostēs repellāmus. 4. Equitēs reprimāmus. 5. Nē fugiāmus. 6. Nē lēgātōs remittāmus. 7. Praesidium collocēmus. 8. Rēs bonās cupiāmus. 9. Nē tēla jaciāmus. 10. Omnēs Caelum cupiāmus. 11. Hominēs bonōs adjuvēmus. 12. Lēgātōs reprimāmus. 13. Nē maneāmus. 14. Imperātōrem moneāmus. 15. Frūmentum portēmus. 16. Fortiter pugnēmus. 17. Lēgem Deī servēmus. 18. Nē mortem timeāmus. 19. Nē barbarīs cēdāmus. 20. Nē bellum gerāmus. 21. Castra hostium incendāmus. 22. Grātiam Deī petāmus. 23. Grātiās Deō agāmus. 24. Marīam laudēmus. 25. Nē oppidum oppugnēmus.

Exercise 22.—1. May you have rewards. 2. May we not be wretched.

3. May they hold the hill. 4. May you not flee! 5. May he conquer.
6. May he not conquer. 7. May he live!

Exercise 23.—1. Pugnet. Utinam pugnet. 2. Utinam nē fugiās.
3. Utinam vincāmus. 4. Mīlitēs adjuvet Deus. Utinam mīlitēs adjuvet
Deus. 5. Nē veniant. Utinam nē veniant.

Exercise 24.—1. Let them drive back the enemy. 2. Let them hurl
back the javelins. 3. Let him press back the enemy. 4. Let him station
a garrison. 5. Let him not lead back the legions. 6. Let him warn the
leader. 7. Let them keep the laws of God! 8. Let them not yield to the
enemy. 9. Let him not kill the king! 10. Let him fortify the winter
quarters. 11. Let him lead back the hostages.

Exercise 25.—1. Obsidēs redūcant. 2. Nē fugiant. 3. Mīlitēs pīla
rejiciant. 4. Servōs remittant. 5. Lēgātus praesidia collocet. 6. Dux
mīlitēs redūcat.

Inscriptions, p. 324.—May you live in God. May you live among
the saints. Sophronia, sweet Sophronia, may you live in God.

Box, p. 325.—Who Is Free? The good man, even if he be a slave, is
free; [but] the evil man is a slave, even if he be a king.

Answer in Latin, p. 326.—1. Did the Gauls come across the river?
(Gallī trāns flūmen vēnērunt.) 2. Did they seize all [of] Gaul? (Oc-
cupāvērunt omnem Galliam.) 3. Did they lead forces through the Alps?
(Dūxērunt cōpiās per Alpēs.) 4. Did they seize part of Italy? (Oc-
cupāvērunt partem Italiae.) 5. Did they contend with the Romans?
(Cum Rōmānīs contendērunt.) 6. Who captured Rome? (Gallī Rōmam
cēpērunt.) 7. Surely the Gauls did not burn Rome, did they? (Gallī
Rōmam incendērunt.)

Box, p. 326.—May the blessing of almighty God, Father, Son, and
Holy Spirit, descend upon you and remain forever. Amen.

Lesson 5

Exercise 26.—A. 1. I ask whether you praise Pilate. (*Laudētis,*
pres. subj. in indirect question in primary sequence, action at same time
as main verb.) 2. I ask whether Pilate was a good and brave man.
(*Fuerit,* perf. subj. in indirect question in primary sequence, action
before time of main verb.) 3. Pilate asked whether Christ was a king.
(*Esset,* imp. subj. in indirect question in secondary sequence, action at
same time as main verb.) 4. Pilate asked why the Jews had taken
Christ (prisoner). (*Cēpissent,* plu. subj. in indirect question in secondary
sequence, action before time of main verb.)

B. 1. I ask whether Columbus came to America. (*Pervēnerit,* perf.

subj. in indirect question in primary sequence, action before time of
main verb.) 2. I ask whether you remember Columbus. (*Teneātis,* pres.
subj. in indirect question in primary sequence, action at same time as
main verb.) 3. Columbus was asking whether the sailors saw land.
(*Vidērent,* imp. subj. in indirect question in secondary sequence, action
at same time as main verb.) 4. Afterwards Columbus asked who had
seen land first. (*Vidisset,* plu. subj. in indirect question in secondary
sequence, action before time of main verb.)

Exercise 27.—1. Caesar quaesīvit num legiōnēs hostēs rejēcissent.
(Plu. subj. in indirect question in secondary sequence, action before
time of main verb.) 2. Caesar quaesīvit num lēgātus obsidēs redūceret.
(Imp. subj. in indirect question in secondary sequence, action at same
time as main verb). 3. Rōmānī quaerunt num mīlitēs servōs represserint.
(Perf. subj. in indirect question in primary sequence, action before
time of main verb.) 4. Quaesīvērunt num Caesar lēgātōs remitteret.
(Imp. subj. in indirect question in secondary sequence, action at same
time as main verb.)

Exercise 28.—**A.** 1. Christ has opened heaven to all men. 2. On the
cross Christ was opening heaven. 3. Christians knew by how much
(what intense) pain Christ had opened heaven. 4. I ask whether Christ
opened heaven. 5. Did the centurion and the Roman soldiers know why
Christ on the cross was opening heaven? (The forms of *aperiō* are,
respectively, perf. indic., imp. indic., plu. subj., perf. subj., and imp.
subj.)

B. 1. What is truth? 2. Do you know what truth is? 3. Pilate asked
what truth was. (The forms of *sum* are, respectively, pres. indic., pres.
subj., and imp. subj.)

C. 1. Why did Christ come into the world? 2. Do you know why
Christ came into the world? 3. Did Pilate know why Christ had come
into the world? 4. Christ came into the world for the common salvation
of all men. (The forms of *veniō* are, respectively, perf. indic., perf.
subj., plu. subj., and perf. indic.)

Exercise 29.—(All the italicized words introduce indirect questions.) 1. We know *who* Christ is. (*Quis,* interrog. pron., sub. of indirect
question.) 2. Did Pilate know *whose* Son Christ was? (*Cūjus,* possess.
adj. modifying *Fīlius.*) 3. We know to *whom* the Jews handed over
(delivered) Christ. (*Cui,* interrog. pron., dat. of indirect obj.) 4. Do
you know *who* handed over (delivered) Christ to Pilate? (*Quī,* interrog.
pron., sub. of indirect question.) 5. I ask *with whom* they led Christ
to death. (*Quibuscum,* interrog. pron., form used for *cum quibus;* abl.

of accompaniment.) 6. Did they all know to (for) whom Christ was opening heaven? (*Quibus*, interrog. pron., dat. of indirect obj.) 7. Do you know whose mother Mary is now? (*Quōrum*, interrog. possess. adj. modifying *māter*.) 8. Do you know whom Christ on the cross called into heaven? (*Quem*, interrog. pron., obj. of *vocāverit*.) 9. Do you know why the Romans did not put Christ to death in the city? (*Cūr*, interrog. adv. modifying *occīderint*.) 10. Do you know where the soldiers led Christ? (*Quō*, interrog. adv. implying motion, modifying *dūxerint*.) 11. They ask how much pain Christ sustained (bore, suffered) on the cross. (*Quantum*, interrog. adj. modifying *dolōrem*.) 12. I ask how many friends were with Christ. (*Quot*, indecl. adj. modifying *amīcī*.) 13. Did Pilate know where Christ's kingdom was? (*Ubi*, adv. modifying *esset*.) 14. Saint Paul knew how many pains (how much pain) Christ sustained (bore, suffered) on the cross for the salvation of men. (*Quantōs*, interrog. adj. modifying *dolōrēs*.)

Exercise 30.—1. Quaerunt num victōriās mīlitum Americānōrum memōriā teneās. 2. Scīsne quis imperātor exercitūs Americānī sit? 3. Scīmus quem Chrīstiānī laudent. 4. Quaerō num Gallī Rōmam cēperint. 5. Scīsne quis Caesar fuerit? 6. Quaerēsne num lēgātus legiōnem prīmam redūxerit? 7. Quaesīvit quot mīlitēs in hībernīs essent. 8. Caesar quaesīvit quot impetūs legiō sustinuisset. 9. Quaesīvimus num Rōmam vīdissēs.

Exercise 31.—1. Let us praise God. (*Laudēmus*, hortatory subj.) 2. Let them not fight in an unfavorable place. (*Locō*, abl. of *locus* used without *in* to express place where. *Nē pugnent*, a negative command in the third person.) 3. May you come. (*Utinam*, particle used with the volitive subj.) 4. Let him not do wrong. (*Nē faciat*, a negative command in the third person.) 5. May God help the unfortunate. (*Adjuvet*, volitive subj.) 6. Let them bravely make an attack. (*Faciant*, a command in the third person.) 7. The life of slaves was often short and full of pain. (*Dolōrum*, gen. w. *plēna*.)

Lucius, a Brave Man (The Valiant Lucius), p. 331.—Once the Romans and the Aquitanians, friends of the Romans, were waging war with the Germans. The Roman army was marching. It came to a difficult and narrow place. Then the Germans, men barbarous and brave, made an attack upon the Roman column. The Romans were fighting in an unfavorable place and there was great danger. Nevertheless the centurions were strengthening (continued to arouse) the courage of the soldiers. "Let us fight bravely! Let us remain strong in the battle line! Let us not yield to the barbarians!"

Among the leaders of the Aquitanians was Lucius, a strong and brave man. Lucius also was arousing the soldiers to battle: "Let us not flee; let us carry on the battle with [our] swords! Let us beat back the barbarians! Press [them] back, conquer [them]!"

Nevertheless, the soldiers on account of (because of their) wounds and the great number of the enemy did not withstand the attack [any] longer. And so the Romans fled. Lucius also was fleeing with the Romans. [His] slaves, however, hastened to Lucius. "The Germans are capturing [your] brother! They are leading him into camp!" Lucius fled no longer. He urged his horse forward toward the enemy; he terrified the enemy with [his] arms and repelled [them]. [His] brother had a great many wounds, and so Lucius placed [his] brother with him on the horse and fled. But the horse was not strong enough, and so he placed [his] brother alone on the horse and urged the horse forward toward the Roman camp. He himself remained in battle (on the battlefield) and awaited the Germans. The enemy hastened swiftly to Lucius. Both the Germans and Lucius fought bitterly. They killed Lucius with swords and darts. He had saved [his] brother; he himself gave himself up to death with great courage. The fortune of war does not always give safety to the brave.

I ask whether Lucius was a brave and strong man. I ask whether you praise the courage of Lucius.

Lesson 6

Exercise 32.—1. Mihi. 2. Tibi. 3. Prō tē. 4. Vōbīscum. 5. Sine nōbīs. 6. Nōs. 7. Meī. 8. Propter virtūtem tuam. 9. Amīcīs meīs. 10. Mēcum. 11. Vōs. 12. In urbe tuā.

Exercise 33.—1. (May) God be with you; and with your spirit (soul). 2. Peace [be] with (to) you. 3. May God give you His grace and peace. 4. Thy kingdom come. 5. May God be with you. 6. After the slaughter of the chiefs we hid (concealed) ourselves in the mountains. 7. Our soldiers have fought for us and for our liberty. 8. Your friends are strong (steadfast, faithful) and brave, and so they will help you. 9. Surely we will not surrender to the enemy? 10. Who will help you in danger? Christ will help you. 11. Because of your victories and your great courage the general will give you great (rich) rewards. 12. He asked whether the soldiers had seen us. 13. We withdrew to a safe place.

Exercise 34.—(All the italicized words are forms of *is, ea, id*, and agree with their antecedents in gender and number.) 1. I ask whether Rome is a great (large, important, renowned) city, for I have not seen it (myself). (*Eam*, obj. of *vīdī*, referring to *Rōma*.) 2. Are there high (lofty) mountains in our territory (land)? Have you seen them? (*Eōs*, obj. of *vīdistī*, referring to *montēs*.) 3. Caesar was a great and brave commander in chief. On account of his victories the Romans praised him. (*Ējus*, used as possess. adj. modifying *victōriās* and referring to *Caesar; eum*, obj. of *laudāvērunt*, referring to *Caesar*.) 4. The consuls and the Roman Senate had great authority among foreign tribes also. All the tribes sent envoys to them. (*Eōs*, obj. of the prep. *ad*, referring to *cōnsulēs* and *senātus*.) 5. Mary, the mother of God, was full of grace, and so all Christians praise her and her name is renowned. (*Eam*, obj. of *laudant*, referring to *Marīa; ējus*, used as possess. adj. modifying *nōmen* and referring to *Marīa*.)

Exercise 35.—1. Gallī fortēs erant. Caesar autem eōs pācāvit et agrōs oppidaque eōrum occupāvit. 2. Rōmānī Chrīstum ad mortem dūxērunt propter Jūdaeōs, nam Pīlātus eōs et prīncipēs eōrum timuit. 3. Rōmānī Rōmam fortiter dēfendērunt. Gallī autem eam cēpērunt et incendērunt. 4. Nostra cīvitās magna et lībera est. Eam semper dēfendēmus. 5. Plūrimī Rōmānī Caesarem laudāvērunt. Quaerō num Deus eum et victōriās ējus laudāverit. 6. Marīa māter nostra grātiā Deī est. Fīliī ējus sumus. Eam laudēmus.

Exercise 36.—1. *Us*, indirect. 2. *Them*, indirect. 3. No reflexive. 4. *Ourselves*, direct. 5. No reflexive. 6. *Your*, direct (adj.).

Exercise 37.—(All the italicized words are forms of *suī*, reflexive pronoun, or *suus, a, um*, reflexive possessive pronoun and adjective.) 1. The cohorts were defending themselves. (*Sē*, direct, obj. of *dēfendēbant*, referring to *cohortēs*.) 2. The Gauls were defending their fields and cities by means of strong garrisons. (*Suās*, direct, modifying *agrōs* and *urbēs*, agreeing in case and number with the nearest antecedent, and referring to *Gallī*.) 3. The consul led the hostages [away] with him. (*Sē*, direct, obj. of the prep. *cum*, referring to *cōnsul*.) 4. For the sake of their liberty the barbarians bravely drove the enemy back. (*Suā*, direct, modifying *lībertāte* and referring to *barbarī*.) 5. The barbarians hid (concealed) themselves in the forest. (*Sē*, direct, obj. of *abdidērunt*, referring to *barbarī*.) 6. The Romans waged war with the tribes nearest to them. (*Sibi,* direct, dat. w. *proximīs*, referring to *Rōmānī*.) 7. The chiefs of the barbarians often led their troops back into the forest. (*Suās*, direct, modifying *cōpiās* and referring to *prīncipēs*.) 8. The general gave to his [men] rewards for courage. (*Suīs*, direct, ind. obj. of *dedit*, referring to *imperātor*.) 9. The Gauls surrendered themselves and all theirs (their possessions) to Caesar. (*Sē*, direct, obj. of *dēdidērunt*,

referring to *Gallī; sua,* direct, obj. of *dēdidērunt,* referring to *Gallī.*)
10. Caesar did not praise himself, did he? (*Sē,* direct, obj. of *laudāvit,*
referring to *Caesar.*) 11. On account of (through) fear the legions withdrew into the city. (*Sē,* direct, obj. of *recēpērunt,* referring to *legiōnēs.*)
12. Renowned generals praise theirs (their own men), don't they?
(*Suōs,* direct, obj. of *laudant,* referring to *imperātōrēs.*) 13. Mary
praised her Son. (*Suum,* direct, modifying *Fīlium* and referring to
Marīa.) 14. The lieutenant sent a message to Caesar about his own
danger. (*Suō,* direct, modifying *perīculō,* referring to *lēgātus.*) 15. The
cohorts fortified their camp. (*Sua,* direct, modifying *castra* and referring
to *cohortēs.*) 16. The legion was bravely defending its standard. (*Suum,*
direct, modifying *signum* and referring to *legiō.*)

Picture caption, p. 338.—I carry all mine (my things) with me.

Exercise 38.—1. Did Pilate know why the Jews had handed Christ
over to him? (*Sibi,* indirect, ind. obj. of *trādidissent,* referring to
Pīlātus.) 2. He asked whether the lieutenant had sent him a dispatch
concerning the danger of the fleet. (*Sē,* indirect, obj. of the prep. *ad,*
referring to the unexpressed sub. of *rogāvit.*) 3. Saint Paul knew by (at
the cost of) how much pain Christ had opened heaven to him. (*Sibi,*
indirect, ind. obj. of *aperuisset,* referring to *Paulus.*) 4. Caesar asked
whether the enemy was terrifying his (his men). (*Suōs,* indirect, obj.
of *terrērent,* referring to *Caesar.*) 5. The leader of the barbarians asked
whether the Romans had withdrawn to the battle line. (*Sē,* direct, obj.
of *recēpissent,* referring to *Rōmānī.*) 6. Caesar asked why his [men]
had withdrawn into the city. (*Suī,* indirect, sub. of *recēpissent,* referring
to *Caesar; sē,* direct, obj. of *recēpissent,* referring to *suī.*) 7. Afterwards
the enemy hid (concealed) themselves in the mountains. (*Sē,* direct,
obj. of *abdidērunt,* referring to *hostēs.*)

Exercise 39.—1. Sē dēfendērunt. 2. Suōs laudāvit. 3. Omnēs hominēs cīvitātēs suās laudant. 4. Marīa sē neque laudāvit neque dēfendit.
5. Cohors sē fortiter dēfendit. 6. Marīa Fīlium suum laudāvit.

Exercise 40.—1. Quaesīvit quis sē dēfendisset. 2. Sciunt quī sē
oppugnent. 3. Quaerit num sē laudēmus. 4. Legiō scīvit Caesarem sē
dēfendisse. 5. Caesar quaesīvit num equitēs suōs vīdissent. 6. Marīa
scit num Fīlium suum laudēmus. 7. Legiō quaerit num ducem suum
sciāmus. 8. Gallī quaesīvērunt num cōnsul obsidēs suōs occīdissent.

Exercise 41.—1. Ego senātum mōnēbō. 2. Marīa māter Deī et mea
est. 3. Quis mēcum veniet? 4. Chrīstiānī Spīritum Sānctum laudāmus.
5. Nōs Americānī cum gentibus nōbīs proximīs multa bella nōn gessimus.
6. Deus nōbīs omnem grātiam dabit. 7. Quaerisne tū num Chrīstus in

mundum propter salūtem nostram vēnerit. 8. Nōs in castra nōs nōn recipiēmus. 9. Viae bonae sunt. Rōmānī eās mūnīvērunt. 10. Eī castra posuērunt. Mīlitēs ea mūnīvērunt. 11. Ea māter Deī est. 12. Magnā (cum) virtūte sē dēfendērunt. 13. Nōs Chrīstum et Marīam mātrem ējus laudāmus. Ea sāncta erat. Deus eī magnum praemium dedit. Omnēs hominēs sānctī eam Fīliumque ējus in Caelō vidēbunt. Omnēs cum eā prō nōbīs ōrābunt. 14. Hominēs sānctī et prō sē et prō nōbīs ōrant. 15. Deus grātiā in nōbīs est. 16. Prō vōbīs pugnābātis. 17. Barbarīs nōs nōn dēdēmus. 18. Nōnne tū mātrem tuam laudās? 19. Caesar scīvit quantō in perīculō (mīlitēs) suī essent. 20. Eī post caedem ducum suōrum Caesarī sē dēdidērunt. 21. Caesar post mortem ducum eōrum barbarōs occīdit. 22. Cohors nova (integra) in oppidum sē recēpit. 23. In silvīs sē abdidērunt. 24. Imperātor multōs lēgātōs sēcum in Galliā habuit. 25. Quaesīvērunt num centuriō Caesarī nuntium dē perīculō suō mīsisset.

Box, p. 340.—Honor thy father and thy mother.

Box, p. 341.—For before Christ's coming the way of life was unknown.

In the Roman Camp, p. 341.—Scene I. In the Roman Camp. Not many (few) cohorts are holding the camp. Caesar is away. On all sides we hear the shouting of the enemy. The enemy are hurling darts and javelins against (at) the Romans from all sides. The Romans nevertheless withstand the attack bravely; they beat back and drive back the enemy. Almost all the Roman soldiers have wounds (are wounded).

A SOLDIER. There is a great number of the enemy. We are not many. They are hurling darts at us from all sides. They will either kill us or capture us.

A CENTURION. We will put hope (will depend upon our) courage. Let us fight to the death. Caesar will know with how much courage we have fought.

S. We have not (no) hope. Large forces of Germans will also cross the river. We have often sent (have sent frequent) messages to Caesar but they have not reached him. The Gauls have either captured or killed our cavalry. Caesar is far away. He will not send help to us nor will he lead us back into the province.

Scene II. The same.

S. We shall not hold the camp [any] longer.

SOLDIERS. Surely we will not surrender ourselves and our standards to the enemy?

C. There is not (no) hope of safety for us. We are not many. Caesar will not come with fresh troops. At dawn the enemy will make an attack and will capture us. What shall we do?

SOLDIERS. They shall not take us!

(They all kill themselves.)

Scene III. In the Roman Camp. At dawn we hear the shouting of the enemy. The enemy approach the camp. They come into the camp and they see the bodies.

THE LEADER OF THE ENEMY. We have captured the bodies of the Romans! (We have captured only dead Romans!) The End.

Answer in English, p. 342.—1. Why did the Romans kill themselves? (Because they did not want to surrender.) 2. We do not praise them for this, do we? (No.) 3. Christian soldiers do not kill themselves, do they? (No.) 4. Why do not Christians kill themselves? (Because God alone is the master of life and death.)

Lesson 7

Exercise 42.—A. 1. They are being hurled down. 2. They are being brought together. 3. He is being left behind. 4. It is being divided. 5. It is being pacified. 6. They are being led back. 7. They are being led. 8. They are being released. 9. They are being hurled. 10. He is being repulsed.

B. 1. The soldiers were being hurled down from the wall. 2. The hostages were being assembled in the camp. 3. A garrison was being left there. 4. The enemy's forces are being divided. 5. Gaul was being pacified. 6. The legion was being led back. 7. The troops were being led out of winter quarters. 8. A dispatch was being sent back to Caesar. 9. Darts were being hurled from all sides. 10. The enemy was being driven into the forest.

C. 1. Our soldiers were cast down from the wall and the rampart by the enemy's darts (fell from the wall and the rampart under a rain of enemy darts). 2. The hostages were brought together from the towns of the Gauls [and] into the Roman camp. 3. A garrison was left behind in the camp by Caesar. 4. The enemy's forces were divided by the leader into many parts. 5. All the tribes of Gaul were pacified (subjugated) by slaughter and with arms. 6. The legion was led back by Caesar from the forest into the camp. 7. The cavalry was led by the lieutenant from the province to the territory of the enemy. 8. The hostages were sent to the city from the camp. 9. Many darts were hurled at ours (our men) from the enemy's camp. 10. The enemy was driven back from the rampart by means of darts and javelins.

Exercise 43.—1. Ex castrīs dūcuntur (dūcēbantur, dūcentur, ductī sunt, ductī sunt, ductī erant). 2. Ā flūmine repelluntur (repellēbantur, repellentur, repulsī sunt, repulsī sunt, repulsī erant). 3. Ex castrīs dīmittitur (dīmittēbātur, dīmittētur, dīmissus est, dīmissus est, dīmissus erat). 4. Moneor (monēbar, monēbor, monitus sum, monitus sum, monitus eram). 5. Pīla in hostēs jaciuntur (jaciēbantur, jacientur, jacta sunt, jacta sunt, jacta erant). 6. Dē colle remittimur (remittēbāmur, remittēmur, remissī sumus, remissī sumus, remissī erāmus). 7. In prōvinciam redūcuntur (redūcēbantur, redūcentur, reductī sunt, reductī sunt, reductī erant). 8. Dē mūrō dējiciuntur (dējiciēbantur, dējicientur, dejectī sunt, dējectī sunt, dējectī erant). 9. In hībernīs relinquuntur (relinquēbantur, relinquentur, relictī sunt, relictī sunt, relictī erant).

Exercise 44.—1. The Helvetians were led from their territory by the chiefs. (*Dē*, prep. w. abl., meaning *from* or *out of*, indicating motion from inside a place; *ā*, prep. w. abl., expressing agent.) 2. The barbarians made an attack upon ours (our men) from the hill. (*Dē*, prep. w. abl., meaning *from*, indicating motion downwards; *in*, prep. w. abl., meaning *upon*, indicating motion toward.) 3. Messages (messengers) were sent to Caesar concerning the lieutenant's danger. (*Dē*, prep. w. abl., meaning *concerning; ad*, prep. w. acc., meaning *to*, indicating direction toward.) 4. The centurions hurled themselves down from the wall. (*Dē*, prep. w. abl., meaning *down from*, indicating motion downwards.) 5. Many of ours were killed. (*Dē*, prep. w. abl., meaning *of*, partitive.) 6. The cavalry fled from the river. (*Ā*, prep. w. abl., meaning *from*, indicating motion away from a place.) 7. The enemy was put to flight by the cavalry. (*Ab*, prep. w. abl., meaning *by*, expressing agent; *in*, prep. w. acc., idiomatic in *in fugam dare*.) 8. The enemy's camp was not far from our camp. (*Ā*, prep. w. abl., meaning *from*, designating separation.) 9. The barbarians were coming out of the river. (*Ex*, prep. w. abl., meaning *out of*, expressing motion from inside a place.) 10. The cavalry withdrew from flight (stopped fleeing). (*Ex*, prep. w. abl., meaning *from*, indicating motion from inside a place; here metaphorical.) 11. The legions withdrew into a safe place. (*In*, prep. w. acc., meaning *into*, indicating motion toward.) 12. Very many horsemen (a great number of the cavalry) fled from the battle (battlefields). (*Ex*, prep. w. abl., meaning *from*, indicating motion from inside a place.) 13. The leader stormed a town [turning aside] from the line of march. (*Ex*, prep. w. abl., meaning *from*, indicating motion from inside a place.) 14. He fled from the city. (*Ab*, prep. w. abl., meaning *from*, indicating motion away from.) 15. The bridge stretches from the town to the [land of the] Helvetians. (*Ex*, prep. w. abl., meaning *from*, indicating motion from inside a place.) 16. Are the Germans far from our territory (land)? (*Ā*, prep. w. abl., meaning *from*, designating separation.) 17. The soldiers recovered from fear. (*Ex*, prep. w. abl., meaning *from*, literally expressing motion.)

Box, p. 346.—Justice for all.

Exercise 45.—1. Cohortēs fugā salūtem petīvērunt. 2. Hostēs dē colle ab equitibus dējectī sunt. 3. Cōpiae ā cōnsule dīvidēbantur. 4. Dē vallō dējectus est. 5. Posteā ex aciē sē recēpērunt et in montibus sē abdidērunt. 6. Dē altō monte iter fēcit et oppidum oppugnāvit. 7. Praesidium in oppidō ā Caesare relictum est. 8. Cōpiae in silvās cōgēbantur et arma parābantur. 9. Concilium ā duce coāctum est. 10. Cōpiae integrae ex prōvinciā ā lēgātō ductae sunt. 11. Barbarī sē ex timōre recēpērunt. 12. Posteā prīmam legiōnem in Italiam redūxit. 13. Frūmentum armaque ex oppidō in castra portābantur. 14. Locō idōneō castra posuērunt. 15. Ā castrīs barbarōrum longē aberant. 16. Nuntius ā prīmā aciē remissus est. 17. Quaesīvērunt num hostēs dē (ex) fīnibus Gallōrum pulsī essent. 18. Omnis Gallia ā Caesare pācāta est. 19. Equitēs ā flūmine repulsī sunt. 20. Ā castrīs hostium (mīlitēs) suōs dūxit. 21. Agmen ex flūmine veniēbat. 22. Pīla dē vallō in hostēs dējiciēbantur. 23. Litterae dē rē gravī ab imperātōre ad cōnsulēs mittēbātur. 24. Nōn multī mīlitēs sē ex proeliō recēpērunt. 25. Caesar ā (mīlitibus) suīs longē aberat.

Exercise 46.—1. Quaesīvērunt num mīlitēs sē ex fugā recēpissent. (*Recēpissent*, plu. in an indirect question in secondary sequence, action before time of main verb.) 2. Cōnsulēs quaerunt num cōpiae ab imperātōre coāctae sint. (*Coāctae sint*, perf. in an indirect question in primary sequence, action before time of main verb.) 3. Quaesīvistī num mīlitēs fugā salūtem peterent. (*Peterent*, imp. in an indirect question in secondary sequence, action at same time as main verb.) 4. Quaerō quī in oppidō relinquantur. (*Relinquantur*, pres. in an indirect question in primary sequence, action at same time as main verb.)

From the Letters of Saint Paul, p. 347.—Paul, an apostle of Jesus Christ, according to the command of God our Savior and of Jesus Christ our hope, to Timothy, beloved son in faith: grace, mercy, and peace [be to you] from God the Father and from Christ Jesus our Lord.

Box, p. 347.—From the East, light; from the West, law.

Lesson 8

Exercise 47.—See Introduction, 3.

Exercise 48.—See Introduction, 3.

Exercise 49.—1. This state is ours (this is our state); these fields and these cities are ours. And so we will fight bravely for this state and we will always defend these fields and these cities. (*Haec*, demons. adj. modifying *cīvitās; hī*, demons. adj. modifying *agrī; hae*, demons. adj. modifying *urbēs; hāc*, demons. adj. modifying *cīvitāte; hōs*, demons. adj. modifying *agrōs; hās*, demons. adj. modifying *urbēs*.) 2. The cavalry was put to flight. They recovered from their fear, however, and were sent back by Caesar to the battle line. (*Hī*, demons. pron., sub. of *recēpērunt*, referring to *equitēs* in preceding sentence; *sē*, reflexive pron., obj. of *recēpērunt*, referring to *hī*.) 3. Both Hannibal and Caesar led great forces into foreign territory for (in quest of) fame. The latter pacified (subjugated) all Gaul; the former, however, was conquered by the Romans. (*Hic*, demons. pron., sub. of *pācāvit*, referring to *Caesar*, used in contrast with *ille*, referring to the person mentioned more recently; *ille*, demons. pron., sub. of *victus est*, referring to *Hannibal*, the person mentioned previously.) 4. The barbarians were exchanging hostages and treating of (discussing) a plan of war. For this reason Caesar led [his] legions against them. They, however, sent envoys to him concerning (to treat of) peace and surrendered themselves and all their possessions to him. (*Sē*, reflexive pron., obj. of the prep. *inter*, referring to *barbarī; eōs*, personal pron., obj. of the prep. *contrā*, referring to *barbarī; illī*, demons. pron., sub. of *mīsērunt*, referring to *barbarī; eum*, personal pron., obj. of the prep. *ad*, referring to *Caesar; sē suaque*, reflexive prons., objs. of *dēdidērunt*, referring to *illī; eī*, personal pron., ind. obj. of *dēdidērunt*, referring to *Caesar*.) 5. God is our father, and so let us love Him in every way. (*Eum*, personal pron., obj. of *dīligāmus*, referring to *Deus*.) 6. The soldiers were sent back to the fields for the sake of (to seek) grain. The enemy's cavalry, however, was sent against them. For this reason they quickly withdrew to the camp. (*Eōs*, personal pron., obj. of the prep. *contrā*, referring to *mīlitēs; hāc*, demons. adj. modifying *causā; illī*, demons. pron., sub. of *recēpērunt*, referring to *mīlitēs; sē*, reflexive pron., obj. of *recēpērunt*, referring to *mīlitēs*.) 7. The Roman cavalry is approaching us; the legions, however, are being held back in the camp by Caesar. Therefore let us send the cavalry against them for these (the legions) because of (their) fear will not come out of camp. 8. Are the Germans far from this territory (land) of ours? 9. A bridge stretched from that town to the [territory of the] Helvetians. 10. Italy is separated from Gaul by high (lofty) ·mountains. 11. There was a Roman province in Gaul. The

Belgians were a long way from this province. 12. High (lofty) mountains separate Italy from Gaul.

Exercise 50.—1. Equitēs in fugam datī sunt, legiōnēs autem in colle mānsērunt (manēbant) et omnēs impetūs pepulērunt. Itaque hīs imperātor praemium dedit, illīs autem praemia data nōn sunt. 2. Americānī in Galliam cōpiās mīsērunt et in Germāniam Germānōs reppulērunt. Hāc dē causā magna cōpia armōrum hīs cōpiīs missa est. Post hoc bellum multī dē illīs mīlitibus in Galliā diūtius mānsērunt. 3. Caesar cōpiās in agrōs frūmentī causā mīsērunt. Contrā eōs dux hostium equitēs mīsit. 4. Deus omnēs hominēs dīligit. Hāc dē causā eōs etiam dīligāmus. 5. Pācis causā inter hominēs populōsque omnī ratiōne amīcitiam cōnfirmēmus. 6. Gallī et Germanī cum Caesare bellum gessērunt. Hōs trāns flūmen reppulit, illōs autem vīcit et pācāvit. 7. Hāc dē causā contrā Germanōs castra posuit.

Picture caption, p. 351.—Isn't he strong?

Mothers, p. 351.—All boys are bad occasionally. Nevertheless mothers praise their sons, [but] do not often praise others' sons. Why do they act so?

Exercise 51.—See Introduction, 3.

Lesson 9

Exercise 52.—1. They are leading hostages to Caesar to strengthen peace (that peace might be strengthened) in this way. (*Ut*, conj. introducing a purpose clause; *cōnfirmētur*, pres. subj. in a purpose clause after a primary tense.) 2. They were holding all the roads by means of strong garrisons lest that new legion should be led (in order to prevent that new legion from being led) through the mountains into Gaul. (*Nē*, conj. introducing a negative purpose clause; *dēdūcerētur*, imp. subj. in a negative purpose clause after a secondary tense.) 3. He stationed strong garrisons in very many places in order that (by which) the province might be defended more easily. (*Quō*, conj. in a purpose clause containing a comparative adv.; *facilius*, compar. adv. modifying *dēfenderētur*; *dēfenderētur*, imp. subj. in a purpose clause after a secondary tense.) 4. The bad soldier fled from battle in order not to receive wounds (to be wounded). (*Nē*, conj. introducing a negative purpose clause; *acciperet*, imp. subj. in a negative purpose clause after a secondary tense.) 5. The leader fortified the camp by means of a ditch and a rampart lest the soldiers be killed by the enemy's attack. (*Nē*, conj. introducing a negative purpose clause; *interficerentur*, imp. subj. in a negative purpose clause after a secondary tense.) 6. He led many fresh legions into Gaul with him in order that this war might quickly be finished. (*Ut,* conj. introducing a purpose clause; *cōnficerētur,* imp. subj. in a purpose clause after a secondary tense.) 7. He leads the cavalry through the forest lest he be observed by the enemy. (*Nē,* conj. introducing a negative purpose clause; *cōnspiciātur,* pres. subj. in a negative purpose clause after a primary tense.) 8. Were those soldiers brave? They were not, for they withdrew from the battle to a safe place in order not to be killed. And so let not a (let no) reward be given to them. (*Sē,* reflexive pron., obj. of *recēpērunt,* referring to *mīlitēs; nē interficerentur,* a negative purpose clause, introduced by *nē,* in imp. tense after a secondary tense; *nē dētur,* negative command in the third person.) 9. May God be loved by all, in every way and always! (*Dīligātur,* volitive subj.) 10. Do you know whether ours (our men) were exhausted by the march (by marching) and by [their] wounds? (*Cōnfectī sint,* perf. subj. in an indirect question in primary sequence, action before time of main verb.) 11. He asked that centurion whether many wounds had been received (sustained) by his [men]. (*Accepta essent,* plu. subj. in an indirect question in secondary sequence, action before time of main verb.) 12. He asked that slave where troops had been led by the enemy. (*Dēductae essent,* plu. subj. in an indirect question in secondary sequence, action before time of main verb.) 13. I ask of you whether all men are influenced by fame. (*Addūcantur,* pres. subj. in an indirect question in primary sequence, action at same time as main verb.) 14. Let both the ditch and the rampart be finished quickly. (*Cōnficiantur,* command in the third person.) 15. Let him not be killed (May he not be killed). (*Nē interficiātur,* negative command in the third person or volitive subj.) 16. After the battle he asked whether the (a) dispatch concerning that battle had been received. (*Acceptae essent,* plu. subj. in indirect question in secondary sequence, action before time of main verb.) 17. May we not be observed! Let us quickly hide (conceal) ourselves in the forest! (*Nē conspiciāmur,* negative volitive subj.; *nōs,* reflexive personal pron., obj. of *abdāmus,* referring to unexpressed sub. of *abdāmus; abdāmus,* hortatory subj.) 18. The military tribune asked whether the enemy's battle line had been perceived by the cavalry. (*Ab,* prep. w. abl., expressing agent; *cōnspecta esset,* plu. subj. in an indirect question in secondary sequence, action before time of main verb.)

Box, p. 353.—Let the whole earth fear the Lord.

Exercise 53.—1. Quaesīvimus num interfectī (acceptī, cōnfectī, dēductī, cōnspectī, adductī, pācātī, captī, audītī, adjūtī, collocātī, incitātī) essent. Quaesīvīmus num interfēcissent (accēpissent, cōnfēcissent, dēdūxissent, cōnspexissent, addūxissent, pācāvissent, cēpissent, audīvissent, adjūvissent, collocāvissent, incitāvissent). 2. Caesar quaerit num captum (cōnfectum, acceptum, cōnspectum, tentum, auditum, cupītum, administrātum, parātum, cōnservātum, datum, occupātum, oppugnātum, comparātum) sit. Caesar quaerit num cēperit (cōnfēcerit, accēperit, cōnspexerit, tenuerit, audīverit, cupīverit, administrāverit, parāverit, cōnservāverit, dederit, occupāverit, oppugnāverit, comparāverit). 3. Quaerimus num contineātur (capiātur, audiātur, interficiātur, addūcātur, pellātur, cōnficiātur, accipiātur, reprimātur, moneātur, timeātur, videātur, dīmittātur). Quaerimus num contineat (capiat, audiat, interficiat, addūcat, pellat, cōnficiat, accipiat, reprimat, moneat, timeat, videat, dīmittat). 4. Caesar quaesīvit num occupārētur (tenērētur, caperētur, audīrētur, cōnficerētur, acciperētur, cōnservārētur, incenderētur, mitterētur, comparārētur, servārētur, administrārētur, darētur, peterētur, pōnerētur, trāderētur, mūnīrētur, vincerētur). Caesar quaesīvit num occupāret (tenēret, caperet, audīret, cōnficeret, acciperet, cōnservāret, incenderet, mitteret, comparāret, servāret, administrāret, daret, peteret, pōneret, trāderet, mūnīret, vinceret).

Exercise 54.—1. In agmen impetum statim fēcit ut bellum celeriter cōnficerētur. 2. Cōpiās coēgērunt atque cōpiam frūmentī armōrumque parāvērunt nē ā Rōmānīs vincerentur et interficerentur. 3. Hic tribūnus mīlitum legiōnēs integrās in Galliam addūxit quō hīberna facilius dēfenderentur. 4. Locō idōneō castra statim posuit nē suī itinere cōnficerentur. 5. Servōs ad Caesarem addūxērunt ut ab eīs quaereret quot virī in prōvinciam dēductī essent. 6. Vēnit ut cōpiās cōgeret. 7. Mīlitēs multa vulnera accēperunt et itinere proeliōque cōnfectī erant. Hāc dē causā imperātor ā (ē) fīnibus hostium in prōvinciam Rōmānam eōs dēdūxit. 8. Dēdūcantur. 9. Nē interficiantur. 10. Vēnit ut rēgem interficeret. 11. Accipiat litterās. 12. Vēnērunt ut legiōnēs integrās in Galliam dēdūcerent. 13. Nē interficiāmur! 14. Amīcitiae Chrīstī causā, omnēs hominēs dīligāmus. 15. Contrā urbem castra pōnāmus. 16. Jūdaeī Chrīstum ad Pīlātum addūxērunt ut interficerētur. 17. Caesar obsidēs et prīncipēs gentis saepe interfēcit ut eam pācāret.

Exercise 55.—1. Let us kill the enemy. (*Interficiāmus*, hortatory subj.) 2. May we not be killed. (*Interficiāmur*, volitive subj.) 3. May he (let him) not kill him. (*Nē interficiat*, volitive subj. or command in third person.) 4. May he (let him) not be killed. (*Interficiātur*, volitive subj. or command in third person.) 5. Let them not kill good men. (*Interficiant*, command in third person.) 6. Let bad men be killed. (*Interficiantur*, command in third person.) 7. A soldier is being sent to kill the boys. (*Ut interficiat*, pres. subj. in a purpose clause after a primary tense.) 8. Joseph fled with Jesus and Mary lest Jesus be killed. (*Nē interficerētur*, negative purpose clause in imp. subj. after a secondary tense.) 9. The Jews led Christ to Pilate in order that He might be killed (put to death) by the Romans. (*Ā Rōmānīs*, abl. of agent; *interficerētur*, imp. subj. in a purpose clause after a secondary tense.) 10. I ask whether the Romans killed him. (*Num interfēcerint*, indirect question in primary sequence; perf. subj. describing action before time of main verb.) 11. I ask by whom he was killed. (*Quō*, interrog. pron., abl. of agent, introducing an indirect question; *interfectus sit*, perf. subj. in indirect question in primary sequence, action before time of main verb.) 12. Did St. Paul know why Jesus was killed (put to death)? (*Interfectus esset*, plu. subj. in indirect question in secondary sequence, action before time of main verb.) 13. Do you know where Christ, the Son of God, was killed (put to death)? (*Ubi*, adv. modifying *interfectus sit* and introducing an indirect question; *interfectus sit*, perf. subj. in indirect question in primary sequence, action before time of main verb.) 14. Did the Romans know who was being killed by them? (*Quis*, interrog. pron. introducing an indirect question, sub. of *interficerētur; sē*, reflexive pron., obj. of prep. *ā*, referring to *Rōmānī*, abl. of agent; *interficerētur*, imp. subj. in indirect question in secondary sequence, action at same time as main verb.)

Exercise 56.—See Introduction, 3.

Lesson 10

Exercise 57.—See Introduction, 3.

Exercise 58.—1. With a good man. (Audācī, celerī, ācrī, dīligentī, līberō, integrō, fortī) 2. We will give rewards to good boys. (Audācibus, celeribus, dīligentibus, līberīs, integrīs, fortibus.) 3. A good boy will receive a reward. (Audāx, celer, ācer, dīligēns, līber, integer, fortis.) 4. The fortune of good soldiers. (Audācium, celerium, ācrium, dīligentium, līberōrum, integrōrum, fortium.) 5. There are good sailors in (with) the fleet. (Audācēs, celerēs, ācrēs, dīligentēs, līberī, integrī, fortēs.) 6. The rewards of a good boy are great. (Audācis, celeris, ācris, dīligentis, līberī, integrī, fortis.) 7. We thank a good leader. (Audācī, celerī, ācrī, dīligentī, līberō, integrō, fortī.) 8. Without good friends. (Audācibus, celeribus, ācribus, dīligentibus, līberīs, integrīs, fortibus.) 9. Through a good servant. (Audācem, celerem, dīligentem, līberum, integrum, fortem.) 10. The king killed many good men. (Audācēs, celerēs, ācrēs, dīligentēs, līberōs, integrōs, fortēs.)

Exercise 59.—1. Rēgēs atque prīncipēs glōriae cupidī saepe sunt. 2. Virī audācēs Germānīs restitērunt et eīs omnī ratiōne nocuērunt. 3. Quis equitibus celeribus praefuit? 4. Caesar, dux audāx et dīligēns, in silvās legiōnēs dēdūxit; equitēs restitērunt. 5. Quem exercituī classique nostrae praeficiēmus? Nōnne praeficiēmus eīs virum dīligentem et audācem? 6. Gallī lībertātī studuērunt, sed tamen ducēs suī audācēs atque mīlitēs ācrēs ab equitibus Rōmānīs celeribus atque audācibus victī sunt. 7. Caesar exercituī Rōmānō praeerat, et omnī ratiōne cōpiīs Gallōrum nocēbat. 8. Erant proelia ācria in silvīs agrīsque Galliae. 9. Omnēs hominēs nātūrā lībertātī student. Multī tamen hominēs miserī servī sunt. 10. Cum barbarīs ācrīs bellum saepe gessimus. Tamen mīlitēs nostrī audācēs eīs fortiter restitērunt.

Exercise 60.—1. Caesar, a bold and eager man, was in command of the Roman army in Gaul. (*Exercituī*, dat. w. *praeerat*.) 2. Many tribes (nations) have resisted both the Romans and the Germans. (*Rōmānīs* and *Germānīs*, dat. w. *restitērunt*.) 3. Caesar often put a careful and courageous lieutenant in command of a legion. (*Lēgātum*, obj. of *praefēcit; legiōnī*, dat. of thing of which w. *praefēcit*.) 4. I ask whether Holy (Saint) Mary strove after her own glory. (*Num*, particle introducing an indirect question; *glōriae*, dat. w. *studuerit; suae*, reflexive adj. modifying *glōriae* and referring to *Marīa; studuerit*, perf. subj. in an indirect question in primary sequence, action before time of main verb.) 5. In war we injure the enemy in every way. (*Hostibus*, dat. w. *nocēmus; ratiōne*, abl. of means.) 6. The Gauls were devoted to (the use of) cavalry. (*Equitātuī*, dat. w. *studēbant*.) 7. For the sake of liberty we will bravely withstand kings and chiefs. (*Lībertātis*, gen. w. *causā; rēgibus* and *prīncipibus*, dat. w. *resistēmus*.) 8. In a good army the general is daring and fierce, the cavalry swift, the centurions and military tribunes exact and eager, and the soldiers brave and bold. 9. The leader stationed careful (alert) guards at every gate. 10. The Roman leaders, men careful and eager, always fortified [their] camps by means of a ditch and a rampart. (*Fossā*, abl. of means.)

Exercise 61.—The Filipinos. In that great war of all the nations (World War) the Filipinos, men daring and brave, resisted the enemy and injured them in every way (by every means possible). Many of them concealed themselves in the forests and the mountains in order not to be taken by the Japanese. From these places (hide-outs) daring boys and men came (went down) to the towns and cities secretly to injure the Japanese. The Japanese stationed careful (alert) guards in every place; nevertheless provisions were burned by the courageous boys; centurions (officers) and soldiers killed; arms seized; camps and bridges set on fire. Thus they did harm (damage) to the Japanese and [then] quickly withdrew to the forests and mountains. They also sent messages to the American leaders concerning the way (progress) of the war and the plans of the Japanese. Afterwards the American general led his forces back to the Philippine Islands. At (during) that time these brave men aided the American soldiers by every means. Finally the Japanese were driven back and conquered.

For this reason shall we not thank these daring and brave men, and praise them, and remember them?

Exercise 62.—A. 1. Frūmentō ab hostibus nocēbātur. 2. Barbarīs ā nostrīs resistēbātur. 3. Lēgātus audāx legiōnī praefectus est. **B.** 1. The cavalry was being bravely resisted by the guards. 2. He ravaged the fields in order that in this way the enemy should be harmed (suffer). **C.** 2. The Germans were resisted and injured in every way by daring men. Germānīs omnī ratiōne ā virīs audācibus resistēbātur et nocēbātur. 5. Who shall be put in command by us of our army and our fleet? Will not an exact and courageous man be put in charge of them by us? Quis ā nōbīs exercituī classīque nostrae praeficiētur? Nōnne vir dīligēns et audāx ā nōbīs eīs praeficiētur? 10. War has often been waged by us with fierce barbarians. They have been bravely resisted by our daring soldiers. Ā nōbīs cum barbarīs ācribus bellum saepe gestum est. Ā mīlitibus nostrīs audācibus eīs fortiter resistēbātur.

Words of Our Lord Jesus Christ, p. 361.—"I have come that they may have life and have [it] more abundantly."

In these words Christ treats of (refers to) the life of grace, for Christ has not come in order that we may live in this world more easily but that by grace we may live in God and God in us.

Lesson 11

Exercise 63.—A. 1. He urges. 2. They fear. 3. They follow. 4. He suffers. 5. They rise. 6. You will speak. 7. He departs. 8. I advance to.

B. 1. The leader was encouraging his men. 2. The Gauls feared the Roman consul. 3. The cavalry was pursuing them swiftly. 4. Christ suffered many things (much) on the cross. 5. Wars were often arising. 6. With whom were you speaking? 7. The fleet was setting out. 8. We were attacking the enemy.

C. 1. The leader strongly urged the cohorts. 2. The Gauls feared the Roman consuls because of their authority. 3. The cavalry pursued the enemy swiftly to kill them. 4. Christ suffered many things (much, intensely) on the cross for our salvation. 5. Wars for the sake of liberty (freedom) have often arisen. 6. With whom did you speak of this matter? 7. The consul departed from the city because of fear. 8. I have attacked the enemy with the remaining cohorts.

D. 1. Let him encourage them. 2. Let them fear God. 3. Let the cavalry follow at once. 4. May you not suffer many pains. 5. May not (no) war arise. 6. Let him not speak of this serious matter. 7. Let him depart. 8. Let us attack the barbarians.

E. 1. The general was killed by a dart while he was urging his men to battle. 2. I ask you whether you fear God. 3. The cavalry, when they had pursued the enemy up to the river and had killed a great number of them, was sent back to the camp. 4. When Christ had suffered many and great (many great) pains on the cross and had spoken afterwards with His [apostles], He was taken back into heaven to [His] Father. 5. When Caesar was speaking with the king of the Germans, the German cavalry approached swiftly and bravely made an attack upon the Roman guards. He (Caesar), however, was neither captured nor killed, for the Roman soldiers withstood with great (magnificent) courage [this] attack and hurled the barbarians back. Caesar therefore arrived safe(ly) at the camp. 6. When a new war for the sake of the common safety of all and of liberty had arisen in Gaul, Caesar set out from the city at once with the remaining cohorts. 7. When the barbarians had advanced to the column Caesar sent the cavalry against them and led the legions safe(ly) back to camp.

Box, p. 364.—If God [be] with us, who [can be] against us?—St. Paul.

Exercise 64.—1. When Caesar had heard about the new war, he set out from the city. (*Audīvisset,* plu. subj. in *cum*-temporal clause in past time, action before time of main verb.) 2. The barbarians received very many wounds when they were attacking the winter quarters. (*Aggrederentur,* imp. subj. in *cum*-temporal clause in past time, action at same time as main verb.) 3. When Caesar had urged his men to battle he drew up the line on a hill. (*Hortātus esset,* plu. subj. in *cum*-temporal clause in past time, action before time of main verb.) 4. When the enemy withdrew from the battle line, the cavalry pursued them swiftly in order that they might not reach camp (to prevent their reaching camp.) (*Reciperent,* imp. subj. in *cum*-temporal clause in past time, action at same time as main verb; *pervenīrent,* imp. subj. in negative purpose clause.) 5. When Caesar had set out for Italy, a new war arose in Gaul. (*Profectus esset,* plu. subj. in *cum*-temporal clause in past time, action before time of main verb.) 6. When Christ had spoken of the Holy Sacrament of His body, very many [of His followers] left Him. (*Locūtus esset,* plu. subj. in *cum*-temporal clause in past time, action before time of main verb.) 7. When (after) Caesar had killed the hostages of (given by) the Gauls, many feared him. (*Interfēcisset,* plu. subj. in *cum*-temporal clause in past time, action before time of main verb.) 8. Christ suffered many pains (much pain) for us. 9. He asked whether a new war had arisen. (*Num,* conj. introducing an indirect question; *ortum esset,* plu. subj. in an indirect question in secondary sequence, action before time of main verb.) 10. He made (built) a bridge on (across) the river in order to follow them more easily. (*Quō,* adv. introducing a purpose clause containing a comparative adverb; *sequerētur,* imp. subj. in a purpose clause after a secondary tense.) 11. Let us pursue them. (*Sequāmur,* hortatory subj.) 12. Let us attack them at once. (*Aggrediāmur,* hortatory subj.)

Exercise 65.—Cum novum bellum in Galliā ortum esset, Caesar ab urbe profectus est et in prōvinciam celeriter pervēnit. Ibi prīncipēs Haeduōrum statim vocāvit ut fidem eōrum cōnfirmāret. Nam Haeduī amīcī senātūs populīque Rōmānī erant et Caesarem saepe adjuvābant. Frūmentum eī cum rogāret dabant et equitēs ad exercitum ējus mittēbant. Cum lēgātī in castra ējus pervēnissent, Caesar dē cōnsiliīs bellī cum eīs locūtus est. Cum lēgātōs cōnfirmāvisset et fidem eōrum laudāvisset, eōs dīmīsit. Cum profectī essent, in fīnēs Haeduōrum cum omnibus equitibus contendit nē injūriās bellī paterentur. Lēgātum legiōnibus praefēcit. Hae equitēs celeriter secūtae sunt. Hostēs, cum Caesar in agrōs Haeduōrum pervēnisset, eōs nōn agressī sunt, nam Caesarem veritī sunt. Itaque sē in fīnēs suōs celeriter recēpērunt et ibi adventum exercitūs Rōmānī expectāvērunt. Caesar eōs nōn statim secūtus est sed cōpiās integrās expectāvit. Hae ab Italiā ā lēgātō adducēbantur.

Box, p. 365.—Their names will live forever.

Exercise 66.—1. Desire. 2. Take. 3. Give. 4. Surrender. 5. Send. 6. Release. 7. Live. 8. Dwell. 9. Open. 10. Flee. 11. Flight. 12. Send down.

St. Andrew Bobola, p. 366.—Andrew Bobola, a priest of the Society of Jesus, traveled throughout Lithuania from town to town to urge all to [accept] the Catholic faith. He spoke to all of the grace of God and of Christ Jesus. He was a very holy man; he helped men in every way and strengthened them in the friendship and grace of Christ. He led many schismatics to the truth. He was neither worn out by [his] efforts (toil) nor terrified [deterred] by dangers; but for Christ's name was ready for all [things].

[Now] the enemies of the Catholic faith were violently aroused by all these things (happenings), and so they sought (hunted) him in order to kill him.

The Cossacks, barbarous men and enemies of the Catholic faith, hastened (went) into Lithuania to ravage the fields and towns and to attack the Catholics. They arrived at a certain town. Bobola had departed from that town shortly before. When the Cossacks heard this, they swiftly pursued him and captured him. When he had been taken to their leader, that unfortunate man (Bobola) suffered many pains for [his] faith and for the name of Christ. Nevertheless he remained strong (staunch) in [his] faith. He was terrified neither by fear of death nor by sufferings. The barbarians therefore killed him by the sword and thus opened heaven for the Saint.

Box, p. 366.—Saint Andrew, pray for us.

Lesson 12

Exercises 67-71.—See Introduction, 3.

Exercise 72.—1. This road is shorter than that. 2. In war the camp is safer than the battle line. 3. A mountain is higher than a hill. 4. We have nothing more noble (glorious) than the grace of God. 5. Caesar was more daring and brave than the leaders of the Gauls. 6. The saints are more like Christ than most Christians, aren't they?

Box, p. 371.—To the brave and faithful nothing is difficult.

Exercise 73.—1. What is more noble than courage? 2. What is holier than our faith? 3. Was Lincoln braver than Washington? 4. What is more common to men than hope? 5. Nothing is more miserable (There is nothing more miserable) than the slave of a bad and harsh master.

Exercise 74.—1. Haec via brevior illā. 2. In bellō castra tūtiōra aciē sunt. 3. Mōns altior colle est. 4. Nihil habēmus nōbilius grātiā Deī. 5. Caesar audācior atque fortior ducibus Gallōrum fuit. 6. Nōnne sānctī Chrīstō similiōrēs plūrimīs Chrīstiānīs sunt?

Exercise 75.—1. Suntne classicī fortiōrēs atque audāciōrēs quam nautae nostrī (nautīs nostrīs)? 2. Estne Rōma nōbilior quam urbs tua (urbe tuā)? 3. Nihil certius est quam mors (morte). 4. Nihil magis dubius quam victōria (victōriā) est. 5. Estne hoc flūmen altius quam illud (illō)? 6. Erantne Rōmānī fortiōrēs quam Gallī (Gallīs)? 7. Estne hic mōns altior quam ille (illō)? 8. Estne hic locus castrīs magis idōneus? 9. Sumusne līberiōrēs quam Rōmānī (Rōmānīs)? 10. Quid est miserius quam servus (servō)? 11. Quid est celerius quam lepus (lepore)? 12. Fuitne Caesar audācior quam Eisenhower (Eisenhower)? 13. Estne Mississippi longior quam Rhēnus (Rhēnō)? **Exercise 76.**—1. What is more uncertain in war than victory? (*Magis*, compar. adv., modifying *dubium; victōria*, nom., same case as *quid* after *quam*.) 2. Caesar was the most daring and the bravest of the Romans. (*Audācissimus*, super. form of *audāx*, adj. modifying *Caesar*.) 3. He proceeded into the territory of the enemy by the longer route. (*Longiōre*, compar. form of *longus*, adj. modifying *viā*.) 4. Nothing is more certain than death. (*Morte*, abl. of comparison.) 5. They informed Caesar of the new war. (*Certiōrem*, compar. form of *certus*, adj. modifying *Caesarem*, in the idiomatic phrase, *certiōrem faciō*, to inform.) 6. They informed the Gauls of Caesar's arrival. (*Certiōrēs*, compar. form of *certus*, adj. modifying *Gallōs*, in the idiomatic phrase, *certiōrem faciō*, to inform.) 7. Is the route through the mountains more difficult than [that] through the forest? (*Difficilius*, compar. form of *difficile*, adj. modifying *iter*.) 8. Caesar, when he had strongly urged his men [on], drew up a battle line at the foot of a hill in a most unfavorable place. (*Colle*, abl. w. prep. *sub*.) 9. He proceeded to the hill with the most daring cavalry. (*Collem*, acc. w. prep. *sub*, expressing motion.) 10. Caesar often spoke among (to) the chiefs of the Gauls concerning a (some) very serious matter. (*Prīncipēs*, acc. w. prep. *apud*.) 11. He fortified the camp by means of a ditch and a rampart in order that the soldiers might be safer. (*Vallō*, abl. of means; *quō*, conj. in a purpose clause containing a compar. adj.) 12. The general asked whether this route was the shortest. (*Esset*, imp. subj. in an indirect question in secondary sequence, action at same time as main verb.) 13. Let us proceed by the shorter way. (*Prōgrediāmur*, hortatory subj.) 14. Let him encourage the soldiers. (*Hortētur*, command in the third person.) 15. In battle soldiers are often uncertain (wavering) between hope and fear. (*Dubiī*, pred. adj. modifying *mīlitēs*.) 16. I ask who is a more certain (sure) friend than Christ. (*Quis*, interrog. pron. introducing an indirect question; *sit*, pres. subj. in indirect question in primary sequence, action at same time as main verb.)

Exercise 77.—1. Caesar, vir audācissimus et fortissimus, suōs saepe cōnfirmābat cum hostēs eōs aggrederentur. 2. Nōnne Marīa sānctissima omnium sānctōrum est? 3. Mīlitēs fortissimī ex aciē in loca tūtissima nōn fugiunt. 4. Gallī lībertātis cupidissimī erant (lībertātī maximē studēbant); prō lībertāte acerrimē pugnābant, sed victī sunt. Itaque erant miserrimī. 5. Vīta hominum brevissima et saepe labōris dolōrisque (dolōrumque) plēna est. 6. Hominēs sānctissimī Chrīstō simillimī sunt. 7. Servī Caesarem dē cōnsiliīs hostium ā saepe certiōrem fēcērunt. 8. Dux hostium, vir audācissimus, locō aliēnissimō sub colle aciem īnstrūxit. 9. Hostēs in locum angustissimum prōgressī sunt. 10. Mors certissima est.

Exercise 78.—Caesar multa itinera trāns montēs altissimōs et flūmina latissima, per loca angustissima et difficillima, in fīnēs barbarōrum fortissimōrum et audācissimōrum faciēbat. Cum gentibus fortissimīs et audācissimīs bellum gerēbat. Cum equitibus celerrimīs et cum virīs fortissimīs et audācissimīs pugnābat.

Ex aciē aut in prōvinciam nōn saepe sē recipiēbat. In fīnēs hostium fortiter et celeriter prōgrediēbātur. Urbēs eōrum oppugnābat; frūmentum incendēbat, obsidēs interficiēbat, et prīncipēs capiēbat. Locīs aliēnissimīs castra pōnēbat. In silvīs, in collibus, sub montibus pugnābat. Gallī miserrimī eum timēbat et, lībertātis et pācis cupidissimī, in eum fortiter et ācriter pugnābant ut eum et legiōnēs ējus ex Galliā pellerent. Victōria maximē dubia et difficillima saepe erat.

Caesar tamen nōn captus est; legiōnēs ējus neque victae sunt neque ex Galliā in prōvinciam Rōmānam pulsae sunt. Et cum (cumque) omnem Galliam pācāvisset et omnēs hostēs vīcisset, interfectus est, nōn in proeliō acrī et dubiō sed in sēnātū Rōmānō; nōn ā barbarīs ācribus sed ā Rōmānīs. Haec erat fortūna misera Caesaris, virī glōriae cupidissimī.

Exercise 79.—See Introduction, 3.

Box, p. 374.—Life has given nothing to men without great (a supreme) effort.

Lesson 13

Exercise 80.—1. Legions from which Caesar was absent did not often begin battle with the enemy, for without a general they had no great hope of victory. The enemy, however, often made an attack with great hope upon those winter quarters in which Caesar was not [present]. For the Romans praised Caesar and the enemy feared him. (*Quibus*, abl. of separation with *aberant*, referring to *legiōnēs; in quibus*, abl. of place in which, referring to *hīberna*.) 2. The Gauls often joined battle with the Germans who lived across the river. For the latter ravaged their fields and burned their towns. (*Quī*, sub. of *incolēbant*, referring to *Germānīs; hī*, sub. of *vastābant* and *incendēbant*, referring to the persons just mentioned, *Germānīs; illōrum*, possess. gen., modifying *agrōs* and referring to the persons previously mentioned, *Gallī.*) 3. When they began battle before the eyes of Caesar, the soldiers who were aroused to courage by hope of rewards fought fiercely and bravely. (*Quī*, sub. of *incitābantur*, referring to *mīlitēs.*) 4. When he was marching through the mountains, Caesar was pressed hard in the defiles by those tribes which dwelt there. (*Quae*, sub. of *incolēbant*, referring to *gentibus.*) 5. Peter, to whom Christ had given the power of His kingdom, fled when the soldiers had taken Christ. (*Cui*, ind. obj. of *dederat*, referring to *Petrus.*) 6. Nearly all of us who are in this world have committed sins. (*Quī*, sub. of *sumus*, referring to *omnēs.*) 7. The Romans who [were] in the defiles [and] held in on all sides, killed themselves in order not to be taken by the barbarians. (*Quī*, sub. of *continē-bantur*, referring to *Rōmānī.*) 8. Herod sent soldiers to kill all the [baby] boys in that town lest Jesus live. Nevertheless Joseph fled with Jesus and Mary to foreign lands. When the soldiers whom Herod had sent came to their town, they killed the children before their mothers' eyes; but Jesus whom they sought was far away. (*Quī*, sub. of *occī-derent*, referring to *mīlitēs* and introducing a relative purpose clause; *occīderent*, imp. subj. in a relative purpose clause in secondary sequence; *quōs*, obj. of *mīserat*, referring to *mīlitēs; quem*, obj. of *quaerēbant*, referring to *Jēsūs.*) 9. The leader said, "Will you give us, who are pressed hard by the difficulties of want, a supply of grain? (*Quī*, sub. of *premimur*, referring to *nōbīs.*) 10. Benedict Arnold, who did not remain in faith with (faithful to) his men (countrymen), went from the camp of the Americans to the British lest he be killed by them (the former, the Americans). (*Quī*, sub. of *mānsit*, referring to *Benedictus Arnold.*)

Exercise 81.—1. Caesar proelium cum mīlitibus quī in angustiīs erant commīsit. 2. Prō castrīs servum cui litterae datae erant inter-fēcērunt. 3. Exercitus quem lēgātus dēdūxit angustiīs premēbātur. 4. Chrīstus illīs quī eum sequuntur, "In rēgnō caelī," inquit, "eritis." 5. Propter peccātum lēgātī quem cohortibus praefēcit plūrimī captī sunt. 6. Propter peccāta nostra Chrīstus, quī Fīlius Deī est, dolōrēs gravēs passus est. 7. Peccāta quae hominēs committunt gravia saepe sunt. 8. Cohors quae in fīnēs hostium missa erat in angustiās pulsa est et ibi victa est. 9. Caesar frūmentum quod in agrīs erat saepe incendē-bat. 10. Servus cui Caesar ante proelium litterās dedit captus et inter-fectus est. Itaque senātus nuntium dē bellō novō quod in Galliā ortum erat nōn accēpit. 11. Ante bellum gentēs omnia quae utilissima ad bellum sunt parābant. 12. Cohortēs quibus cum Caesar flūmen aggrediēbat fortissimae et audācissimae erant. 13. Caesar oppida quae cēperat saepe incendit. 14. Gallī oppidum in quō Caesar obsidēs reliquerat oppugnāvērunt. 15. Montēs trāns quōs Caesar cōpiās saepe dūxit Italiam ā Galliā dīvidunt. 16. Oppidum, ex quō omnēs fūgerant, ā Caesare posteā incensum est. 17. Mīlitēs quōs hostēs in angustiās coēgerant pīlīs et tēlīs interfectī sunt. 18. Caesar, cūjus victōriās omnēs memōriā tenēmus, imperātor audācissimus et fortissimus erat.

Box, p. 377.—Blessed [is he] who comes in the name of the Lord.

Exercise 82.—*Creative work; the following sentences are suggested:*
1. Caesar led back to winter quarters the legions which had fought in Gaul. Caesar in hīberna legiōnēs quae in Galliā pugnāverant redūxit.
2. The soldiers carried javelins with which to injure the enemy. Mīlitēs pīla quibus hostibus nocērent portābant. 3. He built a bridge where the river, beyond which the Haeduans dwelt, was narrow. Pontem fēcit ubi flūmen trāns quod Germānī incolēbant angustum erat. 4. Caesar subjugated the tribes which dwelt across the Rhine. Caesar gentēs quae trāns Rhēnum incolēbant pācāvit. 5. The lieutenant whom Caesar had put in command of the legion drew up the line in a suitable place. Lēgātus quem Caesar legiōnī praefēcit locō idōneō aciem īnstrūxit. 6. The daring barbarians, whose line was drawn up at the foot of the hill, hurled back the javelins. Barbarī audācēs, quōrum aciēs sub colle īnstrūcta est, pīla rejēcērunt. 7. Caesar asked how many soldiers who had come with him from Italy were killed in this battle. Caesar quaesīvit quot mīlitēs quī sēcum ex Italiā vēnerant hōc proeliō interfectī essent. 8. By grace we live in God who is the Father of all. Grātiā in Deō quī Pater omnium est vīvimus. 9. The remaining barbarians, whom the cavalry had pursued, fought fiercely to hurl them back. Reliquī barbarī quōs equitēs secūtī erant ācriter pugnāvērunt ut eōs reprimerent.

The Coming of the Gauls, p. 378.—1. The Gauls Are Coming! The Gauls, who had set out across the Rhine and had seized all the fields of Gaul [and now were]eager for new fields, came into Italy through the Alps. They seized the fields at the foot of the mountains. Then they led troops into the territory of the Clusini to conquer them and take their fields. The Clusini were terrified by this new war. They therefore sent envoys to the Romans to seek help from the Senate and to strengthen [their] friendship with the Roman people. The Romans did not send help but they sent envoys to treat with the Gauls about the safety of the Clusini in the name of the Roman Senate and the people. For the Romans were not eager for war, but were ready for (willing to go to) war for the sake of the friendship of the Clusini.

Those (the Romans') envoys nevertheless were more (unduly) fierce and more like Gauls than Romans. When they had come to the Gauls they treated with them in council. This reply was given by the Gauls: . . .

Then the Clusini and the Gauls joined battle. There the Roman envoys, against (contrary to) the law of nations, took arms and with the Clusini attacked the Gauls. Quintus Fabius, a most brave and noble Roman envoy, killed the leader of the Gauls. The Gauls recognized the Roman envoys. They withdrew from battle at once and, when they had taken counsel concerning this very grave matter, sent envoys to the Roman Senate to treat of this wrong. . . .

And so the Gauls, when they had returned to their own [people], made ready for war against the Roman people.

Answer in Latin, p. 379.—1. Why did the Gauls come to Italy? Gallī in Italiam vēnit ut caperent agrōs novōs. 2. Into whose territory did they lead troops? In fīnēs Clūsīnōrum cōpiās dūxērunt. 3. Why did the Clusini send envoys to the Roman Senate? Clūsīnī lēgātōs ad senātum Rōmānum mīsērunt quod hōc bellō novō territī sunt. 4. Did the Romans send help at once? Rōmānī auxilium nōn mīsērunt. 5. Why were the Roman envoys more like Gauls than Romans? Lēgātī Rōmānī Gallīs magis quam Rōmānīs similēs erant quod ācrēs erant. 6. What did the Gauls desire? Gallī agrōs Clūsīnōrum cupīvērunt. 7. What [offense] did the Roman envoys commit against international law? Lēgātī Rōmānī contrā jūs gentium arma cēpērunt atque cum Clūsīnīs Gallōs aggrediēbantur. 8. Who killed the leader of the Gauls? Quintus Fabius, lēgātus Rōmānus, ducem Gallōrum interfēcit. 9. Why did the Gauls prepare for war? Propter hanc injūriam Gallī bellum parāvērunt.

Lesson 14

Exercise 83.—1. Let us leave behind both the greatest and the smallest (least) sins in order to come to (attain) the highest virtue. 2. Caesar often put greater forces to flight with a small number of soldiers, for he was a very good and a very great leader. 3. Many miserable men are worn out by very great pain. Let us pray for them. 4. Caesar said, "Of the Helvetians Orgetorix was by far the most renowned." 5. Virtue is better than friendship. 6. When the first (men) withdrew from the rampart, the last did not give them a place. 7. Not without great effort did the saints arrive at (attain) the highest virtue. 8. The Romans often pitched camp in higher places and fortified it with a ditch and a rampart in order that the enemy might not easily make an attack upon them. 9. The leader drew up the line on a hill in order that they might hurl javelins upon the enemy from a higher place (position). 10. Sin is the worst thing of all. 11. Let the welfare of the people be the highest law. 12. Caesar was in Italy. When he had heard of the new war he set out from the city and hastened to Farther Gaul. 13. Cicero, a very good and very careful man, delivered many very good (excellent) speeches. 14. What is worse than sin? 15. Was Benedict Arnold a very bad man? 16. Caesar's fortune (fate) was no better than Cicero's. For this one and that one (both) were killed by the Romans. 17. Is virtue better than peace? 18. The soldiers fought with greater courage when praised by Caesar. 19. Both the life and the death of bad men are very bad. 20. Was Herod worse than Pilate? The former sent soldiers to kill the Christ Child; the latter, however, sent Christ the Man to death. 21. Who was the best and greatest of all leaders? [Was it] Caesar? [Or] Napoleon?

Exercise 84.—1. Quid melior et mājor est quam grātia Deī? 2. Caesar saepe minōribus cōpiīs maximās cōpiās vīcit. 3. Sānctus Jōannēs minimus in rēgnō Deī nōn erit. 4. Gallī, cum proelium cum Caesare committerent, saepe maximā virtūte pugnāvērunt; tamen saepe repulsī et superātī sunt. 5. Pessimus omnium hominum erat. 6. Fuitne Caesar maximus omnium Rōmānōrum? 7. Fuitne hoc optimum proeliī cōnsilium? 8. Hominibus partem collis superiōrem (superiōrem collem) complēvit. 9. Eōs in proeliīs superiōribus vīcimus. Eōs nunc vincāmus. 10. Cum Caesar hanc gentem vīcisset, nuntiī dē ējus victōriā usque ad gentēs Germānōrum ultimās missī sunt. 11. Caesar ex Italiā statim profectus est et in Galliam Ulteriōrem celeriter pervēnit. 12. Collem obtinuērunt et dē locō superiōre in hostēs pīla dējēcērunt. 13. Caesar in partēs Galliae ulteriōrēs cōpiās suās dūxit.

Exercise 85.—**A.** 1. They made an attack upon the middle of the enemy (forces). 2. Our cavalry was seen by the enemy on the top of the hill. 3. The top of the mountain was held by Labienus. 4. Camp was pitched at the top of the hill (on the hilltop). He led the soldiers out of camp and drew them up in the middle of the hill at the foot of the camp. 5. These (soldiers) fled to Caesar from the midst of the slaughter (conflict) and informed him of that slaughter. 6. In the last speech (at the end of the speech) he praised them and urged them on.

B. 1. Caesar in summō colle impedīmenta posuit. Lēgātus cum legiōnibus integrīs mediam aciem tenuit. Tum proelium commīsērunt et Caesar equitēs in mediōs hostēs mīsit. 2. Equitēs in medium agmen sē recēpērunt. 3. In mediō colle legiōnēs novās īnstrūxit. 4. In ultimō ponte custōdēs dīligentissimōs collocāvit.

Exercise 86.—A. 1. More grain. 2. More (higher) authority. 3. More (greater) pain. 4. More weapons. 5. With more centurions. 6. Before more (many) envoys. 7. On account of more (many) sins. 8. On account of the mistakes of more (many) leaders.

B. 1. War has more toil and pain than glory. 2. I will not hear more about this matter. 3. The shouting of many men was heard. 4. They were fighting in many places. 5. We are soldiers, and what is more, Romans. And so let us without fear make an attack upon the midst of the camp (upon the center of the enemy's line)!

C. 1. Rōmānī plūs frūmentī rogāvērunt; Gallī autem plūs frūmentī nōn habēbant. 2. Chrīstus apud mē mājōrem āutōritātem habet quam Caesar aut Cicerō, nam Chrīstus via et vēritās et vīta est. 3. Plūribus hominibus grātiās agāmus.

Box, p. 383.—Who has most? He who desires the least of all.

Exercise 87.—1. The chief's mistake harms very many. (*Plūrimīs*, super. form of *multus* used as noun, dat. w. *nocet.*) 2. He asked whether they remembered former victories. (*Tenērent,* imp. subj. in an indirect question in secondary sequence, action at same time as main verb.) 3. He asks whether they fear him. (*Sē,* reflex. pron., obj. of *vereantur,* referring to the unexpressed subject of *rogat; vereantur,* pres. subj. in an indirect question in primary sequence, action at same time as main verb.)

Thanks in Verse, p. 384.—Catullus gives you very great thanks, worst poet of all—worst poet of all in the same degree as you are the best lawyer of all. (Catullus thanks you sincerely, worst of all poets— worst of all poets in the same degree as you are the best of all lawyers.)

Box, p. 384.—The best heritage given by fathers to [their] children [is] the fame of courage and of achievements.

The Coming of the Gauls, p. 384.—The Gauls were incited to war by those wrongs which we have pointed out. They went on the march with all [their] forces. The Romans, when they had been informed of their danger by messengers of the Clusini, were strongly (violently) moved and terrified. Troops were quickly brought together and led out of the city. When they had gone not far (a short distance) from the city, they saw the enemy's forces. The military tribunes who were in command of the Romans neither pitched camp nor prepared a rampart. They drew up a battle line at once. The Gauls began battle with a great shout. The Romans, however (on their part), were violently

terrified and immediately fled. There was a great (terrible) slaughter of
the Romans. The greater part of the Roman troops hastened to Veii; a
smaller part, however, sought Rome in flight (fled toward Rome). The
former did not send a message to the Romans; the latter, when they
reached the city, hastened swiftly to the citadel. Nevertheless the Gauls
did not pursue them at once for they feared an ambush. Afterwards
they marched swiftly to Rome.

The Forgiveness of Sins, p. 385.—"Peace [be] to you," Jesus said,
"as the Father has sent Me I also send you." When He had said this,
He breathed upon [them] and said: "Receive the Holy Spirit. Whose
sins you shall forgive, they are forgiven them, and whose sins you shall
retain, they are retained." . . .

I absolve you from all censures and sins, in the name of the Father,
and of the Son, and of the Holy Spirit. Amen.

Lesson 15

Exercise 88.—1. They went. 2. He crossed the river. 3. Who went
into the camp? 4. They are entering upon new plans. 5. Who went out
by this route? 6. I was going. 7. He will go out on account of fear.
8. They will approach those places. 9. How many soldiers have crossed?
10. The general is going into camp. 11. They are going into the camp.
12. They had crossed the widest river. 13. They will not pass through
the province. 14. He was visiting very many cities. 15. The enemy is
entering upon (beginning) a march. 16. They went into battle. 17. He
was entering upon a new plan of war. 18. Holy men will enter heaven.

Exercise 89.—(All the italized words are accusative of extent of
space and time.) 1. Very many soldiers went (marched) for four hours.
2. The rampart which the soldiers made was ten feet wide. 3. Caesar
was many miles away. 4. The river which they had crossed was ten
feet deep. 5. They went four miles and pitched camp in a favorable
place. 6. For four days they withstood bravely the attacks of the enemy.
7. The camp was a mile from the river. 8. He remained there for ten
days.

Exercise 90.—1. Decem mīlia passuum īvērunt. 2. In hīberna īvit.
3. Caesar flūmina lāta saepe trānsiit. 4. Quattuor hōrās iter fēcērunt.
5. Pōns decem pedēs lātus erat. 6. Multās hōrās mānsērunt. 7. Multās
et maximās urbēs adībimus. 8. Caesar omnia oppida prōvinciae adiit.
9. Cōnsilium novum iniērunt. 10. Castra mīlle passūs ā flūmine erant.
11. Equitēs quattuor mīlia passum ferē ab aciē erant. 12. Fossa quat-

tuor pedēs lāta erat. 13. Flūmen decem pedēs altum erat. 14. Quattuor hōrās hostibus restitērunt.

Exercise 91.—1. He asked who had gone into the camp. (*Iniisset*, plu. subj. in an indirect question in secondary sequence, action before time of main verb.) 2. Do you know whether they have crossed the river? (*Trānsierint*, perf. subj. in an indirect question in primary sequence, action before time of main verb.) 3. I ask whether the enemy is now entering upon a march. (*Ineant*, pres. subj. in an indirect question in primary sequence, action at same time as main verb.) 4. The leader was asking whether the barbarians were approaching the camp. (*Adīrent*, imp. subj. in an indirect question in secondary sequence, action at same time as main verb.) 5. They were building a road in order to go to the province more easily. (*Quō*, conj. introducing a purpose clause containing a comparative; *adīrent*, imp. subj. in a purpose clause in secondary sequence.) 6. Let us pray in order that we may go to heaven. (*Ut*, conj. introducing a purpose clause; *eāmus*, pres. subj. in a purpose clause in primary sequence.) 7. He stationed garrisons lest the barbarians cross the river. (*Nē*, conj. introducing a negative purpose clause; *trānsīrent*, imp. subj. in a purpose clause in secondary sequence.) 8. He sent the cavalry to cross the river and begin battle with the barbarians. (*Trānsīrent* and *committerent*, imp. subj. in a relative purpose clause in secondary sequence.) 9. Let them not cross the river. (*Trānseant*, pres. subj., negative command in the third person.) 10. May you go out. (*Exeās*, volitive subj.) 11. Let us go. (*Eāmus*, hortatory subj.) 12. Let them go out of winter quarters. (*Exeant*, pres. subj., command in the third person.) 13. Let us not go into camp. (*Nē ineāmus*, negative hortatory clause.) 14. The cavalry began battle with the enemy when it had gone out of the forest. (*Exīvissent*, perf. subj. in a *cum*-temporal clause in past time, action before time of main verb.) 15. The soldier was killed by darts when he was coming out of the river. (*Exīret*, imp. subj. in a *cum*-temporal clause in past time, action at same time as main verb.)

Box, p. 388.—Unto (for) the greater glory of God.

Exercise 92.—1. Eāmus. 2. In urbem eant. 3. Nē eant. 4. Ex castrīs nē exeat. 5. Pontem fēcit quō flūmen facilius trānsīret. 6. Cum flūmen trānsiissent, proelium cum equitibus hostium commīsērunt. 7. Scīvit quot virī flūmen trānsiissent. 8. Quaesīvērunt num Caesar per hōs fīnēs trānsiisset. 9. Cum flūmen trānsīrent, tēlīs ac pīlīs interfectī sunt. 10. Lēgātōs vocāvit ut cōnsilium bellī novum inīret. 11. Cum quattuor mīlia passuum iissent aciem hostium cōnspexērunt.

The Coming of the Gauls, p. 389.—The Romans, when the greater part [of them] had gone to Veii from the battle line and had not sent a message to Rome, filled the city with a shout full of pain. They were awaiting without hope the coming of the Gauls. The soldiers withdrew to the citadel to defend it. The others remained in the city and awaited the Gauls. . . .

Then the Gauls killed all those who were not in the citadel and burned the city. Everything (every place) was filled with the slaughter and the shouting.

Lesson 16

Exercises 93-95.—See Introduction, 3.

Exercise 96.—1. Saint Luke said of Christ, "He has done (did) all things well." 2. Not easily did Caesar seize command of all Gaul. 3. Caesar waged war for a long time with the tribes of Gaul. 4. "Many sins are forgiven her," Christ said, "because she has loved much." 5. They came (were coming) into camp safely. 6. He does badly who loves neither God nor man. 7. The Gauls were often terrified by the Roman cavalry. 8. Do you love him more than me? 9. Who was put in command (placed at the head) of our state most recently? 10. Our soldiers in Bataan withstood the attacks of the enemy for a very long time. 11. The Gauls were greatly devoted to [the use of] cavalry. 12. I will remain no longer. 13. Let us desire virtue rather than fame. 14. The Romans asked for more grain but the Gauls had no more grain. 15. The holy man is very often the best man. 16. This place is suitable enough for camp. 17. Have we enough grain? We have too little grain. 18. We Americans have very often been too little prepared for war.

Box, p. 392.—The poor man is not he who has too little, but he who desires more [than he has].

Exercise 97.—1. Caesar bellum bene administrāvit. 2. Gallī saepissimē rēs male administrāvērunt. 3. Adventū Caesaris multum territī sunt. 4. Nūper parum ad bellum parātī erāmus. 5. Caesar bellum administrāvit melius quam Gallī. 6. Laudāsne Caesarem potius quam Cicerōnem? 7. Rōmānī in Galliā diū mānsērunt. 8. Erantne Gallī minus fortēs et audācēs quam Caesar? 9. Hoc optimē actum est. 10. Hae legiōnēs in Galliam nūper dēductae sunt. 11. Deum plūrimum dīligimus. 12. Ad castra tūtō pervēnērunt. 13. Prīnceps, "Rōmānōs," inquit, "facile vincēmus." 14. Satis frūmentī nōn habēbant. 15. Parum frūmentī habuimus.

The Coming of the Gauls, p. 393.—4. The Slaughter of the Gauls.

At dawn the leaders of the Gauls gave a signal to their men, and all the Gauls were drawn up in the Forum. Strongly they made an attack on the citadel, but the Romans thrust them back and hurled javelins down upon them from a higher position. The Gauls, therefore, did not take the citadel.

Then the Gauls stationed guards in order that the Romans who were in the citadel might not get more grain. Meanwhile they carried grain from the fields into the city and ravaged fields and towns far and wide. . . .

Manlius, aroused by their shouting, took arms and hurled down the first Gaul who was already at the top of the mountain. Very many Romans hurried toward (in the direction of) the noise to help Manlius. They disturbed (threw into confusion) the rest of the Gauls with darts and rocks and drove them down. Thus the citadel was saved. . . .

The Gauls, disturbed by the new development, took up (seized) [their] weapons and made an attack upon the Romans [which was inspired] by rage rather than by [any] plan. But both fortune and the counsels of the leaders helped the Romans. At the first onset the Gauls were driven back and put to flight. Afterwards, when the Gauls had drawn up a battle line not far from the city, they began battle again. In this battle the Gauls were defeated. And there a great slaughter was made. The camp of the Gauls was also captured, nor was any messenger of the slaughter left behind (nor was a Gaul left to carry home tidings of the slaughter). Thus both Rome and the glory of the Roman name were preserved by Camillus.

Box, p. 394.—He who desires greater things often gets the lesser.

Lesson 17

Exercise 98.—See Introduction, 3.

Exercise 99.—1. Nūllīus mīlitis. 2. Cum ūnō virō. 3. In nūllam partem. 4. Hūjus rēgis sōlīus. 5. Cum tribus cohortibus. 6. Cum aliō duce. 7. Cum alterō frātre. 9. Utrīque exercituī. 9. In tertiā aciē. 10. In tribus oppidīs. 11. Cum centum equitibus. 12. Sine ūllō timōre.

Box, p. 397.—Add little to little—there will be a great heap.

Exercise 100.—1. The lieutenant filled the whole mountain with soldiers in order that the enemy might not take it. 2. To the only God, King of heaven and earth, be glory forever. 3. We have no other way. 4. Caesar said, "I will not give anyone a route through the province." 5. When Caesar had arrived in Farther Gaul, there was one legion there. 6. The first and second lines fought against those who had with-

drawn to the hill; but the third line began battle with the fresh troops.
7. The Romans held command of other tribes for a long time. 8. Let us
help others by every means. 9. Napoleon and Hitler desired power of
(over) all Europe. Of these [two men] one was a Frenchman, the
other a German; both were conquered after slaughter and suffering.
10. Let him not harm the other. 11. Both the enemy's battle lines were
put to flight. One hid (concealed) itself in the nearest forest; the other,
however, withdrew swiftly to the town. 12. Some desire fame; others,
however, desire influence. 13. Of these two brothers, one is a soldier,
the other a sailor. 14. Some praise certain leaders, others other leaders.
15. For the second day he marched through the province. 16. After the
attack of the cavalry some fled to the mountains, and some hastened
across the river. 17. Napoleon desired power of (over) all of Europe.
18. "Without [doing] any harm," said the chief of the Gauls, "we will
march through the province." 19. When the Japanese had stationed
garrisons in every place, there was no way [out] left for the Americans
who were in Bataan. 20. When the shouting of the enemy had been
heard, the soldiers throughout the entire camp were disturbed and one
asked the other the cause of the shouting. 21. "Therefore one Father,
not three Fathers; one Son, not three Sons; one Holy Spirit, not three
Holy Spirits." 22. When he went out to battle, he left the baggage of
the whole army in the camp. The third legion was left behind in order
that the enemy might not easily enter the camp. 23. All the troops were
collected in one place. 24. The leader stationed two legions on the
mountain top. 25. Caesar waged war with both the Gauls and the
Germans. The one [tribe] he drove across the river out of Gaul; the
other he pacified (subjugated) by arms. 26. In the war some were killed
by darts, some by swords, some by javelins. 27. Some desire one thing,
others another. 28. Ours are terrified neither by any fear nor any danger.
29. He divided the forces into two parts, of which he left one in the
town and led the other into the territory of the enemy. 30. Of these two
centurions one was killed and the other surrendered to the enemy.
31. Cicero said, "Life is nothing without friendship." 32. Let us help
others. 33. Cicero, a very good and very great man, said, "Nothing holds
the republic [together] more powerfully than faithfulness." 34. Christ
said, "The Father and I are one." 35. There was always in them one
spirit and one faith.

Box, p. 398.—Thus passes the glory of the world.

Exercise 101.—1. Kings and leading men are not free from dread
and fear. (*Metū* and *timōre*, abl. of separation without a prep. after

līberī.) 2. Christ will defend us from the enemy. (*Ab hoste,* abl. w. *ab* after *dēfendet*.) 3. The camp, which was pitched on the top of the hill and fortified by a ditch and a rampart, was safe from every danger. (*Summō colle,* abl. of place where; *summō* modifying *colle* and expressing part of the object; *fossā* and *vallō,* abl. of means; *perīculō,* abl. w. *ab* after *tūta*.) 4. The Gauls were warding off the Germans from their territory. (*Fīnibus,* abl. of separation without a prep. after *prohibēbant*.) 5. Caesar said, "I will defend the province from (against) you." (*Ā vōbīs,* abl. w. *ab* after *dēfendam*.) 6. After Caesar's victories Italy was safe from the barbarians for a long time. (*Ā barbarīs,* abl. w. *ā* after *tūta*.) 7. The Alps divide Italy from Gaul. (*Ā Galliā,* abl. of separation with a prep. after *dīvidunt*.) 8. "The Rhone River," Caesar said, "divides our province from the [territory of the] Helvetians." (*Ab Helvētiīs,* abl. of separation w. a prep. after *dīvidit*.) 9. The Gauls were greater in number than the Romans, but they were nevertheless conquered. (*Numerō,* abl. of respect.) 10. The Gauls were superior to the Romans in cavalry. (*Equitātū,* abl. of respect.) 11. The death of the very good is safe from fear; the death of the very bad is most wretched and full of fear. (*Ā timōre,* abl. w. *ā* after *tūta*.) 12. The Helvetians surpassed the rest of the Gauls in courage. (*Virtūte,* abl. of respect.) 13. The boys are swift of foot. (*Pede,* abl. of respect.)

Exercise 102.—1. Mīlitēs tōtīs castrīs territī et pertubātī sunt. 2. Centuriō fortis, "Numerō," inquit, "sed nōn virtūte superātī sumus." 3. Washington et Lincoln virī maximī erant. Uterque nostrae cīvitātī praefuit cum in angustiīs essēmus. Alter et imperātor optimus et praeses optimus erat; alter praeses maximus erat. 4. Per peccātum hominis ūnīus mors in mundum vēnit; per dolōrem ac mortem hominis ūnīus mortem vīcimus. 5. Superābatne Caesar virtūte ducēs Gallōrum? 6. Sine ūllō timōre fidem ac spem nostram in grātiā Deī sōlā pōnāmus. Per eam ā peccātō tūtī erimus. Nūllum (neque ūllum) perīculum nōs terrēbit neque ūllus dolor nōs vincet. Aliōs etiam adjuvābimus et ab omnibus perīculīs dēfendēmus.

Exercise 103.—Mīlitēs nostrī ab hostibus semper nōs dēfendērunt. Aliī Americānī cum hostibus duōs aut trēs annōs pugnāvērunt; aliī relictī sunt ut arma et cōpiam frūmentī parārent. Mīlitēs nostrī fortissimē pugnāvērunt; aliī interfectī sunt, aliī multa atque gravia vulnera accēpērunt, aliī integrī erant. Omnibus grātiās agāmus.

Nūper, duōbus bellīs ācribus, mīlitēs et nautae nostrī fīnibus hostēs prohibuērunt, eōs in agrōs eōrum reppulērunt et ibi eōs vīcērunt. In alterō hōrum bellōrum cōpiās nostrās multa mīlia passuum mīsimus quae cum Germānīs pugnārent. In alterō cum Germānīs et Japōnibus bellum gessimus; utrumque vīcimus. Utrōque bellō in virtūte sōlā mīlitum ac nautārum spem posuimus. Itaque metū ac imperiō gentium aliēnārum līberiōrēs sumus quam multī aliī populī.

Answer in Latin, p. 402.—1. Into how many parts were Caesar's troops divided? Cōpiae Caesaris in trēs partēs dīvīsae sunt. 2. Were the legions the strongest and most useful (effective) of these (parts) for battle? Legiōnēs firmissimae atque ad proelium ūtilissimae erant. 3. Hope of victory was placed in the courage of the legions, wasn't it? Spēs victōriae in legiōnum virtūte posita est. 4. How many men were in a legion? In legiōne ūnā sex mīlia mīlitum erant. 5. How many cohorts were in a legion? In legiōne decem cohortēs erant. 6. Who were in command of the legion? Tribūnī mīlitum legiōnī praeerant. 7. Were the military tribunes who were in Caesar's army very suitable (able) and careful (experienced)? Tribūnī mīlitum quī cum Caesare in exercitū erant maximē idōneī atque dīligentissimī nōn erant. 8. Whom did Caesar put in command of the legions when he began battle? Caesar, cum proelium committeret, legātōs legiōnibus praefēcit. 9. Did the legions have standards? Legiōnēs signa habēbant. 10. What is the legion's standard called? Signum legiōnis aquila vocātur.

Exercise 104.—1. Legiō in decem cohortēs dīvīsa est. 2. Cōpiae Caesaris in trēs partēs dīvīsae sunt. 3. Cīvitās nostra in multās partēs dīvīsa est.

Box, p. 403.—To courage, no way is impassable.

A Christian Prayer, p. 403.—May the Lord bless us, and defend us from every evil, and lead us to eternal life.

Some Things Are Dangers of War; Others Dangers of Peace (The Dangers of War and Peace Are Not the Same), p. 403.—In war men's bodies are wounded by arms; in peace by pleasures.

Lesson 18

Exercises 105-106.—See Introduction, 3.

Exercise 107.—1. Let us refer this matter to the Senate. (*Referā-mus*, hortatory subj.) 2. The enemy came into the province with all [their] forces to bring war upon the allies of the Roman people. (*Īn-ferrent*, imp. subj. in a purpose clause in secondary sequence.) 3. He asked who had reported this. (*Rettulisset*, plu. subj. in an indirect question in secondary sequence, action before time of main verb.) 4. When the enemy had brought war upon [them], the allies did not withstand their force. (*Īntulissent*, plu. subj. in a *cum*-temporal clause in past time, action before time of main verb.) 5. The enemy knew what had been reported to Caesar. (*Relāta essent,* plu. subj. pass. in an indirect question in secondary sequence, action before time of main verb.) 6. He sent the cavalry to inspire very great fear in the enemy. (*Quī,* relative pron. introducing a purpose clause, referring to *equitēs; inferrent,* imp. subj. in a relative purpose clause in secondary sequence.) 7. Let us refer these things to the people. (*Referāmus,* hortatory subj.) 8. Let him betake himself (go) to Italy! (*Cōnferat,* pres. subj. in a command in the third person.) 9. Let foreign tribes not bring war upon us! (*Nē īnferant,* pres. subj. in a negative command in the third person.)

Exercise 108.—1. Quaesīvit num servī satis frūmentī in castra tulissent. 2. Quaerō num dolōrem gravissimum et maximum tuleris. 3. Scīsne quot mīlitēs in secundō bellō omnium gentium arma tulerint. 4. Marīa scīvit cūr Fīlius suus crucem gravem ferret.

Exercises 109-110.—See Introduction, 3.

Exercise 111.—(The time expressed by all the italicized participles is time prior to the main verb.) 1. The Gauls, having been conquered by the Romans, [now] had no liberty. (*Victī,* modifying *Gallī.*) 2. They carried from the camp the bodies of the killed (slain) soldiers. (*Occīsōrum,* modifying *mīlitum.*) 3. He killed the slaves led back by the cavalry. (*Reductōs,* modifying *servōs.*) 4. He brought help to the allies exhausted by effort. (*Cōnfectīs,* modifying *sociīs.*) 5. The Gauls, led on by fear, betook themselves (went) to the town. (*Inductī,* modifying *Gallī.*) 6. The lives of the captured Gauls were saved (spared) by the lieutenant. (*Captōrum,* modifying *Gallōrum.*) 7. The cavalry inspired fear in the enemy disturbed by this affair. (*Perturbātīs,* modifying *hostibus.*) 8. Caesar was informed by the allies of the plans entered upon by them. (*Initīs,* modifying *cōnsiliīs.*) 9. The enemy killed our men, [who had been] forced into the defiles. (*Coāctōs,* modifying *nostrōs.*) 10. The legion, having recently been led into Gaul, was sent to defend from the enemy by force the fields of the allies of the Roman people. (*Dēducta,* modifying *legiō.*) 11. The Gauls' allies, moved by hope of safety, swiftly fled. (*Mōtī,* modifying *sociī.*)

Exercise 112.—1. Gallōs captōs saepe interfēcērunt. 2. Gallī, adventū Caesaris territī, pācem petīvērunt. 3. Castra in colle ab equitibus occupātō posuērunt. 4. Vīs flūminis pontī ā Caesare factō nocuit. 5. Oppidum captum incendērunt. 6. Fortūna sociōrum victōrum miserrima erat. 7. Caesar, certior factus quantō in perīculō sociī populōrum Rōmānōrum essent, equitēs mīsit quī eōs adjuvārent. 8. Gallī, spē victōriae adductī, bellum novum suscēpērunt.

Box, p. 411.—God has sent His only-begotten Son into the world that we may live by Him.—Saint John.

Exercise 113.—1. Those who take part in public affairs take great authority upon themselves; nevertheless, disturbed by fear, they often put off to the next year or refer to the people very serious matters. 2. The allies of the Roman people reported to Caesar many things (much) about the plans of the Gauls. 3. He most surely bears bad fortune (is unfortunate) who has no friends, who has no companions of (in) his sorrow or his fame. For Cicero said, "Without friendship life is nothing." Except for virtue and the grace of God, friendship is the best thing of all. 4. The Romans' slaves often bore very great pain and toil. There were many slaves with Caesar's army. These (they) carried into the camp everything that was useful for war. 5. The centurion reported to Caesar everything which he had found out. 6. The way which bears through the forest and the mountains (a road through forests and mountains) is very often full of dangers. 7. The Romans with their allies inflicted war upon many other tribes. 8. The Mississippi River will carry us past many very great cities. 9. The Roman consuls referred the most serious (very serious) matters to the Senate. 10. Before the battle Caesar brought together (made it a practice to bring) all the baggage into one place in order to defend it from the enemy more easily. 11. The cavalry inspired fear in the enemy routed by the legion. 12. The Helvetians, when they had been put to flight by our men, swiftly betook themselves (went) to the baggage train. 13. The Gauls, aroused to war by the wrongs of (inflicted on them by) the Romans. carried grain into the town from the fields in order to have throughout the war a large enough supply of grain. 14. We Americans, free men, will not bear (tolerate) a king. 15. The slaughter of men who had inflicted no injury upon others was effected contrary to the law of God. 16. The allies of the Roman people, pressed hard by the difficulties of want, often did not withstand the force of the enemy. 17. The enemy, led on by hope of victory, made an attack upon the winter quarters. When the cavalry sent by Caesar had brought help to our men and were warding them off, the enemy retreated. 18. The Romans brought with them on the march a great supply of grain. 19. These were bearing arms. 20. The earth bears crops. 21. Very holy men will bear (win) the reward of glory. 22. The baggage was brought together into one place lest it be taken by the enemy. 23. Very brave men often take upon themselves a great work. 24. These [matters] were reported to Caesar. 25. Caesar, aroused by the wrongs, took the town by force and burned it.

Exercise 114.—See Introduction, 3.

Exercise 115.—1. Mīles ipse vēnit. 2. Eī ipsī vēnērunt. 3. Ipsa hoc ēgit. 4. Ipse hoc ēgit. 5. In hāc ipsā urbe. 6. In ipsō senātū. 7. Propter victōriās hūjus ipsīus virī. 8. Per ipsam illam hōram. 9. Propter hanc ipsam rem. 10. Ipsum rēgem interfēcērunt. 11. Ipsam virtūtem laudāmus. 12. Ipsī rēgī nocuērunt. 13. Mīlitēs fūgērunt, sed ipse dux captus est.

Exercise 116.—1. Caesar, influenced by the dispatch of the Senate, took upon himself [the care of] this matter. 2. Caesar sent an envoy to the Helvetians; he himself betook himself (went) to the province. 3. They captured the king and his allies; the latter they led down to the camp, but they killed him (the king). 4. The king himself was killed. 5. Caesar sent Labienus into the forest; he himself crossed the river by force. 6. In that very battle (both) the enemy was repulsed and their king killed. 7. God Himself loves us. 8. In this very city kings were once praised. 9. God Himself made all things that are in heaven and on earth.

Exercise 117.—1. Marīa ipsa ibi erat. 2. Marīa sē nōn laudāvit. 3. Virtūs ipsa laudātur. 4. Virtūs propter sē laudātur. 5. Gallōs ipsōs laudāvit. 6. Gallī ipsī inopiā pressī sunt. 7. Senātuī Rōmānō ipsī nocuit. 8. Senātus Rōmānus ipse Caesarem laudāvit. 9. Senātus Rōmānus ipse territus est.

Box, p. 414.—Habit is a second nature.

Exercise 118.—1. The cavalry, having pursued the barbarians, inspired fear in them. (*Secūtī*, active in meaning, modifying *equitēs*.) 2. Caesar drove into the forest the Gauls [who had] attacked the camp. (*Aggressōs*, active in meaning, modifying *Gallōs*.) 3. On account of the new war [which had] arisen, Caesar departed for Gaul. (*Ortum*, active in meaning, modifying *bellum*.) 4. Christ, having suffered the greatest pain for our salvation, went to glory. (*Passus*, active in meaning, modifying *Chrīstus*.) 5. The cavalry, having advanced ten miles into the territory of the enemy, saw the enemy's battle line. (*Prōgressī*, active in meaning, modifying *equitēs*.)

Exercise 119.—1. Caesar dē perīculō lēgātī certior factus equitēs mīsit quī hostibus timōrem īnferrent; ipse cum legiōnibus statim secūtus est. 2. Mīlitēs, ab hostibus cōnspectī, impedīmenta in ūnum locum contu'ērunt et, locō idōneō īnstrūctī, vim impetūs fortissimē sustinuērunt. 3. Caesar, prōvinciae praefectus, bellum maximum suscēpit ut Gallōs pācāret et imperium tōtīus Galliae occupāret. 4. Post haec proelia Caesar etiam Germānīs bellum intulit ut ab eīs sociōs populī Rōmānī dēfenderet. 5. Senātus ipse, dē victōriā Caesaris certior factus, eī maximās grātiās ēgit. 6. Haec gentēs lēgibus aliīsque rēbus multīs inter sē distulērunt. 7. Chrīstus homō factus propter nōs maximum labōrem et dolōrem tulit. 8. Classis ā portū profecta in omnēs partēs dīlāta est. 9. Barbarī, in fugam datī, in montēs sē contulērunt. 10. Sēcum magnam cōpiam frūmentī tulērunt. 11. Impedīmenta in hoc ipsum locum collāta sunt. 12. Caesar sociōs mīsit quī hostibus timōrem īnferrent; ipse legiōnēs in fīnēs hostium dūxit. 13. Cōnferāmus vītam Caesaris cum vītā Cicerōnis. 14. Pontem vī occupāvērunt. 15. Cōnferēmusne virtūte Caesarem cum Napoleon? 16. Hanc rem gravem distulit. 17. Vim hostium nōn sustinuērunt. 18. Vīs flūminis pontī nocuit. 19. Gallī virtūte Rōmānōs nōn superābant. 20. Caesar bellum multīs gentibus quae ab imperiō Rōmānō līberae fuerant intulit. Ipse nōmen Caesaris timōrem hostibus intulit. 21. Equitēs Caesarī rettulērunt quae vīderant. 22. In castra sē celeriter contulērunt. 23. Hī virī ipsī arma ferent. 24. Nuntium rettulērunt. 25. Rēs populō Rōmānō relāta est.

Box, p. 416.—The very attempt of (to undertake) noble deeds is noble.

Exercise 120.—1. Hārum omnium urbium maxima erat Rōma. 2. Hōrum omnium mīlitum fortissimus erat Titus. 3. Omnium cōnsulum Rōmānōrum maximus erat Cicerō. 4. Omnium imperātōrum Rōmānōrum maximus erat Caesar. 5. Omnium bellōrum maximum erat secundum bellum omnium gentium.

Answer in English, p. 417.—1. How many soldiers were in a cohort? (600). 2. Why were the standards very useful to the cohorts? (Because soldiers could find their places and move in battle by observing the standards). 3. You understand "signa referre" and "signa īnferre," don't you? (Yes, "signa referre" means "to retreat" and "signa īnferre" means "to attack.")

Box, p. 418.—Each and every man is (himself) the maker of his own fortune.

Man, p. 418.—What is the best thing in man? His reason—for by this he surpasses (is superior to) the animals and follows (imitates) the gods.

Box, p. 418.—The wicked man himself is his own punishment.

The Roman People, p. 418.—Cicero said, "The Roman people are most eminent for [their] greatness of soul."

Lesson 19

Exercises 121-125.—See Introduction, 3.

Box, p. 422.—He carries wood to the forest.

Exercise 126.—**A.** (All infinitives are present active.) 1. The soldier can fight. (*Pugnāre*, obj. of *potest*.) 2. Are you afraid to fight? (*Pugnāre*, obj. of *timēs*.) 3. They are ready to depart. (*Proficīscī*, obj. of *parātī sunt*.) 4. They are preparing to go out. (*Exīre*, obj. of *parant*.) 5. The barbarians tried to cross. (*Trānsīre*, obj. of *cōnātī sunt*.) 6. They began to advance. (*Prōgredī*, obj. of *coepērunt*.) 7. We ought to pray. (*Ōrāre*, obj. of *dēbēmus*.) 8. Aroused by this dispatch, he decided to set out. (*Proficīscī*, obj. of *cōnstituit*.) 9. Influenced by this thing (turn of events), they tried to flee. (*Fugere*, obj. of *cōnātī sunt*.)

B. (All the infinitives are present active.) 1. The Haeduans were unable to defend themselves and their possessions from the Helvetians. (*Dēfendere*, obj. of *poterant*.) 2. The cavalry was trying to cross the river. (*Trānsīre*, obj. of *cōnābantur*.) 3. Having been informed of this thing (move), he determined to unite his forces. (*Conjungere*, obj. of *cōnstituit*.) 4. The Helvetians were not easily able to go out from their own territory. (*Exīre*, obj. of *poterant*.) 5. They determined to carry with them a large supply of grain. (*Ferre*, obj. of *cōnstituērunt*.) 6. Having been informed of the new war [which had] arisen, he determined to levy on the whole province a great number of soldiers. (*Prōvinciae*, dat. w. *imperāre; imperāre*, obj. of *cōnstituit*.) 7. When the Helvetians tried to cross over into the province, Caesar determined to ward them off by force. (*Trānsīre*, obj. of *cōnārentur; prohibēre*, obj. of *cōnstituit*.) 8. He stationed garrisons in order to be able to ward off the barbarians more easily. (*Prohibēre*, obj. of *posset*.) 9. Caesar ought to have defended and helped the allies and friends of the Roman people. 10. The cavalry were not able to pursue them immediately.

C. (All the infinitives are present active.) 1. It is safest to remain in camp. (*Manēre*, w. neut. adj. *tūtissimum;* sub. of *est*.) 2. Is it very useful to prepare arms? (*Parāre*, w. neut. adj. *ūtilissimum;* sub. of *est*.) 3. It is very good to pray always. (*Ōrāre*, w. neut. adj. *optimum;* sub. of *est*.) 4. It is a sin not to love [one's] mother. (*Dīligere*, w. neut. noun *peccātum;* sub. of *est*.) 5. It was difficult to conquer and pacify all the tribes of Gaul. (*Vincere* and *pācāre*, w. neut. adj. *difficile;* sub. of *fuit*.) 6. It is good to help [one's] friends. (*Adjuvāre*, w. neut. adj. *bonum;* sub. of *est*.) 7. To help the miserable is to keep the law of God. (*Adjuvāre*, sub. of *est; servāre*, pred. noun.) 8. It is difficult to unite many states. (*Conjungere*, w. neut. adj. *difficile;* sub. of *est*.)

D. (All the infinitives are present passive.) 1. Could Rome be defended easily? 2. Could the Gauls be easily pacified (subjugated)? (*Pācārī*, obj. of *potuērunt*.) 3. The towns far and wide began to be burned (set afire). (*Incendī*, obj. of *coepta sunt; coepta sunt*, main verb, perf. indic. act. of a deponent.) 4. Mothers and fathers ought to be loved by [their] sons. (*Dīligī*, obj. of *dēbent*.) 5. The enemy could not be hurled back. (*Rejicī*, obj. of *poterant*.) 6. The city will be able to (can) be taken easily. (*Capī*, obj. of *poterit*.)

E. (All the infinitives are present active.) 1. All of us men must love God. (*Dīligere*, w. *oportet*.) 2. Caesar ought to have spared the lives of the hostages. (*Conservāre*, w. *oportuit*.) 3. Soldiers ought to fight very bravely. (*Pugnāre*, w. *oportet*.) 4. Americans ought to defend their state most carefully. (*Dēfendere*, w. *oportet*.) 5. Caesar ought to have kept faith (the pledge) given to the enemy. (*Datam*, perf. part. pass., agreeing with *fidem; servāre*, w. *oportuit*.) 6. Among friends everything must be common (shared equally). (*Esse*, w. *oportet*.)

F. (All the infinitives are present active.) 1. Caesar ordered them to await his arrival. (*Eōs*, acc., sub. of *exspectāre; exspectāre*, w. *jussit*.) 2. The lieutenant ordered the soldiers to remember former victories. (*Victōriās*, acc., obj. of *tenēre; tenēre*, w. *jussit*.) 3. The centurion ordered them to make (build) a bridge. (*Eōs*, acc., sub. of *facere; facere*, w. *jussit*.) 4. Caesar, having been informed of the danger of his men, ordered the cavalry to bring help to them. (*Suōrum*, direct reflexive, modifying *perīculō* and referring to *Caesar* as regards possession; *ferre*, w. *jussit*.) 5. The general ordered them to make an attack at once. (*Eōs*, acc., sub. of *facere; facere*, w. *jussit; jussit*, main verb; perf. indic. act.) 6. The soldiers were ordered to make an attack upon the enemy at once. (*Facere*, w. *jussī sunt*.) 7. The leader was ordered to kill the hostages. (*Interficere*, w. *jussus est*.) 8. The cavalry was ordered to pursue the enemy very swiftly. (*Cōnsequī*, w. *jussī sunt*.)

G. 1. Can boys always be good? (*Bonī*, pred. adj. after *esse*, agreeing w. *puerī*.) 2. Can you be holy (a saint)? (*Sānctus*, pred. adj. after *esse*, agreeing w. unexpressed sub. of *potes*.) 3. We have been ordered by Christ to be holy (saints). (*Sānctī*, pred. adj. after *esse*, agreeing w. unexpressed sub. of *jussī sumus; esse*, w. *jussī sumus*.) 4. Can you be prepared for battle? (*Parātī*, pred. adj. after *esse*, agreeing w. unexpressed sub. of *potestis*.) 5. We ought always to be prepared for death. (*Parātī*, pred. adj. after *esse*, agreeing w. unexpressed sub. of *dēbēmus*.) 6. Among friends everything ought to be common (shared equally).

(*Omnia,* sub. of *dēbent; commūnia,* pred. adj. after *esse,* agreeing w. *omnia; esse,* w. *dēbent.*)

Exercise 127.—A. 1. Prīmā lūce proficīscī parātī erāmus. 2. Manēre possumus. 3. Hae gentēs jūnctae trānsīre poterant.

B. 1. Hanc rem legātō mandāre cōnstituit. 2. Cōnsequī legiōnēs statim nōn poterant. 3. Hīs injūriīs commōtī, conjungere sibi aliās gentēs coepērunt.

C. 1. Bonum et sānctum est aliōs adjuvāre. 2. Difficile est summam virtūtem cōnsequī. 3. Difficillimum est Alpēs trānsīre.

D. 1. Mīlitēs, in angustiās coāctī, tēlīs ac pīlīs interficī coepti sunt. 2. Deus ab omnibus hominibus laudārī et dīligī dēbet. 3. Numerus equitum certus gentī imperārī dēbet.

E. 1. Oportet nōs lībertātem cōnservāre. 2. Oportet nōs lēgem Deī dīligentissimē servāre. 3. Oportuit Caesarem cōpiās suās conjungere.

F. 1. Senātus cōnsulēs legiōnēs contrā hostēs dūcere jussit. 2. Mīlitēs in castrīs ut impedīmenta dēfenderent manēre jussī sunt. 3. Eōs illum capere cōnārī jussērunt.

G. 1. Nōs Chrīstiānī, dolōribus Chrīstī mōtī atque grātiā Deī adductī, sānctissimī esse dēbēmus. 2. Eī quī Deum dīligunt līberī metū mortis esse dēbent. 3. Cupidī glōriae esse coepērunt.

Exercise 128.—1. Oportuit nōs amīcōs nostrōs magis adjuvāre. 2. Oportuit Gallōs fortius pugnāre. 3. Oportuit Pīlātum vītam Chrīstī cōnservāre cōnārī. 4. Oportuit prīncipēs Galliae omnēs gentēs conjungere. 5. Oportuitne Rōmānōs Caesarem in Galliam mittere?

Box, p. 427.—A friend [is] another self.

Exercise 129.—1. The Helvetians, aroused by the speech of the chief, were preparing to go through the territory of allies of the Roman people. 2. The enemy, prevented by force, were unable to cross that river. 3. The chief, eager for glory, said, "We can easily obtain the power (control) of all Gaul." 4. The cavalry, sent very swiftly by Caesar, were able easily to inspire fear in the enemy. 5. When the enemy had been put to flight by our men, the cavalry began to pursue them. 6. Kings very often prepare (plan) to inflict war on others. 7. Driven back from the other route, they determined to go out from their own territory by a very difficult and narrow route. 8. The lieutenant said, "Our fields most certainly ought not be ravaged in sight of the Roman army." 9. Should Caesar have seized the towns and fields of Gaul? 10. Pilate, moved by fear, ordered Christ to be led to death.

Exercise 130.—1. Per grātiam Deī ad summam virtūtem pervenīre possumus. 2. Similēs Chrīstō esse cōnārī dēbēmus. 3. Columbus ad

Indiam viā novā īre cōnstituit. 4. Sānctus Ludovīcus optimus ac sānctissimus rēx esse cōnātus est. 5. Chrīstus, cum in cruce esset, mātrem suam Marīam Sānctō Jōannī mandāvit. 6. Washington omnēs Americānōs jungere et prō lībertāte usque ad mortem pugnāre cōnstituit. 7. Napoleon magnum mīlitum numerum Galliae imperāre potuit. 8. Virī audācēs glōriam maximam cōnsequī possunt. 9. Mīlitēs, cum Caesarem imperātōrem suum in prīmā aciē cōnspexissent, audācius et fortius pugnāre coepērunt. Ita nōs, certiōrēs factī quantum dolōrem Chrīstus prō nōbīs sustinuerit, contrā peccātum ācrius atque audācius pugnāre dēbēmus. 10. Cōnēmur omnēs hominēs adjuvāre nam omnēs frātrēs in Chrīstō sumus.

Exercise 131.—(All the italicized idioms are explained on page 428.) 1. Caesar levied on the province as large a number of soldiers as he could. 2. Caesar hastened to Gaul by the greatest (longest) possible marches. 3. They are collecting the largest forces they can. 4. He attended to these matters as quickly as possible. 5. The cavalry inspired in the enemy the greatest possible fear. 6. Caesar ordered the cavalry to proceed as far as possible. 7. They ravaged the territory as widely as possible. 8. He levied as many hostages as possible.

Selected Quotations, p. 429.—1. The safest thing is to fear nothing except God. 2. Christ said, "He who abides in Me, and I in him, brings forth much fruit, because without Me you can do nothing." 3. Virtue unites man with God. 4. The man who conquers his own desires is braver than he who conquers his enemies. 5. It is more blessed to give than to receive. 6. Saint Paul said, "I can do all things in Him who strengthens me." 7. It is better to receive an injury than to do (inflict) one. 8. I try to subject the thing to me, not (rather than) myself to things. 9. No one will be able to (can) be crowned without a victory.

Lesson 20

Exercise 132.—1. I say that all our soldiers fight bravely. 2. I think that all men seek friendship. 3. I will show that all saints love God very greatly. 4. Caesar was informed that the Helvetians were going out from their own territory. 5. Caesar noticed that his men were being pressed hard by the enemy's cavalry. 6. The general heard that the enemy was in the forest. 7. Caesar saw that the third legion was in very great danger. 8. Caesar knew that the soldiers, forced into the defiles, were with great difficulty withstanding the force of the enemy. 9. The Romans heard that the Gauls were burning all the grain. 10. The Gauls thought that Caesar was far away.

Exercise 133.—1. Sciō decem cohortēs in ūnā legiōne esse. 2. Hominēs bonī nōn negant Deum esse et eum omnēs rēs in mundō optimē administrāre. 3. Caesar vīdit mīlitēs impedīmentīs impedīrī. 4. Dēmōstrāvī tibi tē ad summam virtūtem grātiā Deī pervenīre posse. Quid tē impedit? 5. Sentiō nōn multōs hominēs aliīs nocēre cōnārī.

Exercise 134.—See Introduction, 3.

Exercise 135.—1. I know that the Romans led Christ to death. 2. Do you know that Caesar, a very great and very brave man, conquered and pacified (subjugated) the Gauls? 3. All American boys know that Columbus, having set out from port with the greatest courage, arrived at new lands. 4. The lieutenant said that the enemy had gone across the river. 5. We know that Christ suffered the greatest pains for us.

Exercise 136.—1. They say that the hostages were often killed by Caesar on account of the injustices of (committed by) the Gauls. 2. Caesar remembered that a Roman consul had been overcome by the Helvetians and killed. 3. All Roman boys knew that Rome itself had been captured and burned by the Gauls. 4. We believe that God made everything in heaven and on earth. 5. He said that the enemy had set out at dawn.

Exercise 137.—1. Gallī vīdērunt prōvinciam ā Rōmānīs victam atque obtentam esse. 2. Caesar scīvit Gallōs in Italiam vēnisse et Rōmam ipsam cēpisse et incendisse. 3. Vīdimus Caesarem suōs hortātum in virtūte legiōnum omnem spem saepe posuisse. 4. Reperrimus Caesarem legiōnibus legātum saepissimē praefēcisse. 5. Scīsne centuriōnem centum virīs praefuisse? 6. Vidēbimus multōs Rōmānōs ā Gallīs interfectōs esse.

Box, p. 437.—Life is power.

Exercise 138.—1. Caesar, having been informed of the plans of the Helvetians, did not think that they would march through the province without any wrong (without committing any damage). 2. Caesar answered that this would be a great danger to the province. 3. Caesar heard that the Helvetians would cross the river by force. 4. The Helvetians thought that Caesar would remain in the province. 5. I say that Americans will always defend their state (country) from enemies. 6. I think that the saints will praise God forever.

Exercise 139.—1. Crēdimus Deum nōs omnibus in perīculīs adjūtūrum esse. 2. Caesar scīvit Helvētiōs omnēs cōpiās suās trāns flūmen in prōvinciam ductūrōs esse et perīculum prōvinciae maximum futūrum esse. 3. Dēmōnstrābō tibi Deum optimum esse et eum omnēs hominēs dīligere. 4. Nuntiāvit Helvētiōs prīma lūce flūmen trānsitūrōs esse. 5. Caesar sēnsit legiōnēs sine ūllō timōre hostēs oppugnātūrās esse.

Exercise 140.—1. The Gauls said that they would fight even to the death against the Romans. The Gauls said that they would fight (in company) with them against the Romans even to the death. (*Sē*, sub. of *pugnātūrōs* esse, referring to *Gallī; eōs*, sub. of *pugnātūrōs esse,* referring to persons other than the sub. of the main clause; *sē*, obj. of the prep. *cum*, referring to *Gallī.*) 2. Caesar said that they would fight against him even to the death. (*Eōs*, sub. of *pugnātūrōs esse,* referring to persons other than the sub. of the main clause; *sē*, obj. of the prep. *contrā*, referring to *Caesar.*) 3. The lieutenant perceived that his men, routed by the cavalry, were in very great danger. (*Suōs*, sub. of *esse*, referring to *lēgātus* as regards possession.) 4. I say that I will remain in the faith of Christ even to the last (end of) life. (*Mē*, sub. of *esse,* referring to the sub. of *dīcō.*) 5. Caesar wrote that the Gauls often resisted him most violently. (*Sibi*, dat. with *resistere*, referring to Caesar.) 6. Caesar said he would not go out of (leave) Gaul before a victory was prepared (obtained). (*Sē*, sub. of *exitūrum esse,* referring to Caesar.) 7. Christ affirmed that the Holy Spirit would come. 8. The Romans knew that their men had often been in very great danger. (*Suōs*, sub. of *fuisse,* referring to *Rōmānī* as regards possession.) 9. The Helvetians pointed out that they had routed the Roman army. (*Sē*, sub. of *pepulisse*, referring to *Helvētiī.*) 10. You denied that you had done this. (*Tē*, sub. of *fēcisse,* referring to the sub. of *negāvistī.*)

Exercise 141.—1. Cōnfirmāmus nōs in Chrīstī fidē semper mānsūrōs esse. 2. Helvētiī exīstimāvērunt sē satis frūmentī sēcum ferre posse. 3. Caesar exīstimāvit eōs per prōvinciam sine injūriīs nōn trānsitūrōs esse. 4. Caesar scīvit prīncipēs Galliae sē timēre. 5. Negāvērunt sē prōvinciae nocitūrōs esse. 6. Gallī dīxērunt sē omnī ratiōne Caesarī nocitūrōs esse. 7. Negāvērunt sē eī sē dēditūrōs esse.

Exercise 142.—1. Christ, having been asked by them, replied that He was the Son of God. (*Fīlium*, pred. n., agreeing w. *sē.*) 2. Caesar said the Helvetians were eager for glory. (*Cupidōs*, pred. adj., agreeing w. *Helvētiōs.*) 3. He pointed out that the Belgians were the bravest of all the Gauls. (*Fortissimōs*, pred. adj., agreeing w. *Belgās.*) 4. Do you think that Caesar was better than other leaders? (*Meliōrem*, pred. adj., agreeing w. *Caesarem.*) 5. Others thought that Columbus was very daring. (*Audācissimum*, pred. adj., agreeing w. *Columbum.*) 6. We know that we ought to be holy. (*Sanctōs*, pred. adj., agreeing w. *nōs.*)

Exercise 143.—1. Exīstimāmus omnēs mīlitēs nostrōs audācissimōs ac fortissimōs esse. 2. Crēdimus Chrīstum esse rēgem omnium hominum et Fīlium Deī. 3. Cōnfirmāmus Marīam mātrem Deī ac sānctissimam omnium sānctōrum esse. 4. Omnēs puerī sciunt duo et duo quattuor esse. 5. Gallī scīvērunt prōvinciam, ā Rōmānīs victam, nōn esse līberam. Itaque ipsī cōnstituērunt usque ad mortem pugnāre ut lībertātem suam dēfenderent. 6. Cicerō cōnscrīpsit sē amicītiam esse optimam exīstimāre. 7. Scīmus nōs fortēs esse dēbēre.

God and the World, p. 440.—He spoke—and they were made.

Exercise 144.—1. Caesar thought he should not give the Helvetians a route (passage) through the province. 2. He thought he should prevent them by force. 3. He thought he should prepare everything useful for war. 4. Pilate knew he should try to save the life of Christ. 5. I say that Pilate should have saved Christ's life.

Exercise 145.—1. Caesar arbitrātus est oportēre sē prōvinciam dēfendere. 2. Crēdimus oportēre nōs aliōs adjuvāre. 3. Scīmus nōn oportēre nōs ūllī (cuiquam) nocēre. 4. Putāsne nōn oportuisse Caesarem Gallīs nocēre? 5. Cicerō cōnscrīpsit sē arbitrārī nullam amicītiam esse sine virtūte posse. 6. Scīmus oportēre nōs prō lībertāte pugnāre. 7. Putāsne oportuisse Caesarem cum Gallīs bellum gerere?

Exercise 146.—1. Crēdō Deum esse. 2. Scīmus Caesarem fortem fuisse. 3. Dēmōnstrābimus tibi Caesarem fuisse magnum imperātōrem. 4. Exīstimāmus rēgem bonum facere rēgnum bonum. 5. Senātus Caesaris litterīs certior factus est eum Galliam pācāvisse. 6. Dēmōnstrāvimus mīlitēs Rōmānōs signa sua ācerrimē dēfendisse. 7. Scīs Rōmānōs plūrimōs servōs habuisse. 8. Nōnne putās servōs miserrimōs esse? 9. Exīstimāsne mīlitēs victōriae ac glōriae cupidissimōs esse? 10. Americānī dīcunt sē prō lībertāte ācerrimē semper pugnātūrōs esse. 11. Omnēs hominēs sciunt nōs Chrīstiānōs in grātiā Deī omnem spem nostram pōnere. 12. Caesarī nuntiāvērunt senātum eī propter victōriās ējus grātiās agere. 13. Negāsne rēgēs prīncipēsque agrōs aliēnōs saepe cupere? 14. Vīdimus Rōmānōs cum gentibus proximīs multōs annōs bellum gessisse. 15. Chrīstus dīxit sē in mundum vēnisse ut hominēs Deum Patrem atque Jēsum Chrīstum Fīlium ējus scīrent. 16. Memōriā teneāmus servum peccātī nōn līberum esse. 17. Scīs Germānōs flūmen Rhēnum trānsisse et agrōs Galliae occupāvisse et posteā cōpiās suās in Italiam dūxisse et ibi cum Rōmānīs bellum gessisse. 18. Putō Pīlātum nōn fuisse virum fortem. 19. Putāsne Caesarem fuisse mājōrem quam Napoleon? 20. Vīdimus Caesarem Rōmānīs omnem Galliam aperuisse. 21. Scīsne Perry ad Japōniam cum classī nostrā pervēnisse et haec loca Americānīs aperuisse? 22. Scīsne Jūdaeōs Rōmānīs Chrīstum trādidisse?

23. Caesar dīxit hostēs, cum signa legiōnum vidērent, sē in montēs celerrimē recēpisse. 24. Putāsne Gallōs Caesarem timuisse?

The Roman Army, p. 443.—He who was in command of the whole war and the whole army was called "leader of the war" or "commander in chief." He held supreme power in his own province; he managed everything and was in charge of all matters. . . .

All the lieutenants were of consular rank and were sent (commissioned) by the Senate to the army. Caesar very often placed those lieutenants who were suitable in charge of the legions and the army. Lieutenants were often sent by Caesar to the leading men and the tribes of Gaul to treat with them of the most serious matters. Many of those lieutenants who were with Caesar in the army were very good and very daring men, and of them all the bravest and most careful (competent) was Labienus, whose counsel and reliability Caesar himself praised very highly. . . .

There were six centurions in one cohort. The centurions were so called because they were in command of one hundred soldiers. They were selected from the soldiers themselves (from the ranks) and were the bravest and fiercest of all. They fought with their soldiers in the battle line itself and were very often praised by Caesar himself.

Answer in Latin, p. 444.—1. What was he called who was in charge of the whole army? (Is quī tōtī exercituī praefuit "dux bellī" aut "imperātor" appellābātur.) 2. Who sent the lieutenants to the army? (Senātus lēgātōs ad exercitum mīsit.) 3. Who was the best of all the lieutenants whom Caesar had with him? (Labiēnus optimus eōrum omnium fuit.) 4. How many centurions were there in one cohort? (Erant sex centūriōnēs in ūnā cohorte.) 5. How many soldiers did they command? (Centūriōnēs centum mīlitibus praeerant.)

The Commander in Chief, p. 444.—Cicero said, "For thus I think that these four qualities should be [found] in a supreme general —a knowledge of warfare, courage, authority, and luck."

I Don't Like You, p. 445.—I don't like you, Sabidius, nor can I say why. I can only say this—I don't like you.

I Am a Human Being, p. 445.—I am a human being; I consider nothing human to be foreign to me.

Friendship, p. 445.—Can bad men be true friends? Cicero, a very good man, thought that they could not be true friends, for he wrote these [words]: But I think this first (in the first place), that friendship cannot be (exist) except in (between) the good (good men).

Lesson 21

Exercise 147.—(The time of all the italicized words is prior to the action of the main verb.) 1. *This battle having been reported* (when this battle had been reported), the leader led his troops back to camp. 2. *The war of the Gauls having been finished* (when the war of the Gauls had been brought to an end), Caesar set out for Italy. 3. *The arms having been handed over* (when the arms had been handed over), the Gauls surrendered themselves to Caesar. 4. *The enemy's battle line having been seen* (when the enemy's battle line had been seen), Caesar very quickly drew up a battle line at the foot of the hill. 5. *The bridge having been taken* (when the bridge had been taken), Caesar very quickly led his troops across. 6. *Javelins having been sent* (when the javelins had been hurled down) from a higher place (position), the soldiers made an attack upon the enemy very strongly.

Exercise 148.—(All the italicized phrases are ablative absolutes consisting of two nouns or a noun and adjective.) 1. *Caesar [being] leader* (while Caesar was leader), the Romans overcame the Gauls in battle. 2. *Henry [being] king* (during Henry's reign), Saint Thomas More was led (put) to death for [his] faith. 3. *Cicero [being] consul* (while Caesar was consul), there was great danger of war. 4. *Not a great part of the year remaining* (although little of the year remained), he hastened to set out for Italy. 5. *Washington [being] leader* (under Washington's leadership), the enemy was driven from our territory. 6. *Christ [being] leader* (with Christ as our leader), let us reach heaven with great glory.

Exercise 149.—1. Hīs rēbus nuntiātīs, barbarī fūgērunt. 2. Rōmā captā, Camillus exercituī praefectus est. 3. Hōc magnō bellō confectō, pāx facta est. 4. Ducibus Gallōrum interfectīs, pāx facta est. 5. Cōpiīs hostium cōnspectīs, Caesar castra posuit. 6. Tē duce, omnēs hostēs nostrōs vincēmus.

Exercise 150.—1. A thousand men returned to camp, the rest having been either killed or captured. 2. Exhausted by wounds, he was not able to reach the city. 3. The leading men, having spoken at length among themselves, decided to send envoys to us. 4. Having been ordered to cross the river, they tried very carefully (earnestly) to do that (so). 5. Having abandoned their arms, they fled. 6. This battle having been made (when the battle had been fought), he led the soldiers away to winter quarters. 7. The leader having been killed (when the leader had been killed), the barbarians fled in every direction. 8. The bridge having been swiftly made (when the bridge had been quickly built), he led across the troops which he had with him. 9. Camp having been pitched (when camp had been pitched) in a favorable place, he drew up a battle line. 10. Arms having been taken (when the arms had been taken), he levied on them the greatest possible number of hostages. 11. The barbarians, having been informed (when the barbarians had been informed) of the arrival of Caesar, and troops brought together from all sides, (they) determined to defend their territory. 12. Ariovistus [being] leader (under the leadership of Ariovistus), the Germans waged war with Caesar.

Exercise 151.—1. Oppidīs incēnsīs, barbarī in montēs sē recēpērunt. 2. Caesar dīxit, magnīs cōpiīs coāctīs, hostēs trāns flūmen castra posuisse. 3. Gallī, multīs vulneribus acceptīs, fugā salūtem petivērunt. 4. Proeliō secundō factō, legātus equitēs in castra redūxit. 5. Galliā pacātā, Caesar ad Italiam profiscīscī cōnstituit. 6. Caesar dīxit, hostibus vīsīs, equitēs fūgisse.

Exercise 152.—1. Gallīs victīs, Caesar in Italiam exercitum dūxit. 2. Lēgātī, haec locūtī (hīs dictīs), ē castrīs exiērunt. 3. Pīlīs jactīs, mīlitēs proelium commīsērunt. 4. Urbe vīsā, profectī sumus. 5. Multīs vulneribus acceptīs, mīlitēs in castrīs decem diēs mānsērunt.

Exercise 153.—1. Equitibus hostium cōnspectīs, Caesar castra posuit. 2. Agmen prōgressum quīnque mīlia passuum, ad flūmen lātissimum pervēnit. 3. Lēgātus, cum ad locum idōneum vēnisset, castra posuit. 4. Mīlitēs, cum obsidibus nocuissent, ā centuriōne interfectī sunt. 5. Castrīs fossā vallōque mūnītīs, dux suōs hortātus impetum hostium sustinēre parāvit. 6. Urbe captā, Caesar legiōnēs quae in prōvinciā nūper cōnscrīptae erant trēs diēs exspectāvit. 7. Gallī Rōmam captam incendit. 8. Hāc rē lēgātō crēditā, Caesar ad prōvinciam statim profectus est. 9. Mīlitēs ā Galliā reversī ab amīcīs suīs laudātī sunt. 10. Hōc animadvertō, Caesar cōpiās in proximum collem dūxit. 11. Aciē ab hostibus īnstrūctā, Caesar equitēs mīsit quī impetum sustinērent. 12. Helvētiī, cum omnibus cōpiīs secūtī, impetum prīmā lūce facere parāvit.

Exercise 154.—1. Quod flūmen Gallōs ā Belgīs dīvīsit? 2. Quō annō interfectus est Chrīstus? 3. Cūjus gentis Ariovistus erat rēx? 4. Quī mīles fortissimē pugnāvit? 5. Quae castra vidēmus? 6. Quem lēgātum Caesar legiōnibus praefēcit? 7. Cui obsidī nocuit? 8. Quaesīvit quī mīlitēs hostibus audācissimē restitissent. 9. Quibus mīlitibus litterās dedistī? 10. Quācum gente bellum gessit? 11. Quam urbem maximē laudās? 12. Ad quod flūmen pervēnit?

Exercise 155.—1. Into how many parts was all Gaul divided?

(Gallia erat omnis dīvīsa in partēs trēs.) 2. What tribes dwelt in these parts? (Belgae, Aquītānī, et Gallī hās partēs incolēbant.) 3. In what things did these tribes differ among themselves? (Hī (hae gentēs) linguā, lēgibus, aliīsque rēbus multīs inter sē differēbant.) 4. What river separated the Aquitanians from the Gauls? (Garumna flūmen Aquītānōs ā Gallīs dīvidēbat.) 5. The Marne separated which tribes from which? (Matrona Gallōs ā Belgīs dīvidēbat.) 6. Which tribe was the bravest of all the Gauls? (Belgae fortissimī omnium Gallōrum erant.) 7. Why were these the bravest of all? (Hī fortissimī omnium erant nam ā prōvinciā Rōmānā longissimē aberant et mercātōrēs ad eōs nōn saepe veniēbant.) 8. With which tribe did they very often contend in battles? (Cum Germānīs proeliīs saepissimē contendēbant.) 9. What tribes dwelt across the Rhine? (Germānī trāns Rhēnum incolēbant.) 10. Do you understand that the Helvetians were braver than the Belgians? Doesn't Caesar point out that the Helvetians were the bravest of all the Gauls and that the Belgians were the bravest of all the Gauls [too]? Can this (both statements) be true? (Helvētiī nōn erant fortiōrēs Belgīs. Belgae fortissimī omnium Gallōrum erant; Helvētiī fortissimī omnium Gallōrum tertiae partis Galliae erant.) 11. In what thing (regard) did the Helvetians surpass the others? (Helvētiī virtūte aliōs superābant.) 12. Why did the Helvetians surpass the others? (Helvētiī aliōs superābant quod saepe cum Germānīs contendēbant.) 13. In whose territory did the Helvetians wage war? (Helvētiī in fīnibus Germānōrum bellum gerēbant.) 14. What river separated the Helvetians from the Germans? (Flūmen Rhēnus Helvētiōs ā Germānīs dīvidēbat.) 15. Who of all the Helvetians was the most renowned? (Orgetōrix omnium Helvētiōrum nōbilissimus erat.) 16. Was Oregetorix an Helvetian or a Roman? (Orgetōrix Helvētius erat.) 17. Of what (thing) was Orgetorix very desirous? (Orgetōrix imperiī Galliae cupidissimus erat.) 18. What did Orgetorix do? (Conjūrātiōnem nōbilitātis fēcit.) 19. For what reason were the Helvetians unable to bring war upon their neighbors easily? (Helvētiī bellum fīnitimīs īnferre nōn facile poterant quod locī nātūrā undique continēbantur.) 20. By what rivers and mountains were the Helvetians held (hemmed) in? (Helvētiī unā ex parte flūmine Rhēno, alterā ex parte monte Jūrā altissimō, tertiā ex parte lacū Lemannō et flūmine Rhodanō continēbantur.) 21. The Jura range separated what tribe from the Helvetians? (Mons Jūra Sequanōs ab Helvētiīs dīvīsit.) 22. What river separated the Helvetians from the Roman Province? (Flūmen Rhodanus Helvētiōs ā prōvinciā Rōmānā dīvīsit.) 23. What did the Helvetians very greatly desire?

(Bellī atque glōriae cupidī erant.) 24. Influenced by what things did the Helvetians (what influenced the Helvetians to) prepare to go out from their own territory? (Bellī atque glōriae cupiditāte suā adductī et auctōritāte Orgetorīgis permōtī, dē fīnibus suīs exīre parāvērunt.) 25. What did they prepare for the departure? (Jūmentōrum et carrōrum quam maximum numerum et magnam cōpiam frūmentī parāvērunt.) 26. Because of what (thing)· do you think Orgetorix took upon himself the embassy to the neighboring states? (Orgetorīx lēgātiōnem ad cīvitātēs fīnitimās sibi suscēpit ut eās conjungeret et ita per eās tōtīus Galliae imperium obtinēret.)

Exercise 156.—1. Hāc dē rē per Haeduōs certior factus est. 2. Post caedem centuriōnum (centuriōnibus interfectīs) legiō magnō in perīculō erat. 3. Lībertātem nostram dēfendēmus (prō lībertāte nostrā pugnābimus). 4. Post rēgis mortem multī aliī rēgnum petīvērunt. 5. Hīs dictīs (haec locūtus), profectus est.

Exercise 157.—See Introduction, 3.

The Roman Army, p. 453.—5. The Cavalry. The soldiers who were in the legions were Romans, but there were not (no) Romans in the cavalry. For the cavalry were sent to Caesar from many tribes. Caesar often levied a certain number of horsemen on those tribes which had made peace with the Roman people. Besides Gauls there were Germans in Caesar's cavalry. For, when Caesar had been in Gaul for seven years and was being pressed hard by a scarcity of all things, he called to him (enlisted) horsemen from Germany. These (they) were very swift and brave and easily surpassed the Gauls. After that, therefore, Caesar always had German horsemen with him.

The standard of the cavalry was called "vexillum." He who was in command of the cavalry was called "praefectus."

The cavalry reconnoitered the places (field, terrain, vicinity) and reported everything which the leader ought (needed) to know—in what place (where) the enemy's troops had been collected (massed), how many and what (classes) they were, what they were doing.

In battle they fought with the enemy's cavalry and pursued (those of the) enemy put to flight by the legions.

Answer in English, p. 453.—1. No. 2. From the tribes which had made peace with the Romans. 3. The standard was called "vexillum" and the commander "praefectus." 4. The cavalry served as scouts, fought with the cavalry of the enemy, and pursued troops that had been routed by the legions.

Lesson 22

Exercise 158.—See Introduction, 3.

Exercise 159.—See Gr. 307.

Exercise 160.—1. They were hurling darts upon the enemy as they came out of the forest. 2. The slaves killed the centurion while (as) he forbade them and held them off. 3. The lieutenants killed the messenger as he was arousing the soldiers. 4. The cavalry seized the leading men as they were conspiring among themselves. 5. Caesar, when he had got possession of the enemy's camp, sent the cavalry to pursue the fleeing enemy. 6. There Catulus was killed while fighting most bravely. 7. He gave grain to the Gauls as they asked. 8. The enemy killed the centurion as he was fighting most valiantly. 9. The shouting of the Gauls as they set out was heard by our men. 10. The cavalry pursued the enemy as they fled into the forest. 11. The soldiers made an attack upon the very fiercely resisting enemy. 12. By force he warded off the barbarians as they attempted to cross the river. 13. They killed the man saying (as he was protesting) that he was free.

Exercise 161.—1. Hostēs ex oppidō exīre cōnantēs impedīvit. 2. Fortissimē pugnāns interfectus est. 3. Marīa Chrīstum crucem portantem vīdit. 4. Equitēs magnum hostium fugientium numerum interfēcērunt. 5. Eum ad Italiam revertentem cēpērunt. 6. Ducem suōs hortantem vīdērunt. 7. Servum per silvās contendentem secūtī sunt. 8. Hortāns suōs pīlō occīsus est. 9. Servus equitēs flūmen trānsientēs vīdit. 10. Pīla ab altō locō in hostēs venientēs jēcērunt.

Exercise 162.—1. God helping [us] (with God's help), we can attain the highest virtue. 2. At the beginning of the year, new consuls were made (elected). 3. While the Gauls were forming a conspiracy, Caesar prepared to wage war. 4. As the soldiers were going out, the shouting of the slaves was heard. 5. As our men were fighting (continued to fight) most bravely, the enemy retreated. 6. He thought that with the help of the chief he would get possession of the power. 7. When the soldiers were in fear of the cavalry and were retreating, Caesar himself, having gone forward to the first line, fought with the enemy. 8. They tried to cross the river, although Caesar forbade [it].

Exercise 163.—1. Caesar, castrīs potītus, trēs diēs ibi mānsit. (*Potītus,* perf., action before time of main verb.) 2. Trānsiēns flūmen clāmōrem hostium audīvit. (*Trānsiēns,* pres., action at same time as main verb.) 3. Urbem captam incendit. (*Captam,* perf., action before time of main verb.) 4. Caesarem hortantem suōs vīdit. (*Hortantem,* pres., action at same time as main verb.)

Exercise 164.—1. The Roman leader, when he had seen the king encouraging his men, sent a centurion to him to treat with him concerning the safety of the soldiers. (*Cohortantem*, pres., action at same time as *cōnspexisset; cōnspexisset*, plu., action before time of main verb in secondary sequence.) 2. The enemy, having been put to flight, hinder themselves (get in each other's way). (*Datī*, perf., action before time of main verb.) 3. The centurion, having hurled his javelin at the enemy, killed one of those as he advanced. (*Missō*, perf., action before time of main verb; *prōgredientem*, pres., action at same time as main verb.) 4. The cavalry killed [one of] the enemy as he tried to draw out his sword. (*Ēdūcere*, pres., action at same time as *cōnantem; cōnantem*, pres., action at same time as main verb.) 5. Since a great part (most) of the soldiers were exhausted by wounds, the whole affair was led (brought) into very great danger. (*Cōnfectā*, perf., action before time of main verb.) 6. The soldiers were sent to Caesar with dispatches; of whom (these) many, captured within sight of our men, were killed. (*Captī*, perf., action before time of main verb.) 7. Having received the dispatch, Caesar immediately sent a message to Crassus, whose winter quarters were many miles away. (*Acceptīs*, perf., action before time of main verb.) 8. The enemy captured the envoy as he hastened into Gaul. (*Contendentem*, pres., action at same time as main verb; *cēpit*, perf., main verb.) 9. Leaving a strong garrison at the bridge, he led the remaining troops across the river. (*Relictō*, perf., action before time of main verb.) 10. When these things were known, and the camp had been pitched in a favorable place, he awaited the legion most recently enrolled. (*Cognitīs, positīs, cōnscrīptam*, all perf., action before time of main verb.) 11. After a successful battle, the cavalry pursued the enemy as they fled toward the nearest mountains. (*Factō*, perf., action before time of main verb; *fugientēs*, pres., action at same time as main verb.)

Exercise 165.—1. Territī in proximās silvās fūgērunt. 2. Nostrīs prōgredientibus, hostēs sē recēpērunt. 3. Pugnāns fortissimē in prīmā aciē tēlō interfectus est. 4. Augustō rēge, Chrīstus puer erat. 5. Dē proeliō certior factus, in Galliam statim profectus sum. 6. Equitibus sequentibus, aciem in colle īnstrūxērunt. 7. Deō adjuvante, in fidē Chrīstiānā mānēbimus. 8. Prōgressī quīnque mīlia passuum, aciem hostium vīdērunt. 9. Plūrimīs vulneribus acceptīs multīsque interfectīs, nostrī collem cēpērunt. 10. Caesare cōnsule, Cicerō ex Rōmā exiit. 11. Annō ineunte, Caesar ad Italiam profectus est. 12. Adventū Caesaris commōtī, Gallī in silvās sē abdidērunt.

Exercise 166.—1. When he had said this, he cast himself down from the wall. (*His dictīs.*) 2. When Caesar had taken the city, he burned it. (*Caesar urbem captam incendit.*) 3. When the slave was coming out of the forest, he was captured. (*Ex silvīs ēgrediēns.*) 4. The centurion was killed when (while) he was fighting very bravely in the battle line. (*In aciē fortissimē pugnāns.*)

Exercise 167.—1. Fuitne Caesar maximus omnium Rōmānōrum? (*Maximus*, pred. adj.) 2. Dēmōnstrāvit ubi hostēs essent. (*Essent*, imp. subj. in indirect question in secondary sequence, action at same time as main verb.) 3. Dēfendāmus lībertātem nostram summā virtūte (fortissimē). (*Dēfendāmus*, hortatory subj.; *summā virtūte*, abl. of manner, or *fortissimē*, superlative degree of adverb.) 4. Chrīstus vēnit ut hominēs vēritātem facilius cognōscerent. (*Ut cognōscerent*, purpose clause in secondary sequence.) 5. Caesar dīxit suōs ācerrimē pugnāvisse. (*Suōs*, indirect reflexive, sub. of *pugnāvisse; pugnāvisse*, perf. infin. in acc. w. infin. after *dīxit*, action before time of main verb.) 6. Dīcēns haec (hīs dīctīs; cum haec dīxisset), dē mūrō sē dējēcit. (*Sē*, direct reflexive, object of *dējēcit; dē*, prep. w. abl.) 7. Rōmānī Gallōs eīs resistentēs interfēcērunt. (*Resistentēs*, pres. part. modifying *Gallōs.*) 8. Galliā omnī ā Germānīs victā, Britannī eīs nōn sē dēdidērunt. (*Gallīā victā*, abl. abs.) 9. Nihil melius ac nōbilius quam vēritās (vēritāte) Chrīstī. (*Quam vēritās*, comparison with *quam*, taking same case after as before it; *vēritāte*, abl. of comparison.) 10. Cūjus reī cupidior es quam grātiae Deī? (*Grātiae*, gen., same case after *quam* as *cūjus reī*, gen. after *cupidior.*) 11. Quibus rēbus inter sē differēbant Germānī et Gallī? (*Quibus rēbus*, abl. of respect.) 12. Equitēs, cum hostēs terruissent, in silvās eōs pepulērunt. (*Cum terruissent*, temporal clause; since there is no active past participle of *terreō* and an ablative absolute cannot be used because it would include the word 'enemy,' referred to again as object of 'drove,' 'having terrified' must be expressed by a clause.) 13. Caesar dīxit sē Germānōs ex Galliā pulsūrum esse. (*Pulsūrum esse*, future infin. act. after *dīxit*, action after time of main verb.) 14. Cicerō et Caesar erant virī magnī. Ille multa dīxit; hic multa ēgit (alter multa dīxit; alter multa ēgit). (*Hic* and *ille*, meaning 'the latter' and 'the former,' in which case the position of the English phrases must be reversed; or *alter, alter*, 'one' and 'the other' of two only.)

Prayer, p. 460.—Lord Jesus Christ, who are the way, the truth, and the life, grant gracious(ly) that through the intercession of the Blessed Virgin Mary, Your mother, running the way of Your commands, we may come to eternal life. Who lives and reigns with God the Father in the unity of the Holy Spirit, God, world without end. Amen.

A Riddle, p. 461.—I am unwilling to speak of my own accord, but I give an answer to one speaking.

Lesson 23

Exercise 168.—1. I wish to go. 2. He wished to get possession of the power. 3. We wish to praise God. 4. He points out what he wishes (wants). 5. Christ wishes to save us from death. 6. I wished you to help me with all [your] strength. 7. Our forefathers wished us to be free. 8. The leader wished the soldiers to take grain from the fields. 9. Having considered the time to be unfavorable, he restrained himself (remained) in his own place, nor did he wish to send the cavalry against the enemy. 10. The boy will wish (want) that reward. 11. They were not willing to go by that road. 12. What do you wish to do? 13. He gave rewards to him in order that he might be willing to help him. 14. They wished to decide [upon] a certain time for that affair. 15. The chief said, "What do the Romans wish (want) except to get possession of (to gain) command of all tribes? 16. He asked the envoys what they wished. 17. He said that the Romans wished to defend their allies with all [their] strength. 18. Do you wish (are you willing) to be holy (a saint)? 19. Caesar wished to visit those tribes. 20. He said he wanted to treat with the king concerning all these matters. 21. Men often believe [only] what they wish [to believe]. 22. We readily believe what we wish.

Box, p. 463.—We ought to obey God rather than men.

Exercise 169.—1. Exīre ē castrīs vult. 2. Voluērunt esse līberī. 3. Ostendit eīs quid vellet. 4. Caesarem adjuvāre volēbant. 5. Illa loca adīre volēbant. 6. Quid vīs? 7. Pugnāre prō lībertāte volumus. 8. Vīsne Rōmam vidēre? 9. Fugere voluit. 10. Post tot proelia pācem facere volent.

Exercise 170.—1. As soon as he knew that the Americans had found out that he wanted to aid the English, Benedict Arnold took himself away from (left) the American camp. 2. Caesar returned to the army as soon as he could through the time of year (as soon as the time of year permitted). 3. After Caesar perceived that he was taking (spending) the time in vain and that he could not prevent the enemy from flight (fleeing), he decided to await the fleet. 4. After so many battles, when they perceived that they could not conquer Caesar, the enemy were willing to make peace with him. 5. God has saved us from so many and so great (so many great) dangers! 6. When I perceived that our forefathers had defended liberty with all [their] strength and so handed it over (down) to us, I praised them exceedingly. 7. When the leader noticed that a sharp wind was injuring (damaging) the ships, he held them in the harbor. 8. When Caesar noticed that the last (rear) column was being hard pressed by the enemy, he led all the troops to the nearest hill and pitched camp there. 9. After he understood that Christ had said He was a king, Pilate ordered Him to be led to death. For he greatly feared the Roman emperor. 10. As soon as he reached the new land, Columbus gave God very great (fervent) thanks. 11. As soon as Caesar had reached that town with all [his] forces, the Gauls sent envoys to him to treat of peace and their own safety. 12. After Caesar saw that all the forces of the Belgians, collected into one place, were coming toward him, he hastened to lead [his] army across the river and to pitch camp there on a hilltop. 13. After the barbarians noticed that the Romans had occupied the hill, they hastened to seek safety by flight. 14. As soon as the enemy's battle line was seen, Caesar drew up his men and encouraged [them]. 15. When the Helvetians thought that they were ready for that affair, they burned all their towns. 16. When the Helvetians were informed of Caesar's arrival, they sent envoys to him. 17. When that day came which had been decided [upon] with the envoys and the envoys returned to him, Caesar said he was not able to give a route (passage) through the province to anyone and affirmed that he would prevent them by force. 18. When the leader knew of Caesar's arrival, he hastened against him with all [his] forces. 19. When the standards of the legions began to approach, the barbarians betook themselves (made their way) to the nearest mountains. 20. When Caesar perceived that he could neither check the flight of the enemy from the towns nor injure them, he decided to await the fleet. 21. When Caesar knew in what place (where) the enemy's forces were, he hastened toward them. 22. When all these matters were swiftly arranged, and as soon as he could through the time of year (as soon as the time of year permitted) he hastened to the army. 23. As soon as they caught sight of our cavalry, the enemy, an attack having been swiftly made (made a swift attack and), confused our men.

Exercise 171.—1. Nauta, cum prīmum terram cōnspexit, certiōrem fēcit Columbum, quī statim grātiās Deō ēgit. 2. Ubi prīmum Jāpōnēs impetum in magnum portum nostrum fēcērunt, bellum gerere cōnstituimus. 3. Postquam Caesar Galliam vīcit, erat pāx in Galliā sed nūlla lībertās. 4. Ut prīmum ab hōc perīculō ēreptus est, grātiās Deō ēgit.

5. Ubi hostēs in colle cōnspexit, castra posuit et proelium committere parāvit. 6. Cum prīmum eōs venientēs vīdit, sē in hostēs jēcit.

Exercise 172.—1. Gallī ipsam urbem Rōmam captam incendērunt. 2. Haec locūtus, profectus est. 3. Decem Gallōs captōs ad Caesarem dūxērunt. 4. Duo mīlia mīlitum captōrum in oppidō retentī sunt. 5. Impetū factō, hostēs in fugam dedērunt.

Exercise 173.—1. Why did Caesar think that Gaul was pacified (subjugated)? (Caesar arbitrātus est Galliam esse pacātam quod Belgae superātī erant, Germānī expulsī erant, et Sedūnī in Alpibus victī erant.) 2. Why did Caesar set out for Illyricum? (Caesar in Illyricum prōfectus est quod eās nātiōnēs adīre et regiōnēs cognōscere volēbat.) 3. What was the cause of (what caused) the new war? (Novum bellum in Galliā ortum est quod Venetī et aliae gentēs retinuērunt lēgātōs quōs Pūblius Crassus in fīnitimās cīvitātēs frūmentī causā dīmīserat.) 4. Why was the authority (position) of the Veneti so very splendid (important)? (Hūjus cīvitātis auctōritās amplissima erat quod Venetī nāvēs plūrimās habēbant et scientiā atque ūsū nauticārum rērum reliquōs superābant.) 5. Who made (brought about) the beginning of the war? (Venetī initium bellī fēcērunt.) 6. Why did the Veneti hold the Roman envoys? (Venetī lēgātōs Rōmānōs retinuērunt ut obsidēs suī remitterentur.) 7. Why did other tribes also keep the envoys [sent to them]? (Hae aliae gentēs lēgātōs eādem dē causā retinuērunt.) 8. Did all these tribes desire to be free? (Cupīvērunt hae omnēs gentēs in eā lībertāte quam ā mājōribus accēperant permanēre.) 9. By whom was Caesar informed of this new war? (Ab Crassō dē hōc novō bellō Caesar certior factus est.) 10. What did Caesar order [this] lieutenant to do? (Caesar jussit eum nāvēs longās aedificāre, rēmigēs comparāre, et nautās cōgere.) 11. When did Caesar return to the army? Where had Caesar been in the meantime? (Cum prīmum per annī tempus potuit, ad exercitum reversus est. Intereā Caesar in Ravennā fuerat.) 12. What [things] did the Veneti and their allies especially prepare? (Maximē ea quae ad ūsum nāvium pertinent parāvērunt.) 13. From what places did they summon help? (Ex Britanniā auxilium arcessivērunt.) 14. By what things was Caesar induced to undertake the war? (Multa Caesarem ad id bellum incitābant—injūriae retentōrum equitum Rōmānōrum, rebelliō facta post dēditiōnem, dēfectiō datīs obsidibus tot cīvitātum conjūrātiō nē reliquae nātiōnēs sibi idem licēre arbitrārentur.)

Exercise 174.—1. Why did the Veneti think they could withstand the force of the Romans, after so many other tribes had been conquered, so many chiefs of other nations killed, so many fields laid waste? (The Veneti seemed to have the advantage, in more manageable ships and naval science, in the natural terrain, and in availability of grain and other supplies.) 2. Why did Caesar think he ought to repulse the Veneti with all his strength and conquer them very swiftly? (Because he had to preserve his position for the sake of his political future, and because he must remain supreme in Gaul or withdraw entirely.) 3. Why did Caesar distribute the army more widely before that war? (Because he heard that other Gallic tribes were eager for revolution and recognized the innate desire of all men for freedom.)

Box, p. 467.—God wills [it]!

Exercise 175.—1. Nē commoveāmus perīculō. (*Nē commoveāmus,* hortatory subj.) 2. Deus ā peccātō (peccātīs) nōs ēripiat. (*Ēripiat,* volitive subj.) 3. Lēgātus hanc rem administret. (*Administret,* jussive subj.) 4. Scīsne quis imperātor exercitūs atque classis Americānae sit? (*Sit,* pres. subj. in indirect question, action at same time as main verb.) 5. Dīxit sē sociōs suōs ā Rōmānīs dēfēnsūrum esse. (*Sē,* direct reflexive. sub. of infinitive, referring to sub. of *dīxit; suōs,* direct reflexive, referring to *sē; ab,* prep. w. abl. w *dēfēnsūrum esse.*) 6. Nōs Americānī lībertātī semper studuimus. (*Lībertātī,* dat. w. *studuimus.*) 7. Rōmānī lātissimum atque altissimum flūmen trānsientēs ab hostium equitibus oppugnātī sunt. (*Trānsientēs,* pres. part. modifying *Rōmānī,* action at same time as main verb; *lātissimum* and *altissimum,* superlative adjs.) 8. Suntne montēs nostrī altiōrēs quam Alpēs (Alpibus)? (*Quam Alpēs,* in comparisons *quam* takes the same case after as before it: *Alpibus.* abl. of comparison.) 9. Lēgātus quī legiōnī tertiae praeerat vīdit ducem Gallōrum in proximō et summō colle aciem īnstruentem. (*Legiōne,* dat. w. *praeerat; īnstruentem,* pres. part. modifying *ducem; summo,* adj. referring to part of object, Gr. 851.) 10. Mūnīvit castra fossā quīnque pedēs lātā. (*Fossā,* abl. of means; *quīnque pedēs,* acc. of extent of space.) 11. Mortis metū līberī sīmus. (*Metū,* abl. of separation.) 12. Gallī ipsī ūnum ex suīs tēlīs interfēcērunt. (*Ipsī,* intensive pron. modifying *Gallī; suīs,* direct reflexive referring to *Gallī; tēlīs,* abl. of means.) 13. Poterimusne semper fīnēs nostrōs dēfendere? (*Dēfendere,* complementary infin. after *poterimus.*) 14. Senātus Caesarem mīsit quī prōvinciam dēfenderet. (*Quī dēfenderet,* relative purpose clause in secondary sequence.) 15. Multīs Gallīs interfectīs, Caesar castra vī cēpit. (*Multīs Gallīs interfectīs.* abl. abs.)

Selected Quotations, p. 468.—1. Fortune snatches nothing away except what she has also given. 2. Christ said, "He who wishes to come after Me, let him deny himself and take up his cross and follow Me."

3. Surely we all wish to be happy. 4. In great matters it is enough to have wished. 5. Each is a defect (both are defects)—to believe everyone and to believe no one.

Box, p. 469.—He who speaks what he wishes will hear what he does not wish [to hear]. And he who does what he wishes will suffer what he does not wish [to suffer].

Lesson 24

Exercise 176.—See Introduction, 3.

Exercise 177.—1. Fit. 2. Fīēbat (factus est). 3. Pōns fīēbat. 4. Magna caedēs fīet. 5. Proelium fīēbat. 6. Fīent Americānī. 7. Fīet cōnsul. Rēx nōn factus est. 8. Quid fit? 9. Ostendit eīs quod fierī vellet. 10. Hīs injūriīs factīs, Gallī bellum gerere parāvērunt.

Exercise 178.—1. He ordered the lieutenant to collect as great a number of horsemen as possible. (*Ut . . . cōgeret*, noun *ut*-clause.) 2. He warned them not to flee. (*Nē fugerent*, negative noun clause introduced by *nē* because *monuit* contains the idea of willing.) 3. It happened that the terrified enemy fled. (*Ut . . . fugerent*, noun *ut*-clause.) 4. I wish you to be a friend to me. 5. It often happens that men believe what they wish. (*Ut . . . crēdant*, noun *ut*-clause.) 6. He caused a bridge to be made. (*Fieret*, imp. subj. in noun *ut*-clause in secondary sequence.) 7. He ordered the guards not to harm the hostages. (*Nē*, in a negative noun clause in which the main verb contains the idea of willing.) 8. It happened that the cavalry did not arrive at the camp before that time. (*Ut . . . nōn*, in a negative noun clause.) 9. Orgetorix persuaded the Helvetians to go out of their own territory with all their forces. (*Ut . . . exīrent*, noun *ut*-clause.) 10. Caesar persuaded the Haeduans not to help the enemy. (*Nē . . . adjuvārent*, negative noun clause introduced by *nē* because the main verb contains the idea of willing.) 11. The leader showed the centurions what he wanted done. (*Vellet*, imp. subj. in an indirect question in secondary sequence.) 12. It happened that the wind was not favorable. (*Esset*, imp. subj. in a noun *ut*-clause in secondary sequence.) 13. He persuaded the Gaul by means of rich rewards to carry a letter to Caesar. 14. He persuaded the slave by means of hope (a promise) of freedom and by rich rewards to carry a letter to Caesar. 15. He tried to persuade them not to bring help to his men. 16. Orgetorix persuaded Casticus to seize the royal power in his own state which his father had formerly held. 17. He persuades them easily by this speech. 18. The Helvetians were hemmed in on all sides. It happened through this circumstance that they could less easily inflict war upon [their] neighbors. 19. When two very great tribes had contended for a long time for the power of all Gaul, it happened that one of them called (summoned) the Germans to itself. 20. It happened that the enemy did not bear the first attack of our men. 21. The chief of the Gauls said, "It happens not without [some] cause that Caesar stations (establishes) winter quarters in our state." 22. It happens by nature that men are more violently terrified by new and unknown things.

Exercise 179.—1. Imperāvit equitibus ut hostēs fugientēs sequerentur. 2. Mandāvit mīlitibus ut castra fossā vallōque mūnīrent. 3. Effēcit ut pāx in prōvinciā esset. 4. Factum est ut nūllī custōdēs ibi collocātī essent. 5. Helvētiīs persuādēre cōnātus est nē per prōvinciam trānsīrent. 6. Servum monuit ut litterās ad Caesarem celerrimē ferret. 7. Saepe fit ut hominēs multa peccāta faciant. 8. Persuādeāmus omnibus hominibus ut inter sē dīligant. 9. Volō ut mē adjuvēs. 10. Factum est ut nēmō mīlitēs ex silvīs venientēs vidēret.

Exercise 180.—1. This can be answered with the help of the map on page 74 and the text, pages 81-82. 2. Who was put in command of the fleet? (Decimus Brutus.) 3. This comparison can be found from footnote 21, page 77, and the English passage on page 84. 4. Why did Caesar decide to await the fleet? (Because he was having no success against the foe: he had stormed a number of their towns in vain and could neither prevent their flight nor do them any damage.)

Of Light, p. 474.—And God said: Let there be light and light was made.

Exercise 181.—1. Prōgressī quīnque mīlia passuum, castra idōneō locō posuērunt et sustinēre impetum Germānōrum parāvērunt. (*Prōgressī,* perf. act. part. of a deponent verb modifying the subject of *posuērunt* and *parāvērunt; quīnque mīlia passuum,* acc. of extent of space; *sustinēre,* infin. after *parāvērunt.*) 2. Virtus, inquit, quā nihil nōbilius est, per ipsam laudātur. (*Quā,* abl. of comparison; *ipsam,* intensive pron., acc. w. prep. *per.*) 3. Omnēs memoriā tenēmus miserum illum Benedictum Arnold. Cōnātus est suīs nocēre et, rē scītā Americānīs, ad hostēs fūgit. (*Nocēre,* infin. after *cōnātus est; suīs,* dat. obj. of *nocēre; rē scītā Americānīs,* abl. abs.) 4. Caesar suōs sine ūllō metū et in Gallōs et Germānōs dūxit. (*Suōs,* direct reflexive pron. referring to *Caesar,* obj. of *dūxit.*) 5. Nōn commovēbimur metū mortis ipsīus. (*Ipsīus,* intensive adj. modifying *mortis.*) 6. Gallī hanc urbem ipsam captam incendērunt. (*Ipsam,* intensive adj. modifying *urbem.*) 7. Caesar suōs trāns montēs altissimōs atque flūmina latissima dūcere potuit. Nihil eum impedīvit, nam fortissimus et audācissimus erat.

140 SECOND YEAR LATIN

(*Altissimōs, latissima, fortissimus,* and *audācissimus,* superlative forms.)
Box, p. 475.—Whatsoever is done with courage is done with glory.
Friendship, p. 475.—1. The power of friendship is in this, that one soul, as it were, is made from many. 2. Let this law be ordained in friendship, that we neither ask shameful things nor do them if asked.

Lesson 25

Exercise 182.—1. When this plan was employed, they departed from camp so swiftly that our men were unable to pursue them. (*Ut . . . nōn potuerint,* result clause, perf. subj. used in secondary sequence to emphasize actual occurrence.) 2. Caesar thought that nothing was so difficult that it could not be accomplished by courage. (*Ut . . . nōn posset,* result clause.) 3. In sight of Caesar himself the affair was carried on, so that no rather brave deed could lay hidden. (*Ut . . . posset,* result clause.) 4. There is no one who is able to live well without a friend. (*Quī . . . possit,* characteristic clause.) 5. They were pressed by the extreme difficulties of all things to such a degree that they were forced to lead the troops back to their own territory. (*Ut . . . cogerentur,* result clause.) 6. Our men fought so very bravely that the enemy (actually) fled. (*Ut . . . fūgerint,* result clause, perf. subj. used in secondary sequence to emphasize actual occurrence.) 7. No one is so brave that he is never disturbed. (*Perturbētur,* pres. subj. in result clause.) 8. He is not one to be terrified by fear of death. (*Terreātur,* pres. subj. in characteristic clause.) 9. He is not one to be alarmed by this circumstance. (*Commoveātur,* pres. subj. in characteristic clause.) 10. Ariovistus, king of the Germans, was not the kind to fear the Romans. (*Timēret,* imp. subj. in characteristic clause.) 11. There is no one who wishes to be wretched. (*Velit,* pres. subj. in characteristic clause.) 12. No one will be found who says (to say) he wishes to be wretched. (*Dīcat,* pres. subj. in characteristic clause.) 13. Who will be found who says (to say) that he has enough of everything? (*Quī . . . dīcat,* relative characteristic clause.) 14. Who is there who does not wish (desire) freedom? (*Quī . . . velit,* relative characteristic clause.) 15. He hastened into Gaul so swiftly that the enemy, informed of his arrival, were very violently disturbed. (*Ut . . . perturbātī sint,* result clause, perf. subj. used in secondary sequence to emphasize actual occurrence.)

Exercise 183.—1. Nostrī tam fortēs fuērunt ut vim hostium trēs hōrās sustinuerint. 2. Deus mundum dīlēxit adeō ut Fīlium sōlum in eum mitteret ut hominēs vītam habērent. 3. Quis est quī lībertātem

optimam nōn esse dīcat? 4. Nēmō est quī hoc neget. 5. Marīa tam
sāncta est ut omnēs eam dīligāmus et laudēmus. 6. Illī montēs tam altī
sunt ut nēmō eōs trānsierit. 7. Tot virī interfectī sunt ut Caesar hostēs
fugientēs multōs diēs sequī nōn posset. 8. Metus hostium tantus erat ut
prīmō impetū fugerent (fūgerint). 9. Cāritās Chrīstiāna tālis est ut eā
Patrī, Fīliō, et Spīrituī Sānctō conjungāmur. 10. Tālis est vir quī aliōs
semper adjuvet. 11. Caesar nōn tālis erat quī hostem timeret.

Box, p. 478.—A burden borne well becomes light.

Exercise 184.—Alpēs tam altae et itinera tam difficilia erant ut
Rōmānī exīstimārent Hannibalem in Italiam suōs dūcere nōn posse.
Itaque putāvērunt sē proelium cum Hannibale in fīnibus suīs nōn
commisūrōs esse. Hannibal autem nihil tam difficile esse exīstimābat ut
virtūte fierī nōn posset. Tam dīligenter ac fortiter rem administrāvit
ut cum exercitū magnō Alpēs trānsīre potuerit et cōgere Rōmānōs, ējus
adventū commōtōs et territōs, in agrīs ipsīs Italiae proelium committere
et viās quae ad Rōmam ipsam pertinuērunt dēfendere. Rōmānī tam
commōtī erant ut multōs exercitūs mīserint, virīs summīs ducibus (ā
virīs summīs ductōs), quī Hannibalem sustinērent. Hic autem tam
audāx ac dīligēns erat ut in proeliō saepe vīcerit, Rōmānīs plūrimīs
interfectīs.

Rōmānī tam saepe victī sunt ut intellegerent sē Hannibalem proeliō
vincere nōn posse. Itaque cōnstituērunt novō bellī cōnsiliō ūtī. Cōnstituērunt cum Hannibale in aciē nōn pugnāre sed [potius] oppida
urbēsque suās mūnīre et omne frūmentum incendere. Sine cōpiā frūmentī Hannibal in Italiā manēre nōn poterat, neque cōpiae ējus nōn
tantae erant ut oppida mūnīta oppugnāre possent.

Rōmānī bellum tam bene administrāvērunt et virtūs sua tanta erat
ut Hannibal, mīlitibus labōre et frūmentī inopiā cōnfectīs, ex Italiā sē
recipere coāctus sit. Rōmānī etiam putāvērunt nihil tam difficile esse ut
ā ducibus fortibus et audācibus cōnficī nōn posset.

Exercise 185.—1. On that day all the Helvetians assembled at the
river. (*Illō diē,* abl. of time when.) 2. On the third day he reached the
territory of the Helvetians. (*Diē tertiō,* abl. of time when.) 3. On what
day will grain be given to the soldiers? (*Quō diē,* abl. of time when.)
4. Within four days he will reach camp. (*Quattuor diēbus,* abl. of time
within which.) 5. On the day determined, the envoys returned to
Caesar. (*Diē cōnstitūtā,* abl. of time when.) 6. Caesar waged war with
the Gauls for many years. (*Multōs annōs,* acc. of extent of time.) 7. At
the third hour he reached the river. (*Tertiā hōrā,* abl. of time when.)
8. Fighting very bravely for four hours, they withstood the enemy's at-

tack. (*Quattuor hōrās*, acc. of extent of time.) 9. In what year was Christ put to death? (*Quō annō*, abl. of time when.) 10. Within three years he will return. (*Tribus annīs*, abl. of time within which.) 11. For how many hours did you march through the forest? (*Hōrās*, acc. of extent of time.) 12. For nearly two thousand years the truth of Christ has been announced to all nations. (*Duo ferē mīlia annōrum*, acc. of extent of time.) 13. In ten days we shall receive the dispatch. (*Decem diēbus*, abl. of time within which.) 14. In a short time he will return. (*Brevī tempore*, abl. of time within which.) 15. Reinforcements came at that very time. (*Eō ipsō tempore*, abl. of time when.) 16. At that time Caesar was in the province. (*Eō tempore*, abl. of time when.) 17. They remembered that in battles fought in previous years they had easily overcome the Gauls. (*Superiōribus annīs*, abl. of time when.) 18. He levied a certain number of horsemen on those states which he had pacified (subjugated) in previous years. (*Superiōribus annīs*, abl. of time when.) 19. With Caesar as leader, in many different years they made (had) a great many favorable (successful) battles. (*Multīs annīs*, abl. of time when.) 20. In that year there was a scarcity of grain in Gaul. (*Eō annō*, abl. of time when.) 21. On that day he advanced ten miles. (*Eō diē*, abl. of time when.) 22. On the third day he set out at dawn. (*Tertiō diē*, abl. of time when.) 23. The lieutenant said that within four days he would capture the city. (*Quattuor diēbus*, abl. of time within which.)

Exercise 186.—1. Tertiā diē ad castra lēgātī pervēnit. 2. Tribus annīs eās gentēs pacābimus. 3. Trēs annōs Rōmānīs restitērunt. 4. Diē tertiō cōpiās hostium conspēxērunt. 5. Trēs hōrās ācerrimē pugnātum est. 6. Tertiā hōrā castra in summō colle posuērunt. 7. Duās hōrās mānsērunt. 8. Duōbus hōrīs illud oppidum capiēmus. 9. Multōs annōs Caesar cum Gallīs bellum gessit. 10. Duo mīlia passuum prōgressī sunt. 11. Eō tempore erat inopia frūmentī in Galliā. 12. Fossa decem pedēs lāta erat. 13. Prīmā lūce cum omnibus cōpiīs profectī sunt. 14. Quattuor passūs ab flūmine castra erant. 15. Secundō diē mīlia passuum ab oppidō castra posuērunt. 16. Quattuor diēs barbarōs fugientēs secūtī sunt.

Exercise 187.—1. Rōmānī tam fortēs erant ut multās gentēs vincere potuerint. 2. Ventus tam ācer erat ut classis ē portū exīre nōn posset. 3. Eō tempore tanta inopia frūmentī illō locō erat ut hostēs in suōs fīnēs sē recipere coāctī sint. 4. Mīlitēs Germānōs adeō timēbant ut prīmum impetum nōn sustinuerint. 5. Praesidium tam firmum erat ut hostēs castra capere nōn potuerint.

Exercise 188.—1. Puer celere pede erat. 2. Imperiī cupidī erant.

3. Propter caedem prīncipum suōrum commōtī sunt. 4. Hāc dē rē ā servō certior factus est. 5. Iter ex prōvinciā fēcērunt. 6. Lēgātus legiōnī saepe praefectus est. 7. Vī castrīs (castrōrum) potītus est.

The Love of Christ, p. 481.—Who, therefore, shall separate us from the love of Christ? Tribulation? Or distress? Or hunger? Or nakedness? Or danger? Or persecution? Or the sword? . . . But we will conquer in all matters because of Him who has loved us.

God's Grace, p. 481.—Whether, therefore, little or much, without Him it cannot be done, without whom nothing can be done. (Whether little or much, therefore, it cannot be done without Him without whom nothing can be done.)

Charity, p. 482.—And everyone who loves is born of God, and knows God. He who loves not, knows not God; because God is love. In this God's love has appeared to us, because He sent His only-begotten Son into the world that we might live through Him. In this is love: not as if we had loved God, but because He first loved us and sent His Son as propitiation for our sins. Dear ones, if God has so loved us, we also ought to love each other. No one has ever seen God. If therefore we love each other, God remains (abides) in us and His love is perfect in us. . . . God is love, and he who abides in love, abides in God, and God in him. . . . Let us love God, therefore, because God has first loved us. . . . And this command we have from God, that he who loves God, should love his brother also.

Virtue, p. 482.—Nobody can be happy without virtue, nor can virtue stand firm without reason.

A Saying of Christ, p. 483.—Christ said, "No servant can serve two masters."

Riddle, p. 483.—No one moves me except he who first is moved. What am I?

War, p. 483.—Let war, however, be undertaken in such a way that nothing else except peace seems to be sought.

Box, p. 483.—Time flies—irretrievable.

Friendship, p. 483.—I urge you so to place (esteem) virtue, without which friendship cannot exist, that, except for it, you may (will) consider nothing more excellent than friendship.

Lesson 26

Exercise 189.—See Introduction, 3.

Exercise 190.—1. Leaders came into the town for the sake of speaking. (*Loquendī,* gen. w. *causā.*) 2. A shout having been raised (when a shout arose), the enemy sought safety by fleeing. (*Fugiendō*, abl. of means.) 3. Time for following was lacking (there was no time for following). (*Sequendum*, acc. w. *ad.*) 4. I will not give you one hour for living (to live). (*Vīvendum*, acc. w. *ad.*) 5. The swords were very useful for fighting. (*Pugnandum*, acc. w. *ad.*) 6. Caesar was fierce and brave in acting (action). (*Agendō*, abl. w. *in.*) 7. He thought this place unsuitable for making a sortie. (*Ēgrediendum*, acc. w. *ad.*) 8. They have prepared everything that pertains to departing. (*Proficīscendum*, acc. w. *ad.*) 9. The time of (for) resisting was failing. (*Resistendī*, explanatory gen.) 10. We shall conquer by fighting, not by fleeing. (*Pugnandō* and *fugiendō*, abl. of means.) 11. We shall gain heaven by praying always and by acting bravely. (*Ōrandō* and *agendō*, abl. of means.) 12. Lifted up (elated) by this victory, they immediately betook themselves (made their way) to the other camp. (*Sublātī*, perf. part. pass. modifying subject of *contulērunt.*) 13. At the third hour, a few were ready for departing (to depart). (*Hōrā*, abl. of time when; *proficīscendum*, acc. w. *ad.*) 14. Lifted up (elated) by these happenings, he thought he would finish the whole war within a short time. (*Sublātus*, perf. part. pass. modifying subject of *arbitrātus est; sē*, indirect reflexive pron., sub. of *cōnfectūrum esse; tempore*, abl. of time within which; *cōnfectūrum esse*, fut. infin. in acc. w. infin. construction after *arbitrātus est.*) 15. He took a few days for deliberating (to deliberate). (*Dēliberandum*, acc. w. *ad.*) 16. He wished all fear to be taken away from his state. (*Tollī*, pres. infin. pass. in acc. w. infin. construction after *voluit.*) 17. We shall have no other time for speaking. Now is the time of (for) fighting; now let us drive the Romans with all our strength into the province. (*Pugnandī*, explanatory gen.; *pellāmus*, hortatory subj.) 18. But a plan was not lacking to the barbarians. (*Barbarīs*, dat. w. *dēfuit.*) 19. Cotta failed in nothing for the common welfare. (*Salūtī*, dat. w. *deerat.*) 20. The enemy knew that cavalry, ships, and grain were lacking to the Romans. (*Rōmānīs*, dat. w. *deesse; deesse*, pres. infin. in acc. w. infin. construction after *intellexērunt.*) 21. The enemy is coming! They are in the harbors! Now (this) is the time for fighting, not speaking. We are few, but brave, and what is greater (more), Romans. We will prepare (assure) the victory by fighting very bravely. (*Pugnandī*, explanatory gen.; *mājus*, comparative of *magnus*, pred. adj.; *pugnandō*, abl. of means.)

Exercise 191.—1. Hī virī pugnandī cupidī sunt. 2. Grātiam ōrandō cōnsequimur. 3. Ventus ad proficīscendum idōneus erat. 4. Omnia ad proficīscendum parāvērunt. 5. Ad pugnandum parātī erant. 6. Proficīscendī cupidī erant. 7. Audāx in agendō et dīligēns in loquendō erat. 8. Vītam suam fugiendō cōnservāvit. 9. Ōrandō et hortandō persuāsit eīs nē sē in silvīs relinquerent. 10. Victōriam ācriter et fortiter pugnandō cōnsecūtī sunt. 11. Missus est ad explōrandum.

Exercise 192.—1. Prīmō impetū hostēs fūgērunt. 2. Pīla in hostēs venientēs ab locō superiōre jēcērunt. 3. Multī prīncipēs Gallōrum ā Caesare interfectī sunt. 4. Equitēs in proximum collem celeriter dūxit. 5. Ācriter pugnātum est et magna caedēs facta est. 6. Hostēs prōgredientēs trāns flūmen cōnspexērunt. 7. Cum equitēs pervēnērunt, barbarī sē celeriter recēpērunt.

Exercise 193.—1. Gallum gladiō interfēcit. 2. Fortissimē pugnāvērunt. 3. Castra fossā vallōque mūnīvērunt. 4. Cohortēs, cum lēgātō in silvās pauca mīlia passuum prōgressae, castra posuērunt. 5. Rōmānī cum Germānīs multōs annōs bellum gessērunt. 6. Sine timōre proelium commīsērunt. 7. Multīs hominibus interfectīs, in oppidum sē recēpērunt. 8. Prīmā lūce ad castra profectī sunt. 9. Parvā (exiguā) parte aestātis reliquā, Britanniam adīre cōnstituit.

Box, p. 488.—Do you wish to have great command (power)? Command (rule) yourself.

Exercise 194.—1. Why did Caesar wish to go to Britain? (Caesar in Britanniam īre volēbat ut genus hominum perspiceret et loca, portūs, aditūs cognōsceret.) 2. What Romans were accustomed to visit Britain before Caesar's arrival? (Mercātōrēs Rōmānī ante Caesaris adventum Britanniam adībant.) 3. What did Caesar wish to find out from the merchants? (Ex mercātōribus Caesar reperīre voluit quanta esset īnsulae magnitūdō, quantae nātiōnēs eam incolerent, quem ūsum bellī habērent, et quī essent ad mājōrem nāvium multitūdinem idōneī portūs.) 4. Why did he send Gaius Volusenus ahead? (Gājum Volusēnum quī haec cognōsceret praemīsit.) 5. Why did Caesar set out for [the territory of] the Morini? (Caesar in Morinōs profectus est quod inde erat brevissimus in Britanniam trājectus.) 6. What did the envoys who had come to Caesar from the British states promise? (Pollicitī sunt sē obsidēs datūrōs atque imperāta populī Rōmānī factūrōs esse.) 7. What did Caesar order Commius [to do]? (Huic imperāvit ut adīret quās posset cīvitātēs et eās hortārētur ut cum populō Rōmānō fidem sequerentur.)

Exercise 195.—1. Factum est ut omnēs interficerentur. 2. Monuit puerōs nē sōlī in silvās īrent. 3. Imperāvit ut pōns fieret. 4. Tam ācer in loquendō atque agendō erat ut omnēs eum timuerint. 5. Oportet nōs Jēsum Chrīstum, rēgem nostrum, sequī. 6. Cum prīmum Caesarem vīdērunt, coepērunt dīcere eum interficī oportēre. 7. Illī quī Pīlātō persuādēbant ut Chrīstum interficeret, eum adjuvantem aliōs vīderant.

The Supreme Commander, p. 489.—"Effort in tasks; courage in dangers; diligence in action; speed in bringing things to a conclusion; wisdom in foreseeing." "Neither can that commander restrain (control) an army, who does not restrain (control) himself, nor be severe in judging, who does not wish others to be severe judges of him."

Box, p. 489.—No one gains the highest place by fearing (cowardice).

Friendship, p. 489.—Love and good will taken away (gone), every delight is taken away (gone) from life.

Saint Blaise, p. 490.—Through the intercession of St. Blaise, bishop and martyr, may God free (keep) you from evil (any ill) of the throat and from every other evil. In the name of the Father, and of the Son, and of the Holy Spirit. Amen.

Life's Dangers, p. 490.—

> Our life, full of wars,
> Among enemies, among arms
> After the fashion of war is lived.
> No dawn comes without a fight,
> No night without sorrow
> And a risk of salvation.

Lesson 27

Exercise 196.—See Introduction, 3.

Box, p. 492.—A way is made by force. (Force finds a way.)

Exercise 197.—1. You ought to be praised. 2. A new plan will have to be made. 3. That city must be taken. 4. Those places should be inspected. 5. The fleeing enemy must immediately be pursued. 6. Before the battle the soldiers should have been encouraged. 7. It was necessary to finish this war within a short time. 8. Others must be helped. 9. The enemy crossing the river should be prevented by force. 10. A war will have to be undertaken. 11. It is necessary to prepare everything for setting out (the departure). 12. The lieutenant, a very good and careful man, was to be praised. 13. The war must be inflicted upon them. 14. The baggage was to have been brought together in one place. 15. The Helvetians had to be influenced (persuaded) to go out from their own territory by another route. 16. Very good mothers should be praised.

Exercise 198.—1. Hic vir laudandus est. 2. Interficiendī sunt. 3. Virtūs cōnsequenda est. 4. Illa oppida perspicienda sunt. 5. Castra fossā vallōque mūnienda sunt. 6. Pōns faciendus est. 7. Proelium statim committendum erat. 8. Omnia brevī tempore paranda erant. 9. Hostēs ex silvīs venientēs oppugnandī erant. 10. Agrī hostium vastandī erant nē cōpiam frūmentī habērent. 11. Nōn sequendī sunt. 12. Cōpiae dīvidendae erunt. 13. Labiēnus legiōnibus praeficiendus fuit.

Exercise 199.—1. We must either conquer or die. 2. We must resist those who wish to take away our freedom. 3. It is necessary to go. 4. We will have to set out at dawn. 5. Often it is not necessary to speak. 6. The enemy must be harmed by every means. 7. Cavalry should be striven for. 8. We had to fight very bravely. 9. We must live well.

Exercise 200.—1. Statim pugnandum est. 2. Respondendum est. 3. Proficīscendum est. 4. Barbarīs resistendum est. 5. Classī nocendum erat. 6. Ex castrīs ēgrediendum est. 7. Fortiter moriendum est. 8. Quattuor diēs ibi manendum est. 9. Hōc cōnsiliō ūtendum erit.

Box, p. 494.—No soldier has conquered an enemy without a battle.

Exercise 201.—1. We should fear these things. (*Nōbīs,* dat. of agent w. gerundive.) 2. We must conquer. (*Nōbīs,* dat. of agent w. gerundive.) 3. We should give very great (fervent) thanks to God. (*Deō,* dat. of indirect obj.; *ā nōbīs,* abl. of agent w. gerundive because of the previous dat.) 4. The fleet must be awaited by him. (*Eī,* dat. of agent w. gerundive.) 5. Caesar had to employ this plan. (*Caesarī,* dat. of agent w. gerundive.) 6. You must resist very bravely all those who wish to harm your state. (*Omnibus,* dat. w. *resistendum est; ā vōbīs,* abl. of agent w. gerundive because of previous dat.) 7. The Romans, forced into the defiles, had to fight most bravely. (*Rōmānīs,* dat. of agent w. gerundive.) 8. We must take away (remove) fear from our state. (*Nōbīs,* dat. of agent w. gerundive.) 9. Those places (positions) had to be inspected by Caesar. (*Caesarī,* dat. of agent w. gerundive.)

Exercise 202.—1. Collis lēgātō perspiciendus est. 2. Equitātus ex castrīs Caesarī mittendus est ut legiōnēs adjuvāret. 3. Nāvēs eōrum nōbīs incendendae est. 4. Hostibus ā nōbīs usque ad mortem resistendum est. 5. Hostibus ā legiōnibus fortiter resistendum est. 6. Obsidibus ab eīs nocendum erat. 7. Aut vincendum est aut moriendum. 8. Helvētiīs ā Caesare resistendum erat. Nōnne prōvincia eī dēfendenda erat? 9. Omnibus vīribus ūtendum est ut lībertātem dēfenderēmus.

Exercise 203.—1. He handed the hostages over to the soldiers to be killed. 2. He gave the baggage to the lieutenant to be defended. (He entrusted the defense of the baggage to the lieutenant.) 3. He undertook the collection of ships. 4. He undertakes to wage war.

Exercise 204.—1. He said that the hostages must be killed. 2. He decided he should await the fleet. 3. I think that the camp should be defended and that we should not leave. 4. I think that the enemy should be harmed by the soldiers in every way. 5. He pointed out to the lieutenant that these things must be known. 6. He said that he thought that the Romans should be driven into the province within that time.

Exercise 205.—Caesar had to do everything at one time: display the battle flag which was the sign when they had (for them) to rush together to arms; give a signal with the trumpet; call the soldiers back from the fortification; draw up the battle line; urge on the soldiers; give the signal.

Box, p. 496.—Without sweat and toil no work is finished.

Exercise 206.—1. Haeduī petīvērunt ut Caesar eōs dēfenderet. 2. Ad flūmen iter fēcērunt. 3. Gallīs captīs frūmentum dedērunt. 4. Imperāvit eīs ut pontem facerent. 5. Salūtem meam tibi dēbeō. 6. Cupiunt pācem cōnfirmāre. 7. Lībertātī studēbant. 8. Hoc nōn agendum est. 9. Prōvincia eī dēfendenda erat. 10. Mīlitēs pugnandī cupidī erant. 11. Lēgātī vēnērunt ut pācem peterent. 12. Nōn is est quī Caesarem timeat.

Box, p. 497.—Man must always expect a last (the final) day.

Virtue, p. 497.—For certainly everything must be praised which is joined with virtue.

True Friendship, p. 497.—That is not at all to be called true friendship which is undertaken and kept for the sake of some temporal benefit.

Box, p. 497.—Of the dead, [speak] nothing but good.

Speech, p. 497.—There is a time when nothing [should be said]—there is a time when something [should be said]—but no time when everything should be said.

Extreme Unction, p. 498.—God has spoken to us through St. James thus: "Is anyone sick among you? Let him bring in the priests of the Church and let them pray over him, anointing him with oil in the name of the Lord, and the prayer of faith will save the sick man and God will relieve him, and if he is in (has) sins, they will be taken away from him."

That of which St. James spoke is the sacrament which is called extreme unction.

Box, p. 498.—Of two evils, we must always choose the lesser.

Slavery, p. 498.—Slavery is the very worst of all evils, to be opposed not only by war but also by death.

Selected Quotations, p. 499.—1. We must pray that there be (for) a sound mind in a sound body. 2. We should love some good man and always keep him before our eyes, in order to live as if he were watching and do everything as if he saw it.

Box, p. 499.—It befits a commander to die standing.

Words of Christ, p. 499.—"Heaven and earth will pass away, but my words will not pass away."

Lesson 28

Exercise 207.—1. I am eager for Rome to-be-seen. (I am eager to see Rome.) (*Videndae*, attrib. gerundive modifying *Rōmae*, gen. w. *cupidus*.) 2. He prepares all [things] which are useful for the bridge to-be-burned. (He prepares everything necessary for the burning of the bridge.) (*Incendendum*, attrib. gerundive modifying *pontem*, acc. w. *ad*.) 3. By a bridge being-made, he led the army across the river. (By building a bridge he was able to lead the army across the river.) (*Faciendō*, attrib. gerundive modifying *ponte*, abl. of means.) 4. The soldiers were very eager for battle to-be-begun (to begin battle), but nevertheless the leader held them in camp. (*Committendī*, attrib. gerundive modifying *proeliī*, gen. w. *cupidissimī*.) 5. He considered this time unsuitable for battle to-be-begun (for beginning battle). (*Committendum*, attrib. gerundive modifying *proelium*, acc. w. *ad*.) 6. Caesar was swift in wars being-finished (in bringing wars to an end). (*Cōnficiendīs*, attrib. gerundive modifying *bellīs*, abl. w. *in*.) 7. He considered this hill suitable for camp to-be-pitched (for pitching camp). (*Pōnendīs*, attrib. gerundive modifying *castrīs*, dat. w. *idōneum*.)

Exercise 208.—1. Proeliī committendī cupidī erant. 2. Locus ad aciem īnstruendam nōn idōneus erat. 3. Ad bellum gerendum parātī erant. 4. Frūmentō incendendō cōgere Rōmānōs ex Galliā sē recipere cōnātī sunt. 5. Nunc tempus est Rōmānōrum rejiciendōrum in prōvinciam.

Exercise 209.—1. He sent a lieutenant to pacify those peoples. 2. The Germans crossed the Rhine to fight. 3. He sent the third legion to storm the camp. 4. They came with all the forces to attack the town. 5. The ships of the Veneti were made to bear (constructed so as to withstand) the greatest force of the winds. 6. He sent the cavalry to overtake the enemy. 7. The envoys came to beg for peace. 8. A horseman hastened to the camp to ask for help. 9. The cavalry was often sent to reconnoiter.

Exercise 210.—1. Ad oppidum oppugnandum vēnērunt. 2. Ad prīncipēs illīus gentis capiendōs missī sunt. 3. Frūmentī comparandī causā vēnērunt. 4. Ad explōrandum missī sunt. 5. Ad impedīmenta dēfendenda relictī sunt. 6. Auxiliī petendī causā in oppidum contendērunt. 7. Chrīstus ad omnēs hominēs adjuvandōs vēnit. 8. Deus sōlum fīlium suum in terram vēritātis nuntiandae causā mīsit.

Exercise 211.—1. Caesar Galliae vincendae cupidus erat. 2. Gallī Caesaris occīdendī cupidī erant. 3. Ponte faciendō Caesar hostēs persequī poterat. 4. Servus ad servōs interficiendōs missus est. 5. Locus ad proelium committendum nōn idōneus erat. 6. Nōn erat tempus aciēī īnstruendae. 7. Ad agrōs oppidaque dēfendenda cōpiās coēgērunt. 8. Suīs hortandīs Caesar hostēs saepe vīcit. 9. Servō praemiīs pollicendīs persuāsit ut litterās ad Caesarem ferret. 10. Pugnandō ācriter collem tenuērunt. 11. Vincendō in proeliō Caesar Galliam Rōmānīs aperuit. 12. Caesar audāx in suīs dūcendīs erat. 13. Dīligēns in agendō erat. 14. Dīxērunt Caesarem ex prōvinciā cōpiās dūcere nōn oportēre. 15. Rōmānī vetuērunt Caesarem suōs in Italiam dūcere. 16. Lēgātī et centuriōnēs eī persuāsērunt ut classem exspectāret. 17. Obsidibus retinendīs pācem in Galliā cōnfirmāvit. 18. Gallī cōnservāre lībertātem pugnandō cōnstituērunt.

Box, p. 503.—Christ said, "He who believes in Me has eternal life."

Exercise 212.—1. Barbarī in montibus erant. 2. Brevī tempore illum collem capiēmus. 3. In illum locum maximās cōpiās coēgērunt. (*Cōgō* is construed as a verb of motion.) 4. Ad hostēs prohibendōs duo cohortēs mīsit. 5. Illō annō Caesar cōnsul factus est. 6. Apud suōs ōrātiōnem habuit. 7. Caesar prōvinciae praefuit. 8. Labiēnum duōbus legiōnibus praefēcit. 9. Suōs prō castrīs īnstrūxit.

The Martyrs, p. 503.—God's saints were not afraid, dying for Christ's name. They handed over their own bodies to punishments (torture) because of God.

Circumstantial Evidence, p. 504.—If this [man is] killed by the sword, and you his enemy are caught with a bloody sword in that very place, and no one but you was seen there, and nobody [else] has a motive, and you are always daring, why should we be able to doubt (be in doubt) about the crime?

Box, p. 504.—What nature is better, therefore, in the race of men (human race) than theirs who consider themselves born to help, defend, and preserve [their fellow] men?

Lesson 29

Exercise 213.—See Introduction, 3.

Exercise 214.—See Introduction, 3.

Box, p. 506.—Blessed are all who fear the Lord.

Exercise 215.—1. Hail, Mary, full of grace. 2. O good Jesus, have mercy on us who have committed so many and [such] great sins against you. 3. Hail, Caesar! 4. I will always remember you, my son. 5. Hail, King, we are ready to fight to the death for you. 6. At dawn, soldiers, we will set out and will hasten with all [our] strength to the nearest winter quarters. 7. Soldiers, a war has arisen between me and the Senate. 8. To him who reaches the enemy's camp first, men, I will give great (rich) rewards. 9. Against you and your [people], envoy, we will wage war. Two thousand Gauls are in arms; the Germans are crossing the Rhine and will arrive by the third hour. No time is given (there is no time) either for fleeing or for seeking help. You must hand everything over to us immediately. 10. I wish to persuade you, my friends, to conspire with me against Caesar in order to preserve our liberty.

Exercise 216.—1. Fortiter, mīlitēs, pugnēmus! 2. Eāmus, amīcī meī. 3. Avē, rēx et imperātor! 4. Avē, Jēsū Chrīste, Domine mī et Deus mī! (In ecclesiastical Latin, *Domine meus et Deus meus.*) 5. Cēdē-musne, Rōmānī, barbarīs? Usque ad mortem, mīlitēs, hīs Gallīs miserīs resistāmus. 6. Deus tē servet, fīlī mī. 7. Vēnimus, rēx miser, ut tē occīdāmus propter injūriās ā (abs) tē nātiōnī nostrae illātās. 8. Domine Deus, miserēre nōbīs! 9. Occīdāmus Caesarem, amīcī, Rōmānī, et sīc lībertātem quae mājōrēs nostrī nōbīs trādidērunt cōn-servēmus. 10. Estisne, mīlitēs, ad proelium parātī?

Exercise 217.—See Introduction, 3.

Box, p. 508.—Divide and rule.

Exercise 218.—1. Holy Mary, mother of God, pray for us. 2. Fight bravely, soldiers! 3. Hear [ye]! Your God is one God. 4. Take arms! Bring help! 5. Lead us, O Lord, by Your ways to heaven. 6. Tell us, slave, where the enemy is. 7. Lord Jesus Christ, take away our sins. 8. Lord, make me love You with all [my] strength. 9. Call the soldiers to arms, lieutenant. 10. Christ said, "Follow Me." 11. Attack the enemy! 12. Depart! Get out of the city! Leave us! 13. Go, the Mass is ended. 14. Use this plan! 15. Come with me. 16. Go in peace. 17. Fear God. 18. Persuade them not to undertake war. 19. Love God. 20. Come to help me (to my aid), O Lord. 21. Live, great King.

Exercise 219.—1. Aperīte portās, custōdēs. 2. Dēfende mē, Domine. 3. Adjuvā nōs. 4. Aggrediminī, mīlitēs, fortissimē. 5. Miserēre nōbīs, Domine Jēsū Chrīste. 6. Sāncte Paule, ōrā prō nōbīs. 7. Omnēs sānctī Deī, ōrāte prō nōbīs. 8. Exī ex castrīs. Proficīscere. 9. Pugnāte, mīlitēs, tam fortiter ut nēmō vōbīs resistere possit. 10. Dīc nōbīs, rēx, quod fierī velīs. 11. Dūc, imperātor, et sequēmur. 12. Fer hunc dolōrem, amīce mī, fortissimē. Pōne spem in Deō et ille tibi dabit satis grātiae ut eum ferās. 13. Dux, "Sequiminī mē," inquit, "et Rōmam ipsam capiēmus." 14. Fac hoc tū ipse. 15. Sāncta Mariā, ōrā prō mē in hōrā mortis meae. 16. Loquere fortiter et sine ūllō timōre. 17. Adjuvā aliōs et aliī tē adjuvābunt. 18. Dīlige et dīligēris. 19. Petite et accipiētis. 20. Ī, miser.

Exercise 220.—1. Be unwilling to (do not) place your hope in leading men (princes) and kings. 2. Be unwilling to (do not) fear anyone but God, Christians. 3. Be unwilling to (do not) flee. Remain in battle line. 4. Be unwilling to (do not) flee! Withstand the attack! Place (put) Caesar himself before [your] eyes! Remember the previous victories you got (gained) under his leadership. 5. Do not flee! 6. Be unwilling to (do not) speak (reveal) everything. 7. Do not speak of this matter. 8. Do not leave the battle line. 9. Be unwilling to (do not) trust everyone. 10. Be unwilling to (do not) kill him, for he is not an enemy.

Exercise 221.—1. Nōlī mē rogāre ubi rēx sit. Nē mē rogāverīs ubi rēx sit. 2. Nōlī peccāre. Nē peccāverīs. 3. Nōlī tē dēdere. Nē tē dēdiderīs. 4. Nōlīte pīla jacere. Nē pīla jēcerītis. 5. Nōlī nōs jubēre nōs recipere. Nē nōs jusserīs nōs recipere. 6. Nōlīte cōnārī illud flūmen trānsīre. Nē cōnātī sītis illud flūmen trānsīre. 7. Nōlīte timēre (nē timuerītis) eōs quī corpus occīdere possunt. 8. Nōlī grātiae Deī resistere. Nē grātiae Deī restiterīs. 9. Tenēte. Nōlīte cēdere. Nē cesserītis. 10. Nōlī mē relinquere, Deus mī. Nē mē relīquerīs, Deus mī. (In ecclesiastical Latin, *Deus meus*.)

Box, p. 510.—True praise is owing to courage (virtue) alone.

Exercise 222.—1. Profectī sunt ad Galliam. 2. Iter fēcērunt trēs diēs. 3. Diū pugnātum est. 4. Frūmentum quaesīvit. 5. Pugnandī cupidī erant. 6. Cohortēs nūper cōnscrīptās exspectāvit. 7. Haeduī Caesarem adjūvērunt nam amīcī populī Rōmānī erant. 8. Omnia parāta erant ad proficīscendum. 9. Nuntiāvit collem idōneum esse ad castra pōnenda. 10. Prō tē, rēx, pugnābō. 11. Frūmentī causā lēgātōs ad gentēs proximās mīsit. 12. Ob hanc causam Caesar eōs in prōvinciam venīre vetuit.

Doubting Thomas, p. 511.—But Thomas, one of the twelve, who is called Didymus, was not with them when Jesus came. The other disciples therefore said to him, "We have seen the Lord." But he said to them, "Unless I shall have seen (unless I see) in His hands the mark of the nails, and shall put my finger in the place of the nails, and shall put my hand into His side, I shall not believe." And after eight days, His disciples were again within, and Thomas with them. Jesus came, the doors being closed, and stood in the middle (their midst) and said, "Peace [be] to you." Then he says to Thomas, "Bring hither your finger and see My hands, and bring hither your hand and put [it] into My side, and do not be unbelieving, but believing." Thomas answered, and said to Him, "My Lord and my God." Jesus said to him, "Because you have seen Me, Thomas, you have believed; blessed [are] those who have not seen and have believed."

Box, p. 512.—Give a hand to the wretched!

God's Words, p. 512.—God the Father said of His Son to all men: "This is My beloved Son, hear Him."

Box, p. 512.—Hail, O cross, [our] only hope.

A Saying of Christ, p. 512.—Christ said, "Not everyone who says to Me, 'Lord, Lord,' shall enter into the kingdom of heaven, but he who does the will of My Father who is in heaven will enter into the kingdom of heaven."

Box, p. 512.—Habit is overcome by habit.

A Christian Prayer, p. 513.—Hear, O Lord Jesus Christ, the prayers of Your servants, and have mercy on us: who with the Father and the Holy Spirit live and reign forever and ever. Amen.

Box, p. 513.—Lord, hasten (make haste) to help me.

A Quotation from St. Paul, p. 513.—Saint Paul said, "Bear one another's burdens, and so will you fulfill the law of Christ."

Box, p. 513.—Christ said, "[He] who is not with Me, is against Me."

Christ's Words, p. 513.—Christ said, "And do not fear those who kill the body, but cannot kill the soul; but rather fear him who can destroy both soul and body in hell."

Lesson 30

Exercise 223.—(All the italicized genitives and ablatives are genitives and ablatives of description.) 1. Caesar, a man of great courage, pacified (subjugated) Gaul. (*Magnae virtūtis,* gen.) 2. They were of greater hope (more hopeful) because they had more ships. (*Majōre spē,* abl.) 3. He made a three-foot rampart. (*Trium pedum,* gen.) 4. Oregetorix was a great influence among the crowd (people). (*Grātiā,* abl.) 5. The Romans considered themselves to be magnanimous (high-minded). (*Magnī animī,* gen.) 6. The consul was a man of the greatest influence. (*Maximae auctōritātis,* gen.) 7. We are of this spirit (attitude) toward the Romans that we wish to help them. (*Animō,* abl.) 8. Caesar praised Labienus, a man of great reliability. (*Magnae fideī,* gen.) 9. He made a ten-mile journey. (*Decem mīlium passuum,* gen.) 10. Ariovistus, the king of the Germans, was a man of large body (great size). (*Magnō corpore*, abl.) 11. It was an affair of the greatest danger. (*Summī perīculī*, gen.) 12. He is of small spirit who does not wish to do (accomplish) great things. (*Parvī animī*, gen.) 13. Centurions were often men of the highest courage. (*Maximae virtūtis*, gen.) 14. They came to a river of great depth. (*Magnā altitūdine*, abl.)

Exercise 224.—1. Caesar, vir maximae virtūtis, imperātor erat. 2. Fossam sex pedum fēcērunt. 3. Vercingetorīx vir maximae auctōritātis apud Gallōs fuit. 4. Illī erant mājōre spē quam Gallī. 5. Labiēnus vir maximae fideī fuit. 6. Rēs summī perīculī erat. 7. Homō magnō corpore erat. 8. Cōnsulēs virī maximae auctōritātis apud Rōmānōs fuērunt. 9. Iter quattuor diērum fēcērunt. 10. Erat vir magnā grātiā.

Exercise 225.—1. Eques nuntiāvit pontem in flūmine esse. 2. Impetum in castra fēcērunt. 3. Audīvit oppidum incēnsum esse. 4. Locūtus est dē rēbus gravibus. 5. Dīxit sē tertiā diē perventūrum esse. 6. Audiēns hoc (hīs audītīs), statim profectus est. 7. Hī virī fortēs prō omnibus Americānīs pugnāvērunt. 8. In omnī parte (undique) collēs montēsque erant. 9. Propter hās injūriās bellum in Rōmānōs gerēbant.

A Paralytic, p. 515.—But when Jesus had seen their faith, He says to the paralytic, "Son, your sins are dismissed (forgiven) you."

But there were there certain ones of the scribes, sitting and thinking in their hearts, "Why does this man speak so? He blasphemes. Who can send (take) away sins, except God alone?"

Which (this) being known in his own spirit (mind) that they were thinking thus within themselves, Jesus says to them, "Why do you think those things in your hearts? Which is easier, to say to the paralytic, 'Your sins are taken away (forgiven)' or to say, 'Arise, take up your pallet, and walk?' But that you may know that the Son of Man has power on earth to forgive sins"—He says to the paralytic—"I say to you, 'Arise, take up your pallet, and walk to your home.'"

And he arose at once, and the pallet taken up, he went away before all, so that all marveled and glorified God.

Box, p. 516.—The Jews said to Pilate, "If you send this [man] away, you are no friend of Caesar's; for everyone who makes himself a king speaks against Caesar."

Lesson 31

Exercise 226.—1. These ships returned to harbor because they were unable to hold the course. (*Quod . . . poterant*, indic. expressing the real reason.) 2. Since this is the case, leave the city! (*Cum . . . sint*, subj. w. *cum*.) 3. Our [men] will be confused (in confusion) because they were unable to keep ranks. (*Quod . . . poterant,* indic. expressing the real reason.) 4. Caesar praised Labienus because he had managed everything very carefully. (*Quod . . . administrāvisset,* subj. expressing the alleged reason.) 5. Caesar encouraged his men to prepare (secure) victory in that hour, because it had been come to the end of [their] labors (the end of their labor was in sight). (*Quoniam . . . perventum esset,* impersonal, subj. expressing the alleged reason.) 6. Since he was unable to restrain the enemy's flight, he decided that he should await the fleet. (*Cum . . . posset,* subj. w. *cum.*) 7. Because it is night, I shall send you away. (*Quoniam . . . est,* indic. expressing the real reason.) 8. Because we cannot persuade Caesar to give us a route through the province, we shall make a way by force and with arms. (*Quoniam . . . possumus,* indic. expressing the real reason.) 9. They are able because they seem to be able. (*Quia . . . videntur,* indic. expressing the real reason.)

Exercise 227.—1. Statim revertī nōn poterant quod ventus aliēnus erat. 2. Gallī Caesarem veritī sunt quod audācissimus et fortissimus esset. 3. Cum oppidum capere nōn possent, in fīnēs suōs sē recēpērunt. 4. Vēnērunt ut pācem peterent quoniam sciēbant sē impetūs legiōnum sustinēre nōn posse. 5. Pīlātus imperāvit ut Chrīstus ad mortem dūcerētur quia Jūdaeōs timēbat. 6. Deus Fīlium suum sōlum in mundum mīsit quoniam nōs dīligit. 7. Capere castra nōn poterant quod ea bene mūnīta erant. 8. Hominēs Caesarem laudāvērunt quia in pugnandō fortis et in agendō celer esset. 9. Putāvērunt sē occāsiōnem habēre lībertātis Galliae cōnservandae quia omnēs gentēs conjūnctae essent. 10. Conjūrāvērunt quod Caesar āfuit. Putāvērunt sē capere hīberna posse ante adventum ējus.

Box, p. 518.—If it is [characteristic] of barbarians to live for the day, our plans ought to face (have regard for) an everlasting time.

Of the Death of the Evil and the Good, p. 518.—The death of the good is blessed, the death of sinners, however, is unhappy and wretched.

Friendship, p. 518.—Friendship is given by nature as a helper of virtues (an aid to virtue).

Lesson 32

Exercise 228.—1. The death of the king was a great sorrow to the Germans. (*Germānīs,* dat. of reference; *dolōrī,* dat. of purpose.) 2. He left the cavalry behind as a garrison. (*Praesidiō,* dat. of purpose.) 3. He sent ten cohorts to help Labienus. (*Auxiliō,* dat. of purpose.) 4. One thing was of great use to our men. (*Ūsuī*, dat. of purpose; *nostrīs*, dat. of reference.) 5. He sent Labienus with the third legion to help his men fighting in the defiles. (*Suīs*, dat. of reference; *auxiliō*, dat. of purpose.) 6. Christ came into the world to help us. (*Nōbīs*, dat. of reference; *auxiliō*, dat. of purpose.) 7. That victory of ours was a great sorrow to the enemy. (*Hostibus*, dat. of reference; *dolōrī*, dat. of purpose.) 8. The victories of our soldiers were a very great glory for us. (*Nōbīs*, dat. of reference; *glōriae*, dat. of purpose.) 9. The arrival of Caesar was our salvation. (*Nōbīs*, dat. of reference; *salūtī*, dat. of purpose.) 10. He left them behind to protect the baggage. (*Impedīmentīs*, dat. of reference; *praesidiō*, dat. of purpose.) 11. The centurion said, "Because I am unable to save myself together with you, I will surely save you." (*Vōbīs*, dat. of reference; *salūtī*, dat. of purpose.)

Exercise 229.—1. Mors ējus mihi magnō dolōrī erat. 2. Duās legiōnēs praesidiō relīquērunt. 3. Hoc nostrīs magnō perīculō erat. (Serious = *magnus;* dat. of purpose can be modified only by an adjective of quantity.) 4. Quaesīvit num caedēs prīncipum Gallīs maximō dolōrī fuisset. 5. Nāvēs Caesarī magnō auxiliō erant cum ille bellum cum Venetīs gereret. 6. Equitēs peditātuī auxiliō mīsit. 7. Pugnāns fortiter mortuus est ac ita suīs salūtī fuit. 8. Haec victōria omnibus Rōmānīs glōriae fuit. 9. Dīxērunt victōriās Caesaris Gallīs magnō dolōrī esse.

The Saints, p. 520.—The souls of the saints who followed the footsteps of Christ, rejoice in heaven, and because they poured out their blood for love of Him they rejoice with Christ without end.

Box, p. 520.—Souls are conquered not by arms but by love.

Words of Christ, p. 520.—Christ said to His [disciples], "Ask, and it shall be given to you, seek and you shall find, knock and it shall be opened unto you. For everyone who seeks (asks), receives, and he who seeks, finds, and to one knocking, it will be opened."

The Martyrs, p. 520.—They have indeed died for Christ, and they will live forever.

Continuous Passages for Translation

A. Robert Clive in India, 1.—Multōs annōs Gallī et Anglī Indiā potīrī contenderant. Rēgēs et prīncipēs Indiae dītissimī erant, et Anglī Gallīque ad Indiam propter pecūniam (pecūniae causā) ierant. Bellum tandem ā duōbus virīs audācissimīs et fortissimīs cōnfectum est. Alterī, Gallō, Dupleix nōmen erat; alterī, ducī Anglōrum, Robertus Clive nōmen erat. Dupleix prior ad Indiam vēnit, et repperit Anglōs apud Indōs plūrimum valēre. Cum dēmōnstrāvisset sē audācissimum esse, ab

Gallīs Pondicheri praefectus est. Tredecim annōs sine intervallō summam imperiī in prōvinciā Gallicā tenēbat.

2.—Dupleix autem magnam scientiam reī mīlitāris nōn habuit, scīvit tamen paucōs mīlitēs Europaeōs maximum Indōrum numerum vincere posse. Cognōvit etiam Indōs loca mūnīta capere nōn posse. Itaque Pondicheri cōpiās coēgit et oppidum mūnīvit. Cum annō millēsimō septingentēsimō quadrāgēsimō quartō Anglī cum Gallīs bellum gerere coepērunt, Dupleix impetum Pondicheri exspectāvit.

3.—Classis autem Gallica nāvigāvit ut eī auxiliō esset; ā quā adjūtus Dupleix Madras cēpit quod oppidum maximum Anglōrum erat. Dupleix autem pollicitus erat sē Madras rēgulō ējus regiōnis datūrum esse—rēgulī Indōrum "Nawabs" appellābantur—ut amīcitiam ējus cōnsequerētur; nunc autem, hāc victōriā sublātus, eī eam nōn trādidit. Itaque (quā dē causā) in Nawab exercitum suum dūxit et, hōc victō, Madras prōvinciae Gallicae jūnxit. Novus dux autem Anglicus cōpiās ējus superātūrus erat.

4.—Robertus Clive annō millēsimō septingentēsimō quadrāgēsimō tertiō in Indiam missus est. Optimus imperātor erat et vir dīligentissimus fortissimusque. Repperit Dupleix imperium Gallōrum cōnfirmāvisse et exercitūs Anglicōs saepe superāvisse. Cōnstituit auctōritātem Gallōrum minuere. Itinere celeriter ex Madras factō, oppidum quod Arcot appellābātur oppugnāvit. Hoc oppidum erat in fīnibus Nawab quī Gallōrum amīcus erat. Hōc captō, ille cum paucīs virīs impetūs exercitūs in quō cōpiae Gallicae erant diū sustinuit.

5.—Indī hāc victōriā adeō perterritī sunt ut amīcitiam Clive petīverint et auctōritās Anglōrum in hāc parte Indiae maxima facta est.

Interim Surja Dowlah, Nawab Bengal, Calcuttam oppugnāvit et cēpit quod ea mūnīta erat. Centum quadrāgintā sex Anglī captī sunt. Hōs captīvōs maximā crūdelitāte interfēcit. Jactī sunt in carcerem tam angustum ut ūnā nocte maxima pars perierit. Hic carcer "the Black Hole of Calcutta" appellātur.

6.—Quā rē omnibus Anglīs commōtīs, Clive Calcuttam contendit et eum oppidum cēpit. Brevī autem quīnquāgintā mīlia Indōrum prope eum cōnsēderant; ipse novem centum mīlitēs Anglicōs et duo mīlia Indōrum habuit. Lēgātī suī, conciliō convocātō, petīvērunt ut fugeret. Dē hāc rē ūnam hōram dēlīberāvit; jussit cōpiās prōgredī. Posterō diē ad Plassy ācriter pugnātum est, et victōriā ējus diēī Anglī tōtum Bengal vīcērunt. Ita Clive Gallōs superāvit et Indiam pācāvit.

B. The Boer War, 1.—Caesar omnem Galliam sub imperium populī Rōmānī redēgit; Rhodes Africam Merīdiōnālem prō populō

Anglicō vīcit. Rhodes exīstimāvit populum Anglicum maximam gentem tōtīus mundī esse et Africae Merīdiōnālis multārumque gentium aliārum potītūrum esse. Boers autem, quī Transvaal incolēbant, jam diū resistēbant. Cum in Transvaal esset cōpia aurī, multī Anglī pecūniae causā ibi īerant. Erant brevī in eīs fīnibus plūrēs Anglī quam Boers. Anglī petīvērunt ut ipsī cīvēs fierent. Kruger, quī cīvitātī in Transvaal praeerat, sē id factūrum esse negāvit. "Haec est patria mea," inquit, "hae lēgēs meae sunt. Quī lēgibus meīs oboedīre nōlunt ā patriā meā exeant."

2.—Rhodes Jameson Anglō persuāsit ut quīnque centum virōs cōgeret et ad fīnēs Transvaal prōgrederētur. Crēdēns Anglōs quī in fīnibus Boers sē adjūtūrōs esse, in fīnēs Transvaal statim prōgressus est. Anglī autem eum nōn adjūvērunt et, ab hostibus pressus, sē dēdere coāctus est. Boers autem hōc proeliō commōtī, Anglōs sibi maximam injūriam intulisse dīxērunt; Rhodes etiam apud Anglōs minus valēbat.

3.—Bellum autem ortum est. Boers fortēs et firmī erant. Ducēs eōrum optimā bellī ratiōne ūsī sunt. Cōnstituērunt Anglīs usque ad mortem resistere. Multōs annōs bellum gessērunt et impetūs Anglōrum sustinuērunt, nam Anglī nātūram locī nōn sciēbant neque in fīnibus suīs prō lībertāte suā pugnābant.

4.—Anglī in proeliīs saepe superātī sunt. De la Rey, īnsidiīs collocātīs, Kerwich ducem Anglicum Moedwell Farm superāvit. Hic dux omnēs ad ūnum cōpiās Methuen lēgātī interfēcit et Methuen ipsum cēpit. Kitchener tandem, imperātor Anglōrum, vir maximae virtūtis, uxōribus līberīsque capiendīs et omnī frūmentō oppidīsque incendendīs Boers pācāvit. Mīlitēs Boers inter sē hortātī sunt ut diūtius pugnārent. "Vincendum," inquiunt, "aut moriendum est." Nōn poterant autem impetum Anglōrum diūtius sustinēre et tandem lēgātōs ad pācem petendam mīsērunt. Ita Boers cīvēs Anglicī vī factī sunt.

Classified Review Exercises

1. **Direct Questions, A.**—1. Who is coming? 2. Is not Christ God? 3. Caesar was not killed by the Gauls, was he? 4. Have you visited Italy? 5. Why did Caesar drive back the Helvetians from the province? 6. Where is Rome? 7. Of what was Caesar desirous? 8. By what route did the Helvetians try to go out from their territory? 9. Whom did he place in command of the fleet? 10. Whither will you march?

B.—1. Quibuscum vēnistī? 2. Quis fuit Julius Caesar? 3. Num Caesar ā Gallīs victus est? 4. Cūr Caesarem occīdērunt? 5. Nōnne Caesar

Galliam pācāvit? 6. Num hoc crēdis? 7. Nōnne Caesar multīs hominibus praefuit? 8. Adiistīne montēs?

C.—1. Praefuitne Caesar magnō exercituī? 2. Quibuscum in Italiam iter fēcistī? 3. Nōnne Gallī ā Caesare victī sunt? 4. Cūr Helvētiī in prōvinciam trānsīre cōnātī sunt? 5. Quem legiōnibus senātus praefēcit? 6. Nōnne Caesar multōs Galliae prīncipēs occīdit?

2. **Commands, Wishes, etc., A.**—1. God help me. 2. May our men not be conquered! 3. Let us fight bravely. 4. May you be with me. 5. Let him not go out. 6. Let them make an attack. 7. Go! Depart! 8. Bring help! 9. Fear not. 10. Do not harm others. 11. Let us not flee. 12. Don't believe everything!

B.—1. Deus tē adjuvet. 2. Ex urbe nostrā exeant. 3. Nē eat. 4. Nōlīte oppidum dēdere. 5. Mitte auxilium. 6. Nōlīte ex aciē vōs recipere. 7. Adjuvā amīcōs tuōs. 8. In rēgibus spem nē posueris. 9. Utinam multōs annōs vīvās! 10. Prōgrediāmur. 11. Utinam nullīs noceāmus. 12. Nē capiāminī.

C.—1. Adjuvēmus miserōs. 2. Nōlīte ex aciē vōs recipere. 3. Nōlīte aliīs nocēre. 4. Nē vincantur nostrī. 5. Nōlī timēre.

3. **Clauses of Purpose, Result, Time, etc., A.**—1. He caused large forces to assemble in that place. (*Convenīrent,* imp. subj. in noun clause in secondary sequence, action at same time as main verb.) 2. It happened that the enemy fled. (*Fugerent,* imp. subj. in noun clause in secondary sequence, action at same time as main verb.) 3. He persuaded them to give him hostages. (*Darent,* imp. subj. in noun clause in secondary sequence, action at same time as main verb.) 4. He ordered the cavalry not to injure the hostages. (*Nocērent,* imp. subj. in noun clause in secondary sequence, action at same time as main verb.) 5. Such a great wind arose that he held the ships in the harbor. (*Continuerit,* perf. subj. in result clause; perf. in secondary sequence to emphasize actual occurrence.) 6. The envoys came to ask for peace. (*Peterent,* imp. subj. in purpose clause in secondary sequence; *pācis petendae causā,* gerundive with *causā,* expressing purpose; *ad pācem petendam,* gerundive with *ad,* expressing purpose.) 7. He fortified the camp with a ditch and a rampart in order to withstand more easily and for a longer time the attacks of the enemy. (*Sustinēret,* imp. subj. in purpose clause in secondary sequence, introduced by *quō* before a comparative.) 8. He left the third legion there lest the enemy cross the river. (*Transīrent,* imp. subj. in negative purpose clause in secondary sequence.) 9. Let us pray God to help us. (*Adjuvet,* pres. subj. in noun clause in primary sequence.) 10. Since these things are so (since this is the case), I shall not give you

a route through the province. (*Sint*, pres. subj. in a *cum*-since clause in primary sequence.) 11. When he had caught sight of the enemy's line, Caesar led the legions to the nearest hill and pitched camp there. (*Cōnspexisset*, plu. subj. in *cum*-temporal clause in past time describing the circumstances, action before time of main verb.) 12. The lieutenant, when he was fighting very bravely, was seen by Caesar. (*Pugnāret*, imp. subj. in *cum*-temporal clause in past time describing the circumstances, action at same time as main verb.) 13. We attacked them so bravely that they did not withstand the attack. (*Sustinuerint*, perf. subj. in result clause; perf. in secondary sequence to emphasize actual occurrence.) 14. It often happens that men inflict injuries on others. (*Īnferant*, pres. subj. in noun clause, action at same time as main verb.) 15. As soon as he arrived in the province he ordered new legions to be enrolled. (*Pervēnit*, perf. indic. in temporal clause describing single past action at same time as main verb.) 16. After he conquered them, Caesar led the army back into the province. (*Vīcit*, perf. indic. in temporal clause describing single past action at same time as main verb.) 17. Because they were unable to withstand longer the force of the legions, they sent envoys concerning peace. (*Potuērunt*, perf. indic. in causal clause giving the real reason, action at same time as main verb.) 18. Because it was night, they remained in camp. (*Erat*, imp. indic. in causal clause giving the real reason, action at same time as main verb.) 19. He praised the lieutenant because he had fought very bravely. (*Pugnāvisset*, plu. subj. in causal clause giving the alleged reason, action before time of main verb.) 20. He warned them not to cross the river. (*Trānsīrent*, imp. subj. in noun clause, action at same time as main verb.) 21. I ask you to pray for me. (*Ōrēs*, pres. subj. in noun clause, action at same time as main verb.)

B.—1. Aliīs persuāsit ut Caesarem occīderent. 2. Factum est ut nēmō eum vidēret. 3. Cōnābor omnibus hominibus persuādēre ut pācem servent. 4. Imperāvit nē custōdēs rēgī captō nocērent. 5. Adeō ācriter pugnāvērunt ut hostēs brevī tempore sē recēperint. 6. Caesar Galliam vīcit ut Italiae etiam praeesset. 7. Pontem fēcit quō celerius flūmen trānsīret. 8. Ōrāvī eum nē nōs interficeret. 9. Cum mihi nōn crēdās, nihil tibi dīcam. 10. Cum Caesar in Galliā esset, ab eīs quī amīcī populī Rōmānī nōn erant timēbātur. 11. Ut prīmum rēgem vīdit, gladiō eum interficere cōnātus est. 12. Omnī Galliā pacātā, Caesar cōpiās in Italiam dūxit et brevī tempore Rōmae ipsīus potītus est. 13. Quod Caesarem timēbant, Gallī ējus adventū commōtī sunt. 14. Senātus Caesarī grātiās ēgērunt quod metum Gallōrum ā cīvitāte sustulisset.

15. Caesar eōs monuit nē per prōvinciam iter facere cōnārentur. 16. Cum Caesar eōs omnēs quī sibi resistēbant vīcisset, ab amīcīs suīs interfectus est.

C.—1. Effēcit ut pontem fieret. 2. Imperāvit nē obsidibus nocērētur. 3. Persuāsit eīs ut sēcum īrent. 4. Cum mihi nōn crēdās, tēcum nōn manēbō. 5. Adeō ācriter pugnātum est ut plūrimī occīderentur. 6. Ut prīmum mē vīdit, pugnāre coepit. 7. Caesarī grātiās ēgērunt quod Helvētiōs ā prōvinciā prohibuisset. 8. Tantus ventus ortus est ut portum relinquere nōn potuerit. 9. Deum ōrāmus ut nōs adjuvet.

4. Relative Clauses, A.—1. He stationed halfway up the hill the legion which he had recently enrolled. 2. He who fights without hope is conquered. 3. We are soldiers, and what is more, Romans. 4. Since this is the case, depart! 5. He sent an envoy to treat with them about the welfare of their people. 6. No one wants to be wretched. 7. Who is there that fears you? 8. He sent the leading men to ask for peace.

B.—1. Vir quem Caesar laudāvit erat fortis mīles. 2. Nēmō tam miser est quī nūllam spem habeat. 3. Equitēs mīsit quī Helvētiōs fugientēs occīderent. 4. Nēmō crēdit eī quī Deō nōn crēdit. 5. Ego nōn sum quī sine proeliō oppidum dēdam. 6. Quis est quī prō lībertāte nōn pugnātūrus sit? 7. Nēmō est quī tibi crēdat.

C.—1. Eī quī Japōnēs ab Īnsulā Wakense prohibuērunt fortēs erant. 2. Quis est quī tē vereātur? 3. Lēgātum mīsit quī pācem peteret. 4. Equitēs ēmīsit quī Helvētiōs fugientēs occīderent.

5. Indirect Questions, A.—1. I ask whether you believe that God exists. (*Crēdās*, pres. subj. in primary sequence, action at same time as main verb.) 2. He asked whether Christ was a king. (*Esset*, imp. subj. in secondary sequence, action at same time as main verb.) 3. I ask whether Columbus was the first to reach America. (*Pervēnerit*, perf. subj. in primary sequence, action before time of main verb.) 4. He asked whether Christ had died. (*Mortuus esset*, plu. subj. in secondary sequence, action before time of main verb.) 5. He asked him if he had seen the enemy. (*Vīdissetne*, plu. subj. in secondary sequence, action before time of main verb; the enclitic *ne* introduces the indirect question.) 6. He knew who Christ was. (*Esset*, imp. subj. in secondary sequence, action at same time as main verb.) 7. He asked what they were eager for. (*Cūjus*, gen. modifying *reī*, after *cupidī*; *essent*, imp. subj. in secondary sequence, action at same time as main verb.) 8. We ask whom he killed. (*Occīderit*, perf. subj. in primary sequence, action before time of main verb.) 9. He knew where the guards were. (*Essent*, imp. subj. in secondary sequence, action at same time as main verb.)

10. Do you know why the Jews delivered Christ to Pilate? (*Trādiderint,* perf. subj. in primary sequence, action before time of main verb.)

B.—1. Rogāvimus num Deum esse crēderet. 2. Quaesīvērunt cūr Gallī Caesarī restitissent. 3. Scīsne ubi Rōma sit? 4. Caesar rogāvit num arma servōsque trādidissent. 5. Rogāmus quem classī Caesar praefēcerit. 6. Rogāvērunt quō cōnsiliō ūsus esset. 7. Scīmus quibuscum legiōnibus prōvinciam dēfenderit. 8. Scīsne cuī Caesar arma capta dederit? 9. Lēgātus rogāvit num Germānī Rhēnum trānsīrent. 10. Caesar scīvit quī Helvētiīs ut cōnārentur flūmen trānsīre persuāsisset.

C.—1. Scīsne num Caesar Deum esse crēdiderit? 2. Scīsne ubi Rōma sit? 3. Rogāvit num Germānī Rhēnum trānsīrent. 4. Scīsne cūr Rōmānī Chrīstum ad mortem dūxerint? 5. Scīmus quis prīmus ad Americam pervēnerit.

6. The Genitive, A.—1. He led the army into the territory of the enemy. (*Hostium,* possessive.) 2. He begged for more grain. (*Frūmentī,* gen. w. *plūs.*) 3. Caesar was a man of the greatest courage. (*Virtūtis,* descriptive.) 4. He made a day's journey. (*Ūnīus diēī,* descriptive.) 5. Was Caesar very eager for fame? (*Glōriae,* gen. w. *cupidissimus.*) 6. The Helvetians were desirous of others' fields. (*Agrōrum,* gen. w. *cupidī.*) 7. The town was full of all things. (*Rērum,* gen. w. *plēnum.*) 8. He had enough grain. (*Frūmentī,* gen. w. *satis.*)

B.—1. Imperiī cupidī erant. 2. Simillimus patris est. 3. Habēmusne satis frūmentī? 4. Caesar, vir magnae virtūtis, Galliam pācāvit. 5. Castrōrum hostium potītus est. 6. Inter urbem et collem mūrus decem pedum erat. 7. Nox perīculōrum plēna est. 8. Labiēnus vir maximae fideī erat.

C.—1. Erat vir magnī corporis. 2. Habēmusne satis frūmentī? 3. Erat vir maximae fideī. 4. Simillimus patris est. 5. Multās nāvēs Venetōrum cēpērunt.

7. The Dative, A.—1. The Gauls gave a large supply of grain to the Romans. (*Rōmānīs,* dat. of indir. obj.) 2. The Helvetians were nearest to the Germans. (*Germānīs,* dat. w. *proximī.*) 3. We must all praise and love God. (*Omnibus,* dat. of agent w. gerundive.) 4. That hill was suitable for pitching camp. (*Castrīs,* dat. w. *idōneus.*) 5. The wind often injured the ships. (*Nāvibus,* dat. w. *nocēbat.*) 6. Everyone strives after freedom. (*Lībertātī,* dat. w. *student.*) 7. He levied a great number of cavalry on the Gauls. (*Gallīs,* dat. w. *imperāvit.*) 8. He persuaded them to go out from their territory with all their forces. (*Eīs,* dat. w. *persuāsit.*) 9. He commanded him to explore everything. (*Eī,* dat. w. *mandāvit.*) 10. Caesar often put a lieutenant in command of the legions. (*Legiōnibus*, dat. of thing of which w. *praefēcit.*) 11. Who is in command of this legion? (*Legiōnī*, dat. w. *praeest.*) 12. He sent ten cohorts to help his men [who were] in difficulty. (*Suīs*, dat. of reference; *auxiliō*, dat. of purpose.) 13. I was persuaded to fight for freedom. (*Mihi*, dat. w. *persuāsum est;* impersonal use of an intransitive verb in the passive.) 14. He was persuaded by Caesar to remain with him. (*Eī*, dat. w. *persuāsum est.*) 15. I wish to be like Christ. (*Christō*, dat. w. *similis.*) 16. Caesar took [their] freedom from the Gauls. (*Gallīs*, dat. of separation.) 17. God save me from this danger! 18. Washington's death was a great sorrow to the Americans. (*Americānīs*, dat. of reference; *dolōrī*, dat. of purpose.)

B.—1. Arma Rōmānīs trādidērunt. 2. Helvētiī prōvinciae proximī erant. 3. Ad collem idōneum castrīs suōs dūxit. 4. Magnum obsidum numerum gentibus proximīs imperāvit. 5. Brūtō persuāsērunt ut contrā Caesarem conjūrāret. 6. Lēgātō imperāvit ut cōpiās cogeret quae prōvinciam dēfenderent. 7. Caesar legiōnibus quae in prōvinciā erant praefectus est. 8. Lēgātō tertiam legiōnem auxiliō mīsit. 9. Germānīs ācerrimē ab illīs resistēbant. 10. Mihi ab amīcīs tuīs persuāsum est ut tē adjuvārem. 11. Eratne Marīae similis? 12. Mors Ariovistī Germānīs magnō fuit dolōrī. 13. Quis exercituī praefuit? 14. Nostrīs ab Japōnibus diū resistēbātur. 15. Dīxit mihi quantae cōpiae hostium essent. 16. Lībertās nostra nōbīs semper dēfendenda est.

C.—1. Contendērunt adjuvāre tertiam legiōnem quae ā magnīs cōpiīs hostium equitātūs premēbantur. 2. Pontī ā ventō et vī flūminis graviter nocēbātur. 3. Ab hostibus ācriter resistēbātur. 4. Equitēs Gallīs imperāvit. 5. Magnum exercitum coēgērunt quī prōvinciam dēfenderet. 6. Gallī contrā Caesarem conjūrābant. 7. Oppidō decem legiōnēs praesidiō relīquit. 8. Helvētiī prōvinciae nostrae proximī erant. 9. Equitēs tertiae legiōnī auxiliō vēnērunt.

8. The Accusative, A.—1. Friends killed Caesar (Caesar's friends killed him). (*Caesarem*, dir. obj.) 2. The soldiers called Caesar commander. (*Caesarem*, dir. obj.; *imperātōrem*, pred. acc.) 3. Christ called us friends. (*Nōs*, dir. obj.; *amīcōs*, pred. acc.) 4. Christ is called king by us. (*Rēx*, pred. nom.) 5. The leader led large forces across the river. (*Flūmen*, second acc. w. *trādūxit.*) 6. The lieutenant led all the cavalry across the river. (*Equitēs*, dir. obj.) 7. The cavalry were led across the river by the lieutenant. (*Flūmen*, acc. of the place w. *trāductī sunt.*) 8. He marched two miles. (*Mīlia*, acc. of extent of space.) 9. For three hours they resisted very bravely. (*Hōrās*, acc. of extent of time.) 10. The ditch was two feet wide. (*Pedēs*, acc. of extent of space.)

11. The enemy's camp was a mile away. (*Mīlle passūs*, acc. of extent of space.)

B.—1. Gallī Rōmam ipsam incendērunt. 2. Oportet omnēs Chrīstiānōs Chrīstum rēgem appellāre. 3. Itinere quattuor mīlia passuum factō, castra in colle idōneō posuērunt. 4. Hoc oppidum quīnque mīlia passuum aberat. 5. Decem passūs ā flūmine castra posuērunt. 6. Flūmen centum pedēs latum erat. 7. Caesar equitēs flūmen altissimum trādūxit. 8. Washingtonium patrem patriae suae appellāmus. 9. Trēs hōrās prōgressī, hostēs īnstrūctōs in colle proximō cōnspexērunt. 10. Trēs diēs impetūs sustinuērunt. 11. Quīnque hōrās ācriter et fortiter pugnātum est. 12. Tertia legiō flūmen trāducta est.

C.—1. Ille suīs imperātor appellābātur. 2. Gallī Rōmam incendērunt. 3. Magnās cōpiās flūmen celeriter trādūxit. 4. Mīlle passūs ab hostibus castra posuērunt. 5. Duo mīlia passuum iter fēcērunt. 6. Tria mīlia passuum prōgressī, agmen hostium ex magnā silvā ēgrediēns cōnspexērunt.

9. **The Ablative, A.—** 1. You were absent on that very day. (*Diē*, abl. of time when.) 2. Within a few days we will give (up) the hostages. (*Diēbus*, abl. of time within which.) 3. Ariovistus was of large body (size). (*Corpore*, abl. of description.) 4. All Gaul was pacified (subjugated) by Caesar. (*Ā Caesare*, abl. of agent.) 5. Our state is safe from the enemy. (*Ab hostibus*, abl. after *tūta*.) 6. Rome is a long distance from our land. (*Ā nostrīs fīnibus*, abl. w. *abest*.) 7. The cavalry went forward a rather long way from the camp. (*Ā castrīs*, abl. w. *ab*.) 8. The Romans always fortified [their] camps by means of a ditch and a rampart. (*Fossā vallō*, abl. of means.) 9. Long roads were built by the Romans. (*Ā Rōmānīs*, abl. of agent.) 10. There is nothing better than truth. (*Vēritāte*, abl. of comparison.) 11. The legions fought with great courage. (*Magnā cum virtūte*, abl. of manner.) 12. The Belgians surpassed the rest of the Gauls in courage. (*Virtūte*, abl. of respect.) 13. The camp was full of men. (*Hominibus*, abl. w. *plēna*.) 14. Disturbed by the arrival of Caesar, the Gauls often sent envoys to beg for peace. (*Adventū*, abl. of means or cause.) 15. Having employed this plan, Caesar withdrew (saved himself) from great danger. (*Cōnsiliō*, abl. w. *ūsus; ē magnō perīculō*, abl. of separation or w. *ē*.) 16. They reached camp at the third hour. (*Hōrā*, abl. of time when.) 17. The Gauls resisted the Romans with great courage [and] for a long time. (*Magnā virtūte*, abl. of manner.) 18. By nature all men are eager for freedom. (*Nātūrā*, abl. of cause.) 19. The Gauls tried to prohibit (keep) the Romans from the road. (*Itinere*, abl. of separation.) 20. Friendship, than which nothing better is given to us by nature, cannot exist except

between the good (good men). (*Quā*, abl. of comparison; *ā nātūrā*, abl. of agent; "nature" takes a preposition because it is personified here.) 21. We must resist the enemy. (*Ā nōbīs*, abl. of agent.) 22. There the lieutenant, fighting most bravely, was killed by a dart. (*Tēlō*, abl. of means.) 23. Elated by this victory, the Gauls hoped they would drive the Romans out of Gaul forever. (*Victōriā*, abl. of means or cause.) 24. They went out from their land with all their forces. (*Cum omnibus cōpiīs*, abl. of accompaniment.) 25. Caesar followed them with all [his] forces. (*Omnibus cōpiīs*, abl. of accompaniment without *cum* in a military expression.)

B.—1. Caesarem gladiīs interfēcērunt. 2. Brevī tempore amīcōs nostrōs vidēbimus. 3. Sumusne ab omnibus hostibus tūtī? 4. Gallī ā nōbīs longē absunt. 5. Metus ex cīvitāte nostrā ā Washingtōniō, vir maximae virtūtis, ēreptus est. 6. Via per prōvinciam ā Rōmānīs mūnīta est. 7. Hīberna fossā quīnque pedēs lāta mūnīvērunt. 8. Quis Caesare fortior ac audācior erat? 9. Tertiō diē certior factus est hostēs castra ad silvās posuisse. 10. Maximā cum virtūte nōbīs restitērunt. 11. Hominēs nātūrā glōriae student. 12. Hominēs bonī līberī ā metū sunt. 13. Victōriīs quās Caesar cōnsecūtus erat commōtī sunt. 14. Superantne nostrī aliōs virtūte et fidē? 15. Quō cōnsiliō ūteris? 16. Vī prōvinciā eōs prohibuit. 17. Hostibus ā nōbīs omnī ratiōne nocendum est. 18. Gallī cum omnibus cōpiīs in Italiam vēnērunt ut agrōs novōs occupārent. 19. Pīlīs multōs Gallōs venientēs occīdērunt. 20. Secundō diē nuntius ad castra Caesaris pervēnit. 21. Suntne montēs nostrī altiōrēs Alpibus?

C.—1. Ā Rōmānīs viae optimae mūnītae sunt. 2. Collis mūrō mūnītus est. 3. Cum lēgātīs rex Germānōrum etiam vēnit. 4. Ab omnī impetū tūtī sumus. 5. Ā virō pessimō interfectus est. 6. Magnus numerus Gallōrum in Italiam vēnit ut agrōs eōrum quī ibi incolēbant occupārent.

10. Pronouns, A.—1. We have conquered these (the latter). We shall make an attack on those (the former). (*Hōs, illōs*, used in contrast.) 2. He who fights most bravely is praised. (*Is*, used as antecedent of the relative.) 3. Let us storm this city. (*Hanc*, adj.) 4. Rome is a great and noble city. Have you seen it? (*Eam*, pron.) 5. Orgetorix killed himself. (*Sē*, direct reflexive.) 6. Caesar praised his [men]. (*Suōs*, reflexive possessive pron.) 7. The envoy said he would set out on the third day. (*Sē*, indirect reflexive, sub. of *profectūrum esse*.) 8. The enemy fled lest the cavalry harm them. (*Sibi*, indirect reflexive, dat. w. *nocērent*.) 9. He ordered the cavalry to go with him. (*Sē*, indirect reflexive, abl. of accompaniment.) 10. He praised the envoy because he had sent cavalry to help him. (*Sibi*, indirect reflexive, dat. of reference.)

11. They praised themselves. (*Ipsī*, intensive pron. strengthening obj. *sē* but in nom.; *sē*, direct reflexive.) 12. He sent the cavalry into the forest; he himself hastened across the river. (*Ipse*, intensive pron.) 13. On that very day the message reached Caesar. (*Ipsō*, with the demonstrative *eō*, to be translated "very.") 14. Virtue is praised for itself. (*Ipsa*, intensive pron. strengthening obj. *sē* but in nom.) 15. Those who commit sin harm themselves. (*Ipsī*, intensive pron. strengthening *sibi* but in nom.; *sibi*, direct reflexive, dat. w. *nocent.*) 16. One praised Caesar; another praised Pompey. (*Alius . . . alius*, of more than two.) 17. Some think one thing, others another. (*Aliī alia*, idiomatic expression, Gr. 825.) 18. One group fought against the Gauls; the other against the Romans. (*Alterī . . . alterī*, of two groups.) 19. Of these two brothers one is a sailor, the other a soldier. (*Alter . . . alter*, of two only.) 20. He was wounded in one (the other) foot. (*Alterō*, of two only.) 21. We ought to help others. (*Aliōs*, pron., direct obj.) 22. Brothers ought to love one another. (*Sē*, direct reflexive, acc. w. *inter.*) 23. The Gauls gave one another (exchanged) hostages. (*Sē*, direct reflexive, acc. w. *inter.*) 24. These peoples differ among themselves. (*Sē*, direct reflexive, acc. w. *inter.*) 25. The cavalry recovered from fear. (*Sē*, direct reflexive, obj. of *recēpērunt.*) 26. The enemy withdrew into the mountains. (*Sē*, direct reflexive, obj. of *recēpērunt.*) 27. The enemy surrendered themselves and all their possessions to Caesar. (*Sē*, direct reflexive, obj. of *dēdidērunt; sua*, direct reflexive possessive pron., obj. of *dēdidērunt.*)

B.—1. Petrus et Jūdas discipulī Chrīstī erant; alter autem negāvit sē Chrīstum scīre, alter eum prōdidit. 2. Tertia legiō, in angustiās coācta, pressa est. Itaque Caesar duās cohortēs mīsit quae eam adjuvārent. 3. Negāvit eōs arma dedisse. 4. Dīxērunt sē contrā Rōmānōs bellum gestūrōs esse. 5. Marīa sē nōn laudāvit. 6. Rōma ipsa ā Gallīs incēnsa est. 7. Mātrēs nostrās laudāmus. 8. Ipse in urbe mānsit. 9. In hāc urbe ipsā Caesar ā Rōmānīs interfectus est. 10. Eō diē ipsō ad fīnēs hostium pervēnērunt. 11. Imperāvit equitibus ut statim sē sequerentur. 12. Ōrābant et prō sē et prō amīcīs suīs. 13. Hominēs malī sibi nocent. 14. Alius alium imperātōrem laudat. 15. Homō bonus sē nōn laudat, sed aliōs. 16. Caesar audīvit Gallōs inter sē obsidēs dare. 17. Rōmānīs sē dēdidērunt. 18. In castra sē recēpit. 19. Habuit magnum equitum numerum quī sē dēfenderant.

C.—1. Grātiās eīs ēgit quod sibi praesidiō essent. 2. Dīxit sē brevī tempore flūmen perventūrum esse. 3. Orgetorīx sē occīdit. 4. Hominēs malī sibi nocent. 5. Sua omnia dēdidērunt.

11. **Adjectives, A.**—1. God helps the brave. (*Fortēs*, used as noun.) 2. Caesar praised his men. (*Suōs*, reflexive possessive adj. used as noun.) 3. Our men were braver than the enemy. (*Nostrī*, possessive adj. used as noun.) 4. He spoke the truth. (*Vērum*, adj. used as noun.) 5. The soldiers arrived in camp safely. (*Tūtī*, adj. expressing condition of body or soul, used in adverbial sense.) 6. He collected the baggage at the top of the hill and left the legions recently enrolled to protect it. (*Summō*, adj. meaning part of the object.) 7. Columbus was the first to reach America. (*Prīmus*, equivalent to a relative clause, Gr. 850.) 8. There are many large cities in America. (*Et*, joining *multus* w. another adj.) 9. This mountain is higher than that. (*Altior*, comparative adj.) 10. The river is somewhat wide. (*Lātius*, comparative adj.) 11. Mary is the holiest of all the saints. (*Ūna omnium sānctōrum sānctissima*, *ūna* and *omnium* used to express the absolute superlative.) 12. Caesar was the bravest and most daring of all the Romans. (*Omnium Rōmānōrum fortissimus*, absolute superlative.) 13. They were resisting them with the greatest courage. (*Maximā*, superlative of *magnus*.)

B.—1. Nihil fortibus difficile est. 2. Quis prīmus in castra vēnit? 3. Erant duae legiōnēs in summō colle. 4. Fortissimus erat. 5. Tempus brevius erat. 6. Flūmen lātius erat. 7. Ille fortissimus omnium mīlitum erat. 8. Labiēnus audācior erat quam ceterī lēgātī. 9. Prōvincia in Galliā Ulteriōre erat. 10. Ad nōs tūtī reversī sunt. 11. Caesar audācior erat quam Pompējus.

C.—1. Eratne Caesar audācissimus? 2. Quis prīmus ad Americam pervēnit? 3. Reversī sunt tūtī. 4. Fortēs nōn semper vincunt.

12. **The Gerund and Gerundive, A.**—1. By acting bravely we overcome unfavorable things (adversity). (*Agendō*, gerund, abl. of means.) 2. He went with me for the sake of speaking. (*Loquendī*, gerund, gen. w. *causā*.) 3. They were sent to explore. (*Explōrandum*, gerund, acc. w. *ad*, expressing purpose.) 4. He gave (devoted) himself to praying. (*Ōrandō*, gerund, dat. of indirect obj.) 5. Our men were very eager to begin battle. (*Committendī*, gerundive, gen. w. *cupidissimī*, agreeing w. *proeliī*.) 6. This place is suitable for pitching camp. (*Pōnendīs*, gerundive, dat. w. *idōneus*, agreeing w. *castrīs*.) 7. Virtue is useful for preparing (is conducive to) friendships. (*Comparandās*, gerundive, acc. w. *ad* after *ūtilissima*, agreeing w. *amīcitiās*.) 8. He led the army across by building a bridge. (*Faciendō*, gerundive, abl. of means, agreeing w. *ponte*.) 9. They came to beg for peace. (*Petendae*, gerundive, gen. w. *causā*, agreeing w. *pācis*.) 10. They came to beg for peace. (*Petendam*, gerundive, acc. w. *ad*, agreeing w. *pācem*.) 11. He

sent the cavalry to pursue the enemy. (*Sequendōs*, gerundive, acc. w. *ad*, agreeing w. *hostēs*.) 12. They fled from the town by another gate for the sake of their own safety. (*Cōnservandī*, gerundive, gen. w. *causā*, agreeing w. *suī*.) 13. Others must be helped. (*Adjuvandī*, gerundive as pred. adj. to express necessity, agreeing w. *aliī*.) 14. Christ said that all men should be loved by us. (*Dīligendōs*, gerundive as pred. adj. to express necessity, agreeing w. *hominēs*.) 15. The lieutenant asked whether the fleet should be awaited. (*Exspectanda*, gerundive as pred. adj. to express necessity, agreeing w. *classis*.) 16. We must either conquer or die. (*Vincendum* and *moriendum*, gerundive of transitive verbs used impersonally w. *est* to express necessity.) 17. A new plan had to be employed. (*Ūtendum*, gerundive of ablative verb used impersonally w. *fuit* to express necessity.) 18. He said it was necessary to resist even to the death. (*Resistendum*, gerundive of intransitive verb used impersonally w. *esse* to express necessity.) 19. We must make use of God's grace. (*Ūtendum*, gerundive of ablative verb used impersonally w. *est* to express necessity.) 20. They had to resist the enemy. (*Resistendum*, gerundive of intransitive verb used impersonally w. *erat* to express necessity.) 21. He asked whether they had had to injure (damage) the ships. (*Nāvibus*, dat. w. *nocendum; ā sē*, abl. of agent; *nocendum*, gerundive of dative verb used impersonally w. *esset* to express necessity in a subordinate clause.) 22. He undertook to wage war. (*Gerendum*, gerundive as pred. adj. w. *suscēpit*, agreeing with *bellum*.) 23. The city was handed over to the soldiers to be burned. (*Incendenda*, gerundive as pred. adj. w. *trādita est* in passive, agreeing w. *urbs*.)

B.—1. Germānī pugnandī cupidī erant. 2. Ad explōrandum missī sunt. 3. Ācer in loquendō erat. 4. Proeliī committendī cupidī erant. 5. Ad aciem īnstruendam hic collis idōneus est. 6. Mūrō faciendō collem mūnīre poterat. 7. Ad pācem petendam vēnērunt. 8. Omnia ad proficīscendum parāta erant. 9. Collis idōneus est ad castra pōnenda. 10. Suī cōnservandī causā fūgērunt. 11. Deus nōbīs omnibus laudandus est. 12. Omnibus hostibus ā nōbīs resistendum est. 13. Pāx nōbīs cōnservanda est. 14. Hōc cōnsiliō ūtendum est. 15. Hāc ratiōne nōbīs ūtendum est. 16. Obsidēs occīdere nōn oportuit. 17. Omnia unō tempore facienda erant. 18. Trībus diēbus eis perveniendum est. 19. Labiēnus classī ā Caesare praeficiendus erat. 20. Caesar cōnstituit classem exspectandam esse. 21. Caesar dīxit ab eīs illā ratiōne ūtendum esse. 22. Rōmānī putāvērunt Gallōs pācandōs esse.

C.—1. Novō et meliōre cōnsiliō nōbīs ūtendum est. 2. In cōnsiliīs capiendīs audāx erat, in agendō celer et fortis. 3. Collēs castrīs pōnendīs

idōneī sunt. 4. Ad pācem petendam vēnērunt. 5. Mīlitēs ad proficīscendum parātī erant.

13. Infinitives, A.—1. To praise God is to pray. (*Laudāre* and
ōrāre, used as sub. and pred. nom.) 2. It is good to help others. (*Adjuvāre*, used as pred. nom. w. neuter adj. *bonum*.) 3. We are ready to
fight. (*Pugnāre*, used as obj.) 4. We must praise God. (*Laudāre*, infin.
w. *oportet*.) 5. He had to go. (*Īre*, infin. w. *oportuit*.) 6. By praying and
by acting bravely we can overcome unfavorable circumstances. (*Super-
āre*, obj. of *possumus*.) 7. The Gauls were unable to defend themselves.
(*Sē*, reflexive, obj. of *dēfendere; dēfendere*, obj. of *potuērunt*.) 8. We
ought to help others. (*Adjuvāre*, obj. of *dēbēmus*.) 9. Soldiers ought to
be very brave. (*Fortissimī*, pred. adj.) 10. He ordered a bridge to be
built. (*Pontem fierī*, acc. w. infin. after *jussit*.) 11. He ordered them to
withdraw to camp. (*Eōs sē . . . recipere*, acc. w. infin. after *jussit*.)
12. Christians have been commanded to love one another. (*Sē*, obj. of
prep. *inter; dīligere*, obj. of *jussī sunt*.) 13. The soldiers wished to begin
battle. (*Committere*, obj. of *voluērunt*.) 14. I wish you to be my friend.
(*Tē*, sub. of *esse; amīcum*, pred. nom. after *esse*.) 15. I wish that you
would not flee. (*Fugiās*, pres. subj. in a negative noun clause after *volō*,
action at same time or after time of main verb.) 16. He was informed
that all the Gauls were in arms. (*Gallōs . . . esse*, acc. w. infin. after
certior factus est.) 17. He said he would arrive within a few days.
(*Sē . . . perventūrum esse*, acc. w. infin. after *dīxit*.) 18. I know that
Caesar pacified Gaul. (*Pācāvisse*, in acc. w. infin. after *sciō*.) 19. I think
you are a very good man. (*Tē*, sub. of *esse; virum optimum*, pred.
nom. w. adj. after *esse*.) 20. I know that Rome itself was burned by the
Gauls. (*Incēnsam esse*, in acc. w. infin. after *sciō*.) 21. I think that our
state is praised by many. (*Cīvitātem . . . laudārī*, acc. w. infin. after
arbitror.) 22. They said they ought to surrender. (*Eōs . . . dēbēre*,
acc. w. infin. after *dīxērunt; sē dēdere*, obj. of *dēbēre*.) 23. Orgetorix
was said to be seeking royal power. (*Rēgnum*, obj. of *petere; petere*,
infin. after *dīcēbātur*.) 24. The king of the Germans is thought to have
been killed by the Romans. (*Occīsus esse*, infin. after *putātur*.)

B—1. Semper ōrāre optimum est. 2. Oportet nōs Deum dīligere.
3. Estisne prō lībertāte pugnāre semper parātī? 4. Putāsne Gallōs fortiter
pugnāvisse? 5. Jussit equitēs hostēs sequī. 6. Jussit castra statim mūnīrī.
7. Dīligere amīcōs est bonum. 8. Oportuit Gallōs inter sē conjungī.
9. Volumus omnēs amīcōs nostrōs fortēs et bonōs esse. 10. Dēbēmus
vēritātem petere. 11. Dīxit sē brevī tempore ventūrum esse. 12. Jussit

eōs statim sē dēdere. 13. Caesar putābātur rēgnī glōriaeque cupidus esse. 14. Sēnātus certior factus est Galliam ā Caesare pācātam esse.
C.—1. Dēbēmus prō lībertāte pugnāre. 2. Ōrāre nōn est difficile. 3. Oportuit Gallōs statim inter sē conjungī salūtis commūnis ac lībertātis dēfendendae causā (ut salūtem communem ac lībertātem dēfenderent). 4. Dēbēmus omnēs adjuvāre aliōs. (Aliī omnibus nōbīs adjuvandī sunt.) 5. Putō tē optimum esse.

14. Participles, A.—1. They burned the captured city. (Captam, part. modifying urbem.) 2. He was killed [while] fighting very bravely. (Pugnāns, part. modifying sub. of interfectus est.) 3. These things having been said, he departed. (Hīs dictīs, abl. abs.) 4. With Caesar as leader, the Romans pacified (subjugated) the Gauls. (Duce, noun in abl. abs.) 5. The cavalry pursued the fleeing enemy. (Fugientēs, part. modifying hostēs.) 6. Having set out at dawn, they reached the town at the fourth hour. (Profectī, part. modifying sub. of pervēnērunt.) 7. Winter being entered upon (in the beginning of winter), he led the legions into winter quarters. (Initā, part. in abl. abs.) 8. By force he warded off the enemy trying (as they tried) to cross the river. (Cōnantēs, part. modifying hostēs.) 9. Having said this, he died. (Locūtus, part. modifying sub. of mortuus est.)

B.—1. Hōc bellō cōnfectō, Caesar putāvit Galliam pācātam esse. 2. Caesare duce, Rōmānī Gallōs vīcērunt. 3. Brevī tempore relīquō, sē in castra recēpit. 4. Fortiter pugnāns tēlō interfectus est. 5. Oppida capta incendērunt. 6. Hoc Gallīs victīs magnō dolōrī erat. 7. Rēgem resistentem occīdērunt. 8. Illī venientēs ā servō cōnspectī sunt. 9. Ponte captō, cōpiās trāns flūmen trādūxit. 10. Haec locūtus statim jussit eōs impetum facere. 11. Gallī nōn poterant loca mūnīta facile capere.

C.—1. Hōc cognitō, Caesar in Galliam statim profectus est. 2. Bellō Helvētiōrum cōnfectō, prīncipēs omnis Galliae ad Caesarem vēnērunt. 3. Suōs hortātus statim jussit impetum in oppidum fierī. 4. Exeuntēs ex castrīs, ā Gallīs oppugnātī sunt. 5. Equitēs Gallōs fugientēs secūtī sunt. 6. Rōmānī venientēs ex silvīs hostēs cōnspexērunt. 7. Bellō initō, Caesar in Italiā erat.

15. Prepositions, A.—1. He is in camp. 2. He arrived in camp at the third hour. 3. They fled into the woods. 4. He was on the bridge. 5. They made a very brave attack against them. 6. In war very many are killed. 7. Caesar had great courage. 8. He brought the baggage together in one place. 9. May God save us from this danger. 10. He set out from camp. 11. He was a long distance from the river. 12. He was killed by him. 13. He recovered from fear. 14. He came down from the

mountain. 15. They were preparing to go out from their own territory with all their forces. 16. He was informed of that victory. 17. For which reason (therefore) they surpassed others in courage. 18. They came to the river. 19. They came to seek peace. 20. We are ready for all things. 21. That place is suitable for pitching camp. 22. They fought until night. 23. He drew up the battle line in front of the camp. 24. He arrived at camp before night. 25. He delivered a speech in the presence of the soldiers. 26. He had the greatest influence among the Gauls. 27. He is coming with me. 28. He fought with courage. 29. A few of our men received wounds. 30. Between the hill and the river there was a large forest. 31. I will give no one a route through the province. 32. He was informed of this affair by messengers. 33. As soon as he could through the time of year (as soon as the time of year permitted), he set out for the army. 34. He left the enemy behind him. 35. After that battle the enemy withdrew into the forest. 36. He led the army past the camp of the enemy. 37. This was done contrary to the law of God. 38. He fears no one except God. 39. He stationed guards in front of the gates. 40. Pray for me. 41. We will fight for liberty. 42. Because of these wrongs they undertook war. 43. They are fighting without hope. 44. Fight without any fear. 45. He drew up the battle line at the foot of the mountain. 46. He arrived at the river about nighttime. 47. They advanced up to the mountain. 48. The Germans dwelt across the river.

B and C.—1. Ā flūmine iērunt. 2. In castra vēnērunt. 3. In grātiam Caesaris vēnit. 4. In Labiēnō magna virtūs erat. 5. In ūnum locum magnās cōpiās coēgērunt. 6. Nautae in flūmine erant. 7. In flūmine pōns erat. 8. In eōs impetum fēcērunt. 9. Deus nōs ab hāc morte (huic mortī) ēripiat! 10. Fugā salūtem petīvērunt. 11. Rēx Germānōrum ā Rōmānīs interfectus esse putābātur. 12. Dē mūrō dējectus est. 13. Per litterās hoc cognōvit. 14. Estisne ad mortem parātī? 15. Ob hanc causam Caesar ab aliīs Rōmānīs timēbātur. 16. Prō portīs aciēs īnstrūcta est. 17. Maximā cum spē pugnāvērunt. 18. Inter urbem et flūmen mūrus altissimus erat. 19. Per maximās silvās iter fēcērunt et trāns flūmen lātum trānsiērunt. 20. Ante noctem proelium cōnfectum est.